A STORY OF H[...]

RESURRECTED

ANDREW & ZOE CULLEN

READEX
By Reading We Experience

Title: Resurrected
Subtitle: A story of Hope
A story of overcoming PTSD and spiritual enlightenment
Authors: Andrew and Zoe Cullen
Edited by Linky Muller

● ●

The views of the author do not reflect those of the Defence or government
policy and the military responses referenced within are not necessarily a
true and accurate reflection of current or precious Defence procedures.
Matters of operational security have been amended where necessary.
This book contains names and details surrounding the deaths of Australian
Defence personnel Killed In Action (KIA) in the Afghanistan War between
the years 2008 and 2012. Details of these events may cause emotional
distress to some readers.

Resurrect

rɛzəˈrɛkt/

verb

past tense: resurrected; past participle: resurrected

restore (a dead person) to life.

"he queried whether Jesus was indeed resurrected"

synonyms: raise from the dead, restore to life, bring back to life, revive

"on the third day Jesus was resurrected"

revive or revitalise (something that is inactive, disused, or forgotten).

Resurrected

Foreword

by Major-General (Retired) John Cantwell AO DSC

Best-selling author of "Exit Wounds: One Australian's War on Terror"

It takes courage to deliberately walk up to a bomb rigged to explode at a touch or possibly connected to a trigger device in the hands of a hidden insurgent. It also takes courage to relive the devastation caused by such bombs when soldiers or civilians stumble onto them. It demands a special form of courage to speak openly and fully about the toll such experiences exact on the heart and mind.

Andrew and his wife Zoe have recounted their shared journey through the fear, exhaustion and loneliness that comes with combat deployments to fight Australia's wars on foreign soil. Deadly events from multiple deployments to Afghanistan are described with brutal clarity. As an explosives expert, Andy confronted some of the toughest days a soldier can endure, rendering safe lethal roadside bombs and unexploded munitions, or picking through the shattered remains of humans blown apart by devices that detonated. For her part, Zoe describes their personal battle to overcome the emotional damage suffered by Andy and the growing strain placed on their relationship.

Finally driven to seek professional psychiatric care, Andy found support and comfort in his religious beliefs. While I do not share that faith, I have shared his path back from the black abyss of post-traumatic stress and emotional wounds. I applaud Andy and Zoe for speaking so honestly about their struggles and for helping other Australians understand the human cost of the duty rendered in their name by the extraordinary men and women of our Defence Force.

Resurrected

Resurrected

A story of hope

For those suffering from PTSD and the loss of identity that comes with it. For those who want to overcome the life sentence of mental illness and have the courage to step out on the journey of coming to terms with finding their new identity. A story about a man whose love for adventure and loyalty to his country leaves him completely broken but finds him unexpectedly stumbling upon spiritual enlightenment. A story about the wife of a serviceman who faces the challenges of single parenthood and then has to deal with the consequences of a trauma- tised loved one coming back from the war zone. This story is a raw account encompassing both viewpoints of Andy and of Zoe his beloved wife, and their journey through the dark times, the hurt, the fears and challenges that are very real for a couple and a family dealing with the trauma of modern warfare and the continued battle and casualties that rage on at home.

Andrew and Zoe Cullen

Dedication

We dedicate this book to all the servicemen, women and their families who sacrifice so much for the protection of others. We acknowledge the great commitment required to fulfil your duty. Know that you are not defined by what you do or have done in your past, but rather are defined by who you are.

We salute you.

"Greater love hath no man than this, that a man lay down his life for his friends." John 15:13 (KJV)

Contents

Prologue

Promises made from a hospital bed

I woke up in a hospital bed staring at the ceiling, the flickering fluorescent lights bouncing off of the stark white walls, the feeling of clean starchy sheets on my skin. I could feel the frame of the hospital bed through the thin mattress. I couldn't hear anything for a few moments as I wondered how on earth I had arrived here. My mind was clouded by the morphine and other drugs in my system and I felt a tightness on my chest like a vice compressing my lungs underwater as I struggled to breathe. It felt as though my heart was also being pressed from all sides as sharp pains shot through my chest. As I slowly gained consciousness, I felt the tubes in my arms and patches on my body, I heard the low electrical buzz of the machines next to the bed. I tried to sit up but had no energy at all. Gazing out the window trying to orient myself, I recognised the familiar coastline and buildings of Coolangatta on the Gold Coast, and it all came flooding back.

I was in a very bad way having been brought into the emergency room at John Flynn Hospital the night prior by ambulance and then taken to the cardiac ward for further treatment and monitoring. I was diagnosed with blood clots on my lungs and pleurisy.

I knew I was dying.

As I lay in bed confronted by my own mortality I had an overwhelming feeling of despair and the thought that I had destroyed everything good in my life raced through my mind like an out of control freight train. I felt no desire to go on living and was relieved at the thought that I might die in a hospital bed from some bizarre medical condition and not have to go through with the act of ending my own life, a plan that had plagued my thoughts for some time now. I also felt more at peace with the idea of my wife and children hearing the news of my passing in this way, rather than finding my lifeless body at home or disappearing in the ocean never to be seen again. At least this way they would have a body for the funeral and they could hold their heads up and not have to live with the shame in the knowledge that their husband and father had committed suicide.

As I lay there staring at the ceiling I found myself asking the question: "how did I get here?" A little while ago I was in a position of pain, suffering and despair. To end up in hospital at this time in my life was not altogether unexpected as I had been suffering from Post-Traumatic Stress Disorder (PTSD) and major depression for some time and I had been medicating with alcohol and Valium® as well as numerous anti-depressants and anti-psychotics. In addition to this my family situation was extremely strained to say the least. My wife was losing strength in her will to support me through this difficult time as she was burning out raising four kids on her own and dealing with my mood disorders. My children didn't know which father was going to greet them from one moment to the next and it was driving a wedge between us, that if not repaired soon, would tear the bond forever.

I had significant anger issues and was abusing alcohol as a self-medicating tool in order to sleep; not the best drug to consume if you're already depressed, can't sleep and on a fist full of pills every day. I did this in a desperate attempt to block the vivid and horrific hallucinations and dreams I would be confronted with each night. These events were a constant reminder of my time spent in Afghanistan. The nightly torment became unbearable over time and wore me down to a state of mental and physical exhaustion. All in all, I was doing my best to simply hang on from day to day.

Allow me to share my journey with you, a normal everyday Aussie bloke, whose life became consumed by darkness and through the darkness found purpose again.

In recounting a number of events that shaped my life and revealing the way I viewed the world and my part in it. These pages provide an insight into my personality, values and philosophy. They take a look, unashamedly, at mental illness and bear witness to the problems faced by many returning veterans in the hope of shining some light and understanding on an illness that is plaguing our society.

As anyone that has been deployed in any combat zone will tell you, 'it's not all beer and skittles'. This book takes a look at the good, the bad and the ugly of deploying to war on the modern battlefield of Afghanistan, through the eyes of an Australian soldier, and the mental scars that are carried long after returning home.

It is also an autobiography about a boy who wanted nothing more in life than to become a proud and honourable man with a story to tell, at least a story that was worth telling.

I have included a number of specific military incidents from my time in Afghanistan. Most accounts are taken from my personal diary or drawn from memory so if my dates are slightly out or details missing I apologise up front, one thing I have learned through this journey is that our memories are not always as reliable as we might hope.

1

Genesis

I am the son of Mick and Carmel Cullen, born in Camden NSW. We were your typical Aussie family with an Irish Catholic heritage. My family has been in Australia for over two hundred years as the first Cullen's to land were Irish convicts amongst the first fleet so you don't get much more Australian than that; other than our Aboriginal brothers.

Mick was a Bankstown brawler, he joined the Royal Military College (RMC) at the age of 17, continuing a proud military service tradition held by his father and his grandfather before him. He would complete 50 years of service, an incredible achievement of service, to his nation and one that I am extremely proud of.

Carmel was a young country girl from Crookwell, a small farm town West of Goulburn NSW. My parents met in Ingleburn after my mother finished teacher's college in Wagga Wagga and Dad completed his Officer training at Duntroon and Puckapunyal. Home was wherever Dad's job took us and I was blessed with loving, yet strict parents.

I am the second son of four boys and had a disciplined upbringing - not that we avoided our run-ins with the law. A family of four boys always taught to defend themselves and never be pushed around is bound to run into hiccups from time to time.

My father was the RMC (Royal Military College) boxing champ and carried his badge of honour with pride. I remember sitting around at family BBQ's listening to my uncles tell stories of their big brother Mick getting into all sorts of strife as a kid. I guess that's where the fiery side comes from, that and Irish blood.

Dad was as tough as they come, he was firm and never allowed us to talk back or argue but he was also capable of expressing deep love. I remember getting the occasional cuddle from my Dad that made me feel incredibly safe and comforted. I never feared anything when I was with him and he brought a great stability to our family home.

Mum was simply always there through every scratch, bump and brush of my childhood, picking me up dusting me off and getting me back on my feet. As a child I loved spending time with her watching her cook or sew. I just wanted to be around her as much as I could as she was a constant source of comfort and grounding.

Much of my childhood was spent travelling from one school to another, following my father on posting after posting, including a stint in Sydney, Canberra, England and even the USA. I actually miss those days as I found it quite easy to transition between schools and friends. A scrawny kid with big ears and an even bigger attitude. I loved adventure and was always looking for fun.

Religion was introduced from a young age and we attended a Catholic church for the obligatory Easter and Christmas Mass. I was baptised as a child and went through confirmation, 'to protect my immortal sole' and that was that. We were what you would call nominal Catholics at best. My father didn't really seem to harbour any deep spiritual beliefs but my mother had a faith that burned quietly inside her and would get her through the difficult times in her life, particularly when my father was away for extended periods of time.

The Catholic Church always felt like a cold place to me and I often wondered why God would choose to reside in these buildings with smelly old priests rather than hang out at the beach or in the mountains. Internally, I have always had a sense that God was with me however, I never really felt a personal connection to him or thought of him as my own personal saviour. Little did I know that this relationship would later prove to be the most powerful and meaningful relationship I would ever form.

Some of my earliest memories of primary school were not that pleasant. I was outgoing and happy to play with anyone, physically strong and mentally tough and a quick study at anything I put my mind to, other than English. Superman had Kryptonite and I had the English language as my nemesis. Spelling was my main issue as words just didn't seem to make sense, however, I developed a love of numbers that soon offset my deficiencies in English.

Emotionally I was all over the place, I had a very thin skin when it came to bullying or teasing and as a result I would often find myself in trouble. I was very fortunate, in that I had no health concerns, social disadvantages, or emotional abuse issues to overcome and life generally came easy to me.

Most people thought I had ears that were too big for my pre-pubescent head though and the occasional taunts of 'Dumbo', 'wing nut' and 'Big Ears' would ring out across the playground making me feel an anger rise in me like a kettle to the boil. I didn't react well to the teasing, often punching some smart lipped kid in the face or pushing his head into a wall. I remember feeling very proud of myself the first time I broke a kids nose with my fist. I was particularly quick to anger and violent in my response to teasing, which was not what I would consider a good trait and not something I encourage in my own children, but that was who I was then, as I made violence my friend.

My ears would be the main cause of trouble for a number of years until my parents got sick of being called to school to pick me up after receiving yet another suspension or cane from the school headmasters. My parents made the decision to have my ears tucked, a simple little operation designed to bring the ear back flatter against the head. For many years, I would continue to be quite ashamed of the operation, as I considered it a sign of weakness and personal failure in my inability to deal with my own problems.

It was overwhelmingly the right decision for me as it had the desired effect, in that the teasing stopped and I stopped punching people in the face, at least for the reason of teasing me about my ears. I do think my right hook suffered as a result of less practice though. The truth was, my ears would be the defining factor of my childhood and my developing personality. I developed an utter hatred for bullies, a burning desire in my heart to always help the afflicted, and a very fiery temper.

During the periods of time Dad was home, we would live in Sydney. From as early as I can remember I enjoyed the excitement of the city, friends nearby and the ocean, which I was drawn to, at our fingertips. I always felt like we had the best of both worlds as kids. We played rugby in winter and did athletics and surfing in summer.

The majority of school holidays and any period that Dad was deployed for any length of time, Mum would pack us all up and take us to stay on her parent's farm. The farm was a sheep and cattle station in the harsh NSW interior about an hour west of Goulburn. My mother had grown up and lived there with her 9 brothers and sisters. The farm remained in the family, handed down to my uncle and then back to my own parents who still reside there today. The place has a majestic feel to it. Stunningly beautiful in its harshness, blisteringly hot summers, bitterly cold winters and it would seem like nothing in-between.

My childhood moments on the farm were spent riding horses, motorbikes, milking cows, collecting eggs, cleaning up in the shearing shed, sorting wool and feeding the dogs. I learned to drive a car at about the age of 10 and was mustering sheep and cattle on horseback soon after.

My uncles would spend long hours with my brother and me at their feet, eagerly learning everything we could about farm life. From drenching and shearing to birthing and castrating of animals. I felt a real connection to the animals especially the horses, and I am drawn to horses in a way that is difficult to explain, even today. Their company simply helps me find peace and it grounds me.

My uncles did not always teach us lovingly and on occasion would take advantage of our ignorant city slicker upbringing. I remember on one occasion, we were given a lesson in how to castrate sheep. My uncle grabbed a lamb's balls and indicated we were to take a firm grasp, latch on with our teeth and in one swift motion, bite the little buggers off. At which point my brother and I looked at each other, horrified at the idea of biting the nuts off of about fifty odd lambs. My uncles laughed as we readied ourselves for the task and only stopped us just shy of placing some poor lamb's balls in our mouths, handing us some rubber bands to attach around the little feller's family jewels instead.

There was never a dull moment at the farm as we had so many cousins to play with. Each of my mother's brothers and sisters had large families, so we literally had between twenty to thirty kids around at any given time.

We would build forts in the hay bales, ride horses until we couldn't walk properly, shoot rabbits, ducks and kangaroos from the back of the ute and ride around on anything with wheels that we could get moving. We would spend hours catching yabbies (freshwater crustacean) in the creek and fishing for trout in the dams, constructing makeshift rafts out of anything we could find, only to sink within minutes of launching them in the middle of the freezing dams.

I was given all the freedom in the world to explore and seek adventure to my heart's content with one simple rule to obey, 'be home before dinner.' It was the life on the farm that makes me ensure my own children spend time out in the elements fending for themselves, learning and exploring, it is our connection with nature that awakens the adventurer in all of us.

My brothers and cousins and I would walk for miles along the dusty roads covered in flies that relentlessly tried to burrow into the corner of your eyes and mouth. We would cool off by jumping into the creek and play games with electric fences and large bulls. Although we would get hurt on a regular basis we never ran home or cried about it we would simply dust ourselves off, get up and continue on.

One day whilst riding a quad bike we decided we would see how many people we could fit on it at one time and managed to get six of us on, riding flat out around the grain silos when my cousin Davie rolled the bike throwing bodies in every direction with the only injury, a broken arm to himself. We were genuinely more concerned with how my Poppa (grandfather) would react to the dings on the bike.

My Poppa, Russell Croker, was a tough, but extremely loving man, he had suffered from polio from a young age and lost about 50% use of his right leg. He didn't go to war as a result of his illness and was refused service in the Army, as I understand it, this was something that he regretted for much of his life and he often expressed how proud he was of all those that served this great nation of Australia.

He was a true Aussie battler, working the land his entire life, the farming backbone of a great nation. His polio never slowed him down; he would be up from the crack of dawn and work like a mule until dusk.

Many nights he would gather his multitude of grandchildren, sleeping in all areas of the farmhouse, together for a story and he would arrange sing-alongs and poetry readings whenever he could. He had an incredible love for life and would express his love for others in the most beautiful way by making you feel like you were the only person in the world when he spoke to you. He was deeply engaging and interested in your point of view.

My Nanna (grandmother) was one of the smallest people I have ever met, I was taller than her by the time I was ten years old and I loved spending time with her. She was not an overly happy person, suffering from depression for most of her life. I think having ten kids would send any mother around the bend.

She was very reserved and never really showed emotion or expressed love easily. I think my own mother inherited some of her tough exterior in raising four boys on her own for long periods whilst Dad was away. She loved all her boys to bits and was always there for us but developed a tough exterior to compensate, as a single parent being the disciplinarian and loving mother. It didn't leave a lot of time for hugs and kisses.

Life for us kids was more about survival, I think. I believe it had to do with the skills I learned spending endless days on the farm, free to explore, that gave me the independence and courage I would need later in life.

My older brother Tim and I became very close as a result of our narrow age gap of 18 months and our families constant travelling. I was in his shadow for much of my early life as most younger siblings are, however, Tim was an extremely talented sportsman and I envied his natural abilities as I found it awkward trying to emulate his achievements.

We did everything together. He had the same adventurous spirit as I did and was fiercely protective of his little brother.

I remember one day at the school bus stop in Canberra. A kid twice my size was picking on me so my brother, full of confidence in my fighting abilities, organised an impromptu punch up.

He placed a twenty-cent piece in my hand just before the fight and told me to hold it tight in my fist between my knuckles when I hit the bloke. He had heard about it somewhere and assured me it would fell this 'child giant' I was about to face.

Unfortunately, my brother must not have been paying close attention when he heard this advice as it was supposed to be a roll of coins not a single coin. When I hit the fella I nearly broke my hand. I dropped my head and my hands and started to take a few hits, at which point Tim jumped in and made swift work of the bigger kid. He then took me home, apologising for his obvious error in advice.

We told Dad about it when we got home and he gave me some advice I will never forget. "No matter how much pain you are in, keep swinging and never give up!" It was a motto that he would use for everything from long distance running, to football and life, "Keep on moving and never give up!"

We finally stopped moving around and settled in an Army married quarter in Sydney's affluent suburb of Mossman. I loved high school and made a small group of friends I would cherish for life. However, I couldn't wait to get out into the real world and prove myself as a man. I got into the odd bit of trouble now and then, "hanging out with the wrong crowd" my mum would say, but the truth was I was just as much a bad influence on my friends as they were on me.

We weren't bad kids just very naughty, as one of my mate's mums would later tell me at his funeral. Although I had a great sense of adventure, I lacked a good moral compass at times. I shoplifted and even stole a car once, smoked pot and went to strip clubs all before the age of 16. Alcohol became a large part of my life from a very young age and was the precursor to all sorts of mischief. We would get into fights while roaming the streets of Sydney, spend our nights trying to impress pretty girls and enjoy long summer days on the beach.

Tim and I went through childhood together thick as thieves, riding bikes, playing footy and competing at everything. We would be the very best of friends and the worst of enemies constantly scrapping with each other over a borrowed T-shirt or girlfriend.

We very nearly killed each other on a few occasions smashing furniture over each other when Dad was away and Mum could not quite control us. I even threw a few bricks at his head on one occasion. Including the time I accidentally broke his back whilst wrestling on the streets of North Sydney whilst heavily intoxicated.

This was in the days before Mixed Marshal Arts (MMA) and we would have a great time trying to best each other. Nine times out of ten he would win until I eventually overtook him in stature.

A very uncomfortable cab ride and a long wait at the hospital ensued with the news that Tim had broken one vertebra and had damaged multiple disks. It's safe to say I felt bloody awful at that point.

Tim was a star football player and was set for a life in grade football with the North Sydney Bears; he also had an opportunity with the Australian Institute of Sport for sprinting. However, to his credit he did not let the injury stop him from succeeding in life and is an extremely successful businessman today.

High school was a blast, I had a very close group of friends which included the ever vigilant level-headed Mick Glacken, who got me out of more scrapes than I care to remember. This was often helped by the fact that he was a man mountain at over 6ft tall and around 85kg in high school. I believe his maturity beyond his age came from the sad fact that he had lost his mother to cancer at the age of 13. The reality was that, although he looked quite fearsome, even at a young age, he was and still is a gentle giant. He didn't even like playing footy that much through fear of hurting someone by accident. He was very aware of his own physical strength and kept it under control through self-discipline. I only really remember Mick losing his temper on one occasion.

My other mate was the loveable larrikin Andrew Scott (Scotty), a redheaded freckle faced fire ball, so full of energy he never stopped moving. We spent years surfing and getting into trouble together. We started drinking at the age of 14 when Scotty would steal his grandfather's expensive bottles of wine from his cellar and we would sneak out to meet up at the local park. We would push the cork into the bottle with a stick and drink a bottle between us, talking about girls, school, fears and dreams, and then we would roll down the grassy hills laughing until the early hours of the morning before ending the night throwing up.

At the age of 25, Scotty was found swinging from a rope in his Dad's garage. He had tied a perfect knot using the skills we learned and practiced together in Scouts. I felt a darkness as I entered into the garage that day, an eerie sense of utter tragedy. I looked around the garage that we had spent many hours in over the years, searching for answers in the objects around me, looking for a clue that could explain why this had happened. It was a sad and tragic end to a life tormented by drugs, alcohol and depression. Scotty's death would become a constant reminder to me of how dark life can get and how incredibly helpless one must feel to reach the point of suicide. I never could understand Scotty's decision to kill himself that day and I registered it as a desperate act of a young man in extreme mental anguish.

Scotty called me the night he died and wanted to meet up to talk. I was working in the Army in Liverpool at the time and we were completing some very physical, long days. I told him I would pick up a six pack and come and see him after work, but I was tired and I put off the visit telling myself I would drive out to see him after having a rest.

A few short hours later and my best mate was dead. I never got to say goodbye, and I never got to tell him that I loved him and that everything would be okay. I knew he was struggling with a failed relationship and was using various drugs, but I didn't think for a moment he was suicidal. I blamed myself for many years for not being there for my friend when he needed me and for not being a good enough friend to know how much pain he was in.

I still remember him, even today, greeting me in the early hours of the morning with a huge grin on his freckled face, surfboard under his arm, so excited to get into the water. The surf was truly his happy place. We shared the same love for the ocean and the waves.

I spoke at his funeral and felt such grief at the loss of my best mate under the tragic circumstances of his death. It haunted me for a long time.

The third member of our small crew was the loyal to a fault, Johnny Taylor. John was a loveable handsome and intelligent young guy. He had more natural ability academically than the rest of us put together, though, he more often than not chose to ignore his intellect in place of the opportunity to get into trouble and enjoy life a little more dangerously.

He was the first of the group to get a license and quickly developed a lead foot and dangerous driving technique that nearly killed the lot of us on more than one occasion.

One of my fondest memories of my friends growing up was taking a trip to Durras, on the East coast of Southern NSW, a small sleepy surf beach community where we would camp, drink, play cards and tell stories around the campfire.

Our days were filled with adventure and our nights an endless party of trying various drugs. We thought we were just embracing our youth however, life would later teach me we were playing a very dangerous game and setting into motion life choices that would have catastrophic consequences.

Every innocent choice we made in our youth lead in some way to justifying another and another and yet another, until some of us were so deeply entrenched into the seedy drug culture of Sydney's underbelly that the only way out was nigh on impossible. I still believe that if I had not chosen to join the Army and Mick the Navy, when we did, none of us would be alive today.

Johnny would later be found dead, at 38, living on a couch, in a single car garage in Sydney's outer West. Dead as a result of living a life of extended drug use and dangerous choices.

He left behind three failed relationships and four beautiful kids whom he did not see enough. John loved his children and his family and friends very much. However, the shame of his self-imposed circumstance in life, often drew him into a life of isolation, avoiding the people he loved and pushing them away.

His funeral was small and uneventful, I remember feeling the weight of his life as though he never reached anywhere near his potential and it reminded me not to waste any opportunity but to grab on with both hands and never let go. To try and live a life without regret because regret in the grave is useless.

I placed a very high regard on friendship and to this day would drop almost anything to help a mate in need.

We spent summer holidays on the Northern Beaches chasing waves and winters playing footy. Life was great, full of one crazy adventure after the next. We would go on surfing and fishing trips up and down the NSW East Coast eating nothing but baked beans for dinner each night and catching fish during the day as we had no cash between us.

I worked various jobs throughout high school from being a KFC cook to a shelf packer at the local supermarket. I even took a job as an assistant in a fruit shop where the owner would pay me partly in cash and partly in pot.

Although I would smoke pot occasionally I never really liked it, as it would make me paranoid and self-conscious. As a result of my experience with pot I would tend to be more cautious with most drugs than many of my friends during my early teenage years although there was never lack of opportunity.

I thought the world was my oyster, just one adventure after the next, and that's exactly how I pursued life. Schoolwork came fairly easy to me; I never really applied myself and simply did the bare minimum to get through without attracting unwanted attention from my parents or teachers. I would wag the occasional day if the surf was up or a new movie we really wanted to see was out. I was naturally bright and had a gift with numbers, although English was still my nemesis and I, still to this day, can't spell to save myself. However, I have never let it stand in the way of achieving my goals, including writing this book.

I studied for a total of five days leading up to my High School Certificate and only because my mother hounded me until I applied myself. I finished with a respectable score and although I was not interested in going to university my mother insisted on applying for a number of universities on my behalf and when I received the acceptance, I quickly deferred for a year. She had great wisdom and foresight to push me and it is only through her belief in me that I ended up with a degree and later as an officer in the Army.

I knew exactly what I wanted to be from a young age and that was an Officer in the Army. When I was a boy I was introduced very early on to what it meant to be an ANZAC. My father was in the Australian Army when I was born and only retired recently after completing 50 years of service, a phenomenal feat in any trade let alone the Military. I often looked up to him as he went off on operations around the world, Peacekeeping and the like. My grandfather on my father's side had also served in the Second World War and I had numerous uncles and aunts who served. I saw a world of great adventure, and I thought members of the military should be looked up to and respected for the sacrifices they were making. My father would leave for long periods of time and then return to tell my mother, my brothers and I the details of his last adventure.

A real turning point for me in my adolescence was when I was arrested alongside a number of my close friends, soon after completing high school, for doing burnouts on an oval at Middlehead.

My mates and I had been drinking beers and decided it would be fun to tear up the local sports oval and test the limits of Johnny's car, we drove down the road and onto the oval taking turns doing figure eights and laughing hysterically. The only issue with the plan was, it was right next door to an Army barracks that had a 24 hour guard.

The Army barracks also happened to be where my father was the Commanding Officer. The Duty Officer sent out a few trucks to block the exit of the oval until the police arrived and arrested us for wilful damage to public property, underage drinking and driving a motor vehicle whilst intoxicated.

As I was fortunate enough not to be driving at the time the police arrived, I didn't cop the last charge. Suffice it to say, some community service later and a very angry father who kicked my butt into gear to sort out my life, I could see it going in only one direction, if I stayed around Sydney and the scene I was in.

I applied for the Royal Military College Duntroon and although my grades were sufficient I was knocked back at officer selection for immaturity and advised to enlist as a private soldier or reapply after I had secured a tertiary degree.

I was ashamed not to be selected as an officer however, I knew I still had some growing up to do and I understood the decision of the panel.

It was no surprise to anyone when I decided to enlist as a private soldier. With a keen sense for both adventure and trouble, it would prove to be a decision that would change my life forever, and test my mind, my body and my spirit.

I read stories of great ANZAC legends, winners of the esteemed Victoria Cross, and I imagined myself alongside those great men. I was wrapped up in a feeling of patriotic pride and a great sense of belonging to something of value. Something so much bigger than myself. Something with real purpose.

2

The Search

I enlisted into the Australian Army on the 16th of January 1996; I had just turned 18 and headed off to Kapooka for basic training. I found Kapooka difficult at times and anyone that has been through there would agree the place was not for the faint of heart. But I found the mateship and physical work extremely rewarding. I was still just a scrawny kid, all skin and bone, tough and sharpwitted with an uncanny ability to get myself in and out of trouble at the drop of a hat.

This experience proved to be difficult both mentally and physically but I loved pushing myself and quickly forged a reputation as one of the fittest and toughest members of the platoon. I loved everything the Army would teach from basic soldiering, to weapons, navigation, and first aid.

The only thing I didn't like was discipline for the sake of discipline. I would often speak up when I witnessed something I didn't think was right, like a NCO belittling a recruit for no good reason, or someone whom I saw as simply being on a power trip, taking advantage of their authority. It was the same indignation rising up in me from when I was a schoolboy, not simply happy to let things go without saying something. My attitude would often find me standing at attention in front of the Platoon Commander or doing turns on the parade ground with a heavy pack on my back in the early hours as a form of punishment to realign my thinking.

I understand the whole "break you down as an individual and build you back up as part of the organisation" mentality the Army threw at its recruits, and to be honest I swallowed the entire patriotic pill, choosing to put my own personal feelings aside for the greater good as it were. I felt like I was now part of something bigger than myself, involved in something with real importance and value. I couldn't wait to get into the real job and left Kapooka without looking back. I was assigned to Corps of Infantry and posted to Singleton to complete my Infantry Basic Training.

Singleton was a lot tougher than Kapooka and I needed to focus all my efforts on getting through the training. I got through largely unscathed as I had learned to keep my mouth shut and toe the line as far as discipline was concerned. I also thrived at the tough physical work and loved pushing my body to its limits during physical training and field exercises. Quickly mastering any weapon I was given and applying myself to develop my skills at survival, navigation and first aid. Aggression was my friend and I was now in an environment where I was encouraged to show it. I embraced screaming at an imaginary enemy, whilst driving my bayonet into sandbags and wooden stakes on the bayonet assault course. Really thriving in the teamwork and mateship it required for my Section to complete the school's obstacle course in record time.

I had found my groove and the infantry fitted me like an old pair of boots. Still seeking some extra regimental excitement outside work hours, sneaking into town for a few beers and the opportunity to even speak to a girl.

We would apply all the skills taught to us regarding stealth and obstacle clearance when sneaking back into the barracks undetected, ready for work the next day. Other than getting into the occasional brawl and losing a few teeth, Singleton was fairly uneventful.

I graduated Singleton and was posted to the D (Delta) Company, 6th Battalion Royal Australian Regiment in Brisbane as a Private Rifleman in the Royal Australian Corps of Infantry. I wore my beret and "Skippy badge" with honour and walked around with a new sense of pride in the knowledge that I had earned my position.

*****

Settling into life as a Rifleman, I deployed to Malaysia late in 1996, for jungle warfare training and what I saw as an awesome adventure overseas. We would spend weeks in the thick jungles of Malaysia and then cause chaos in the small bars in Penang whenever we were given leave.

I spent Christmas and the New Year travelling with mates through Thailand, drinking and partying 'till all hours of the morning. The days were spent recovering from the night prior on the beaches or exploring the many sights of the cities and eating anything I could try that sounded exotic, like snake and buffalo. We entered chilli eating contests against local Thai men only to lose convincingly.

The jungle intrigued me and I respected it as one of the harshest environments on the planet to survive in. We had completed a number of difficult training camps prior to deploying, including the Jungle Warfare Training Centre at Canungra, but even that was nothing compared to the dense jungles of South East Asia. I was fascinated by everything that crawled and was convinced we had gone back in time, to some prehistoric land, as the insects were bigger than anything I had ever seen back in Australia. Mosquitos the size of small dragon flies, scorpions the size of dinner plates and bird-eating spiders, not to mention the very real threat of tigers.

During the quiet moments I would let my mind drift, thinking about my grandfather surviving in the jungles of Borneo fighting the Japanese and the struggles he must have endured. The thought of his time at war would carry me through any difficult or uncomfortable circumstance I was in, and I developed a strong ability to endure difficulty, understanding that it was more of a battle of the mind, as our bodies could cope with so much more than we ever thought possible.

Under the jungle canopy at night, I could not see my hand in front of my face. The environment amazed me and I could not get enough of the challenge of living in this hot, wet, and humid environment.

We would spend days patrolling through the thick jungle moving faster at times on our stomachs than standing. I witnessed a giant python being killed, as it was responsible for killing a local rubber tree tapper. We watched ants the size of match box cars fighting giant centipedes and would spend hours betting on match-ups between any animal we could find including rats, scorpions, ants and spiders.

I loved the thick smell of the jungle air and daily downpours of monsoonal rain; the heaviest rain I had ever seen in my life. It would fall in sheets of thick droplets so heavy you could not hear anyone speak next to you and visibility would decrease to a few meters. Nothing stayed dry and we quickly put our survival skills to the test to remain healthy and strong in such a challenging environment.

I enjoyed the silence of working in the jungle, no one talking unless absolutely necessary; all communication done through hand signals. We spent hours just sitting and watching the environment around us, looking for our enemy, waiting to conduct an attack, or move to the next location. I developed a very healthy respect for the jungle from my time in Malaysia and it was to be an experience that sparked a fire in my heart for more adventures in the future.

During our Christmas leave we visited Hell Fire Pass. Known by the Japanese as Konyu Cutting, a railway cutting on the former Burma Railway in Thailand, which was built with forced labour during the Second World War, in part by Allied prisoners of war. Sixty-nine men were beaten to death by Japanese guards in the six weeks it took to build the cutting, and many more died from cholera, dysentery, starvation, and exhaustion. Over 22 000 Australians were captured by the Japanese when they conquered Southeast Asia in early 1942. More than a third of these men and women died in captivity. This was about 20 per cent of all Australian deaths in World War II.

The magnitude of the sacrifice and loss of life faced by the Australian POWs hit home to my patriotic spirit and solidified my commitment to the Australian Army. It was only after learning more about the atrocities committed by the Japanese that I began to understand my grandfather's distrust of Japanese people back in Australia. Something I always found strange and confronting as a child. It was at that point that I was challenged to do something more substantial and meaningful with my military career.

Before leaving Thailand my friend Dan and I would have a few more crazy adventures, many of these focused around alcohol and poor judgment.

One particular morning we woke up in our hotel room late, realising we had missed our flight off a remote island somewhere in the Gulf of Thailand and we needed to get back to Penang Malaysia the following day or would face an Absent Without Leave (AWOL) charge.

We quickly packed our bags and headed to the airport only to find there were no more planes for another two days. We headed to the ferry port and boarded the first ferry back to the mainland, landing in a small fishing village in the north of Thailand. They didn't even have sealed roads, so after speaking with some locals to determine how to get to Bangkok we started walking and eventually reached a road with a bus stop. We waited for what seemed like a very long time, although it was likely only an hour or so, slowly realising we would most likely not make it back to the base on time for our morning parade.

It was not long when a bus pulled up and we boarded it for a crowded drive back to Bangkok city, arriving in the main bus exchange just as the sun was setting. We enquired for a bus to Penang; however, were informed there were no more buses that night and would have to wait until the morning. Realising that was not an option for us, we walked around and befriended another person travelling south and convinced him to split a cab for the 1,100km drive to get us to Butterworth.

An expensive activity, but one that would save us from being charged and potentially costing us a lot more. We struck a deal with a local driver insisting he make record time to get us to our destination on time, I think he thought all his birthdays had come at once as he made enough in that one transaction to last him six months' wages.

We eventually arrived on base at 6am on the Monday morning having travelled for nearly 24 hours straight across two countries and had just enough time to dump our bags, get dressed and report on parade. Dan and I looked at each other exhausted and laughed at the fact that we had made it back.

It was only a few short weeks later that I did get charged for AWOL after sneaking off base with a mate to attend a local bar for a few drinks. We were caught at gun point by a number of Malaysian military personnel scaling the razor wire fence getting back into the base in the early hours of the morning. As a result, I would spend my first few days back in Australia in the cells in Gallipoli barracks Brisbane, polishing brass and cleaning grout lines with my toothbrush.

After my short stint in the cells, I decided I would focus on being the best soldier I could be. I had a goal of being accepted to the Royal Military College (RMC) as an Officer. I had seen how officers were respected in the units and had the authority to make decisions and make a difference. I knew my ability to make an impact was limited as a soldier, at least until I reached the rank of Sergeant, and I could not see myself staying out of trouble long enough for that to happen. I simply didn't have the patience for it.

I decided, if I wanted something more from my career I would need to study, so my next adventure was university. Under the Army Ready Reserve program, I attended tertiary schooling and completed a Bachelor of Science Architecture at the University of Newcastle. I completed my studies in the same way I completed my schooling with minimal effort. My motto was 'P's get Degrees' and that's all I needed to get me in the door at RMC.

My university holidays were not enjoyable like most university students, as I would pack up and report for duty with the Army. I put more effort into my military career than my university studies and took on the role of instructing new Reserve Officer Recruits in Infantry tactics, weapons and basic first aid. I graduated university three years later with average grades in all subjects. However, it was during my reserve time that I started to excel. I completed an Assault Pioneer course, an infantry version of basic military engineering, where I was first exposed to explosives. Let's just say I had found my calling, as it turned out, I loved 'blowing stuff up.'

After completing University, it was time to re-evaluate life. University had taught me that I loved design, but I could not sit behind a desk and feel any fulfilment in life. My desire to be an Architect was dead. I simply longed for adventure. I stayed up at night planning a trip through South America and saving my money for a plane ticket. Having saved enough for a one-way ticket to Argentina and after spending weeks failing to convince one of my friends to join me I decided it was time to go solo. With no real plan and no real money, I bought a 'Learn Spanish book', and hopped on a flight out of Sydney with a backpack and the fever of adventure in my blood.

Argentina was a myriad of colours, sounds and flavours I had never experienced before. I spent hours, people watching in the large open squares, and quickly developed a passion for understanding and studying cultures. Music seemed to move these people in a way I had never experienced back in Australia. People, young and old were dancing in the streets and celebrating life. The overt displays of happiness seemed so far removed from the streets of Sydney, people smiled at me and even engaged in polite conversation. I wanted to learn more about these people, what made them tick and what they held dear.

The truth is, I was still trying to find my own identity, and I wanted to put it together from as large a tapestry as possible. I saw travel as the perfect way to educate myself and to better understand the world around me and my part in it. I was not so much on a spiritual journey, as one of physical indulgence in all that the world had to offer. I wanted to soak up the atmosphere and assimilate into the cultures around me as best I could. I quickly made friends with an Argentinian local named Gabriel, he wanted to travel through Brazil, and we teamed up. I agreed to teach him English and he would teach me Spanish.

My South American adventure would see me travel throughout Argentina, north to Iguazu Falls on the border of the Argentine province of Misiones and the Brazilian state of Paraná. The falls were a spectacular site and unlike anything I had ever seen in Australia. I was immediately taken back to a childhood visit to Niagara Falls in Canada where I had visited whilst travelling with my parents. The sheer power of the water filled my mind with excitement and wonder, and I would spend my day dreaming about how the world was created and all the incredible majesty that existed within it.

Continuing my travels south-east across Brazil into Sao Paulo and on to Rio de Janeiro. The sights and sounds were incredible but my desire was to be in nature and not stuck in the bustling cities and chaos. I travelled on a very low budget of a few dollars a day, and I had managed to pick up a few labouring jobs from place to place to supplement my meagre belongings wherever I could; this gave me the opportunity to fund each leg of my journey.

Mostly, I just looked for opportunities to make money and get food anyway I could and in most instances it worked out fine. I befriended people and they would invite me into their homes for dinner and a place to rest for a night or two, only resorting to backpacker hostels when I absolutely had to. We hitch-hiked, caught buses and trains and spent days walking from town to town across Brazil. It was in Rio that I learned about the Amazon River tours and expeditions and my love for the jungle and adventure were sparked again.

I had no way of affording a ticket on one of these expensive tours so I hatched a plan to complete the Amazon adventure on a shoestring budget and do it my own way. My new friend and I bartered two tickets on a local passenger ferry from the port of Belem at a very cheap rate in exchange for labour tasks on the boat. The next week was spent with us crammed in like sardines, sleeping on hammocks pressed tightly against each other, surrounded by various animals and eating a very unhygienic meal of rice, beans and chicken every day.

The cramped and unhygienic conditions rapidly deteriorated to the point that everyone on board was fighting off bouts of diarrhoea and vomiting, and the boat developed a stench I would rather forget. I decided to relocate my hammock to a new airier location and tied it above the top deck of the boat between two masts making for a much more enjoyable journey.

My first indication that we may have chosen the wrong boat was almost immediately upon departure from Belem, when the boat was surrounded and boarded by local police, resulting in the captain running around collecting cash from passengers to pay a bribe to the armed police. After a little digging around, we realised the main purpose of this vessel was to transport Cocaine, and the passengers were simply a convenient cover for the real operation of drug trafficking.

I spent hours soaking up the sun on the top deck of the vessel, staring out into the vast expanse of the Amazon River, catching glimpses of pink dolphins and incredible bird life. The magnitude and beauty of the place amazed me.

Arriving in Belem my new travelling companion and I stayed with a local family we met, on board the drug boat and I was fortunate enough to experience life as a local. The following days were spent hatching plans to make money and we were blessed by the loving hospitality of this local family who fed and sheltered us for the next week. We eventually came up with a way to secure some much needed funds by rowing down the river to a local logging area and purchasing a large drum of petrol with our last remaining cash. Our one-day paddle downstream turned into a three-day physical paddle back upstream, with our now heavily laden canoe. We spent the next few nights deep in the Amazon jungle, being feasted on by mosquitos and other insects, but we made it back to the village and spent the next few days selling petrol out of empty coke bottles to motorcyclists on a street corner. I had made enough money to secure a ticket on a small sea plane to take me further into the jungle of this incredible country. It was at this point that my new friend and I parted ways and I was on my own again.

My first look at the seaplane I had purchased a ticket for, was a little concerning. It was small with blackened wings from the twin engines on each side. It looked old and in very poor condition and I questioned the wisdom of my decision. However, I pressed on, driven by the lure of the next adventure and where it would take me. We attempted take off three times before the small plane eventually lifted off the river with its heavy load and we slowly climbed. As we gained altitude, I became even more aware of the incredible expanse of the Amazon Jungle below. The plane followed the river for some time before cutting overland and the winding snake like shape of the river was revealed in its full beauty. The turbulence was severe to say the least and even the locals seemed significantly distraught at times. We continued to climb over a mountain range only to take a rapid decent on the other side of the mountain. The plane dove sharply jerking all the passengers back into their seats. A number of people began to scream and pray in Portuguese, frantically crossing their bodies with the sign of the cross and kissing small crosses tied around their necks. The pilot seemed to struggle with the controls and for the first time in my life I thought that I could very easily die. The realisation of how remote we were hit me, and I realised we could crash, never to be seen or heard of again. I remember the feeling of pure fear followed by thoughts of regret that I had not lived a full life as yet and I started praying along with my fellow passengers.

Fortunately, the pilot was able to wrestle the plane under control and conduct an emergency landing on the river below. We anchored the plane and spent the next few nervous hours listening to the pilot and co-pilot banging away at one of the small engines on the wing. My mind was filled with thoughts of having to trek for days through the interior with the few people on-board desperately trying to find civilisation again. After anxiously waiting, the pilots prepared the plane for flight again, we freed anchor and drifted down a section of the river until we found a long straight stretch that would serve as a take-off location.

This experience haunted me for days as I considered my mortality in a way I had never considered it before. I normally felt immune to danger and thought bad things like plane crashes and death only happened to other people. However, during this experience I had no control over the outcome and my life, and I was completely at the mercy of the pilots. For the first time in my life I felt completely helpless. I was so used to taking control of the situations that were presented to me, being the master of my own destiny, or at least believing that I was. I very quickly felt much smaller in the world and realised that I was not really in control of much at all.

I also pondered on the fact that I had turned to prayer in the very instant that I realised that I was not in control of the events unfolding. I was certainly not a religious person at this point in my life, although I did believe in God, and even though I had been given a Catholic upbringing, I was a nominal believer at best. I certainly didn't feel like a religious person. I did however, at that moment, feel a very real and powerful connection to the creator that I was praying to and I was praying with all my heart that he would hear my prayer and somehow intervene to protect all the people on board. I remember praying for the forgiveness of my sins and simply for help. I did not feel like I had a personal relationship with God but I did find peace in the chaos and was able to think clearly as soon as I had prayed. The very real physical and emotional response I had at that point was not lost on me and it served to create a deeper relationship with God and arm me with a tool to face many difficulties in my life. I realised prayer was my comforter and gave me strength in the face of whatever situations life presented.

Before long we were back in the air and soon had reached Manaus, which is located in the middle of the Amazon rainforest. It is known as the "Heart of the Amazon" and "City of the Forest". It was to be the launching pad for my next adventure. I planned to travel deeper into the Amazon Jungle, to experience something not on any Lonely Planet Travel Guide. I knew how to survive in a jungle environment, how to navigate, and how to protect myself. All I needed was a little local knowledge. So, I found a guide willing to take me on a five-day Jungle Safari on a tight budget to teach me the ropes. I can't recall his real name but I called him Smiley on account of him never being without one. We purchased supplies including food, live chickens, some simple fishing equipment, a machete and a detailed map. I already had my sleeping gear, clothing, and basic first aid and navigation equipment. My military training would come in handy as far as navigation, and basic survival such as, keeping my feet dry and avoiding insects and the ability to apply first aid in the event of injury, but I needed to learn more about my specific environment and that is where you just can't beat local knowledge. We headed off in a small canoe with an outboard motor and before long there was no sign of civilisation and I was loving the peace that the river provided.

My goal over the next week with my guide was to ensure I was capable of surviving on my own and to do that we focused on the five keys to survival: water, food, shelter, fire and first aid. Water could be sourced from the river and boiled before drinking and I also carried a fabric filter for added protection against waterborn parasites. I was shown how water could be obtained inland in good quantity through specific vines that grew as thick as your arm. When the vines were cut with a machete they would run like a tap for a few minutes providing sweet clean water. Shelter was easy as I had a 'hootchie' (small plastic sheet), hammock and mosquito net to keep me dry and off the ground and protected from insects. As for fire I simply resorted to my trusty Zippo and waterproof matches for backup. First aid really came down to personal hygiene and an education about the local flora and fauna to better understand how to avoid potential dangers. I needed to know what could kill me and how to avoid it, including poisonous plants and animals such as the arrow frog, jaguars and particularly nasty insects. The week spent with my guide proved to be critical to my survival, as I was introduced to many things I would never have been able to work out on my own, including safely hunting for food such as caiman crocodile, fishing, including catching and eating piranha, anaconda, and even monkey. I was educated on the likely locations of dangerous animals such as tarantulas and scorpions and how to avoid them. We looked for coconuts, squash, cucumber, peanuts and citrus fruits, all of which are plentiful in the Amazon.

At the beginning of my trip I had mentioned to Smiley that I wanted to try a drug known as Ayahuasca. It is traditional medicine brew made out of Banisteriopsis caapi vine, often in combination with various other plants. The brew is used as a traditional spiritual medicine in ceremonies among the indigenous Amazonian peoples. I had heard reports from people who have consumed Ayahuasca that they had spiritual revelations regarding their purpose on earth and the true nature of the universe. In addition, it is often reported that individuals feel they gain access to higher spiritual dimensions and make contact with various spiritual or extra-dimensional beings that can act as guides or healers. It's basically magic mushrooms on steroids and known as the most powerful natural hallucinogen on the planet. This all sounded really amazing to me and I thought I'm only going to have this opportunity once so I might as well find out for myself. Smiley explained to me that the process for making Ayahuasca was difficult and only known to few Shaman or witchdoctors. So our first journey was to a small local village to meet a Shaman. He agreed to make the brew for a small price and we were told to return to the village in four days for the drinking ceremony.

The following week was filled with adventure including swimming with piranha, hunting caiman by night with a machete, fishing and learning about the jungle. My guide, Smiley, and I got along well and quickly developed a friendship enjoying each other's company. Our second last day was spent travelling back to the Shaman's village and meeting the local community. They had arranged to bring a number of people in for the ceremony including five other tourists and some village elders. We were shown to the village communal hut and set up our hammocks. We were treated to a traditional feast with dancing and singing and very excited kids running around. As darkness fell the women and children left and we were moved into a common area and seated in a tight circle on the ground around the Shaman who had poured his black concoction into a two-litre water bottle. He then explained to us that he would conduct the ceremony which would be followed by the offering of the drink. He explained the ceremony was an important part of the process in gaining approval from the spirits to enter into their world.

I was a little concerned, but more intrigued than anything, and I turned to see Smiley sitting close behind me. He lent forward and told me he would watch over me through the entire process and that I would be fine. I trusted my guide and felt at ease with the situation. Looking around the circle I saw a number of American and English tourists and a number of older indigenous men all eagerly excited and soaking up the atmosphere.

The Shaman then broke into a chant and conducted a tobacco smoking ceremony whilst gently hitting everyone in the circle with leaves and blowing smoke in our faces, we were then required to smoke a cigarette and wait while the Shaman poured out a small cup of the black liquid for each individual in the circle. I smelled mine and thought there is no way I would normally drink anything that looked or smelled like this; however, looking around I could see some people had already begun to drink it. So I sent caution to the wind and threw it down the hatch not sure what to expect. The Shaman continued to smoke and chant. It did not take long for the effects of the drug to show themselves on individuals in the circle. One after another they would lie down or role over to throw up violently.

I thought 'what the hell have we drunk? It's poison. I turned to ask Smiley. He reassured me that the throwing up was normal and that the effects would come on soon after. I sat and watched everyone in the circle throw up and move off, or simply lie down in a drugged out haze; however, other than a few stomach rumblings I felt nothing. After ten minutes I again turned to Smiley and said I didn't feel anything so he asked the Shaman for another glass. I drank the second glass and watched, as everyone around me seemed to go into a coma of sorts but still nothing. After another ten minutes or so I asked Smiley to intercede again. The Shaman was nervous and did not want to give me a third glass and some discussion broke out between the locals and my guide. Eventually after some laughing and pointing I was renamed "Iron Stomach" and given a third glass. The effects were almost instant.

I rolled over and crawled to a nearby bush to throw up and could barely get back to my spot. Smiley helped me to lie down and get comfortable and as I lay there looking up at the thatched roof of the community hut above I felt my body get very light. What happened next blew my mind and all I can say is that this drug is extremely potent. I felt my body lift up and float; as I looked back towards the ground I saw myself still lying there. I realised I was out of my body and my initial thought was, 'Oh No! What if I can't get back?' I felt really peaceful and just released myself to go with what was happening and I looked back towards the sky. I passed through the thin roof of the hut and my eyes were drawn to the millions of stars above. I continued higher into the sky until I was about 40 feet off the ground, then I turned and looked back to earth I was flying over the river and I could see all the creatures under the water. I dove down into the water feeling the splash of the warm water as I entered into this world. I swam without the need for oxygen and explored for what seemed like an hour. Then I came up and was immediately drawn to movement on the jungle floor. I chased the animal and felt like I entered into the body of a jaguar, I felt its muscles and heartbeat as I ran across the jungle floor and with ease I was chasing down some small prey and as I caught the animal in my jaws I was ejected back into the sky above. I felt drawn to the earth and entered into it travelling through layers of rock and dust travelling to a location I didn't know.

I spent the next few hours drifting in and out of semi-consciousness at one point waking enough to realise I was in my hammock and that Smiley was sitting up in a chair next to me.

When I finally woke the next afternoon I was told I had slept for nearly 12 hours and I needed to eat something. I arose, ate and washed down in the river to shake off the cloud that surrounded my head. I spoke to a few of the other tourists about their own experiences and all reported having significant hallucinations. I can't say I felt spiritually enlightened by the experience however, I felt like the spiritual world was more real to me in that moment than it had ever been to me prior. I had a lot more questions after this experience than I had answers.

Back in relative civilisation, I had arranged to purchase a canoe from one of the villagers for my week long solo adventure and I was eager to get going. I had marked on my map where I was and the small villages I wanted to travel to, including the village from where I could get my boat ride home. So I set off confident in my abilities and my newly honed skills.

After two days enjoying my independence and surroundings I couldn't shake off the very uncomfortable feeling that I had somehow become very lost in one of the remotest locations on the planet. I tried to reassure myself I would soon come across a village as I continued down river. It wasn't until late in the afternoon that I saw some kids playing on the riverbank and I was flooded with feelings of relief and elation. I honestly don't think I have ever been happier to see another soul. I called out to them but they saw me and ran into the bush.

Paddling over to the bank I dragged the canoe up onto secure ground and headed off on foot to locate my little friends. I quickly came across a very small village of around ten huts and was greeted by a cautious group of men and children. I spoke in my best Portuguese but it didn't seem to help much as I tried to explain how I needed to find a village that received supplies from the city where I could get a boat back to Manaus. The villagers were very friendly and set me up in a communal hut. We ate and drank and laughed trying to communicate as best as we could. I was just happy to have found some people and they just seemed amazed to see a strange white man in their village.

That night I slept for the first time since my solo journey had begun. The next day I spent alongside the village fisherman checking his fishing nets, repairing small holes and watching the slow and tranquil life of the Amazon go by. I remember thinking of all the hustle and bustle of life back in Sydney and how far removed I was from it. I was fascinated and intrigued by the fisherman, who seemed to be the happiest person in the world, living what I considered to be a very simple yet content life; the monotony of this life seemed almost alluring to me. However, I knew I could not stay and after two short days of Amazonian Bliss in the most relaxed village on earth I headed downriver managing to trade my canoe for a lift back to the city where I was able to continue my journey.

My South American Journey was far from over and I would soon travel through some incredible places that quenched my appetite for culture, food and architecture. I visited the city of Cuzco, and walked the Inca trail to the ancient city of Machu Picchu in Peru. I spent a day, free-climbing to the very peak of the mountain that overlooked the ruins below, I took a short detour to a site known as The Temple of the Moon, a ceremonial temple cave carved from the mountain Huayna Picchu near Machu Picchu. The cave is thought to have been used to store mummies and is said to house the three planes of the Inca religion including the world above (Hanan Pacha), the earth and physical life (Kay Pacha) and the underworld (Ukju Pacha). These three planes are also represented respectively by three animals; the condor, the puma, and the snake. It was a rather eerie place thought to be the site of ritual sacrifices. The exhilaration of the climb was enhanced by the thin mountain air that was so cold in comparison to the humidity of the Amazon. I loved being in nature on my own, no limits, no responsibilities or distractions, simply time to embrace the environment and my adventurous spirit.

From Cuzco I travelled further down the Peruvian coast and eventually onto Bolivia, stopping at the highest inland lake in the world, Lake Titicaca. I caught a small boat to an island in the middle of the lake and spent a few days resting from over exertion and altitude sickness brought on by excessive trekking. I eventually decided to stop walking and took a bus South into Bolivia and transferred onto a crowded train for a few days' travel through the harsh Bolivian desert. I was surprised to come across a large number of tall white blonde -haired blue-eyed people in the desert of Bolivia all speaking German and dressed in what I considered very modest traditional clothing not dissimilar to Amish People. I would learn these people were known as Mennonites, a Christian faith descended from German and Dutch people who settled in the region in the 1950's and 60's. I found these people much less hospitable than the Bolivians and they didn't want to have anything to do with me. Unlike in other towns where the locals had opened their homes to me I was forced to sleep in the street through a cold night as I waited for another train to continue my journey South, back to where it had all begun in Argentina.

My journey had quenched the burning desire for adventure within me, at least for a while. I returned to my life in Newcastle; living with a girlfriend, working at the local Army reserve unit a few days a week, and at the pub pouring beers most nights to make enough money to cover rent and food. I started a small business as a Landscape Designer drawing residential landscape designs and completing the physical transformations.

It satisfied both urges in my mind, the mental challenge of design and the physical challenge of labouring. I felt some satisfaction that I was at least using the skills I had gained at University and I enjoyed working for myself. After some initial success I began to look at growing my small business into something bigger; however, I ended up losing a substantial sum of money on a job that went bad and my insurance failed to cover the loss.

Added to this was that my relationship with my girlfriend was breaking down and I wanted out but didn't know how to break it off. I needed to make some money fast to resolve my situation and I immediately looked back to the Army as a way out.

I started working more and more at the Army reserve unit, training Officer Recruits and the Commanding Officer (CO) offered me as much work as I wanted. I enjoyed the training job and quickly made a name for myself at the unit. One evening after a long day and night of training I was speaking with the CO about my desire to go to the Royal Military College (RMC), he wrote me a letter of recommendation on the spot and a week later I had the letter of offer to attend a selection interview. With a letter of recommendation from my Commanding Officer and a degree under my belt it looked like this time I might get in.

I attended the interview and excelled in all areas except my essay writing, my poor spelling and grammar had not gone unnoticed; however, the selection board approved my enlistment and told me I would need to work on my written English skills whilst at RMC. Intakes were happening in a few weeks and I saw this as the opportunity I was looking for to get out of Newcastle and out of a failing relationship so I went home, told my girlfriend I was re-joining the Army, packed a bag and left, never looking back.

I spent my final weeks, prior to going to Duntroon, back in Sydney catching up with family and friends. I enjoyed the time seeing my brothers and I was so impressed with how they were all doing. Mum and Dad were ecstatic at the news of my re-enlistment and could not be happier for me seeing the Military as a very stable and reliable career choice. They were truly happy at the prospect of me becoming an officer and so was I.

Scotty and Johnny, two of my closest school friends had fallen even deeper into the seedy underworld of Sydney's drug scene and were struggling to hold down jobs and girlfriends. I hated seeing my friends struggle and would offer assistance whenever I could but most of the time it was met with an impervious response of everything was fine and I was the one with the issue. The writing was on the wall, my mates were changing and it was clearly for the worse.

Mick on the other had joined the Navy shortly after I left for the Army and was now excelling in his career as a Submariner. We would often talk about the dangerous path our close friends were treading and lacked the ability to help them as we were both travelling all over the country with our employment. It weighed heavily on my soul.

My thoughts were now vastly consumed by my desire to graduate from The Royal Military College, Duntroon. Although I had ended up attending some four years after I had initially applied, I was now there.

Somewhat by chance, a little older, wiser and more mature. I believe I was always destined to be an Officer as I had always been drawn to it from a young age. The urge to join came from a deep burning desire to serve my country, make my parents proud and achieve something of value, that was bigger than myself. I wanted to prove to everyone that I could succeed as an Officer and a leader. My desire to serve my country had only grown over the past few years and I entered into this period of training with a preconception that as a former soldier I knew how an officer should behave, lead and command and I was chomping at the bit to finish my training and get stuck into the real job of leading soldiers.

The next eighteen months were both extremely challenging and rewarding. I made friends quickly and still hold those friendships today. Although we see much less of each other the bond shared through completing RMC together is a strong one only understood by people who go through life-changing situations together. Some of my best mates were much like myself, eager to learn, seeking both adventure and adrenalin, and are just a little bit crazy. We also enjoyed a drink and a party and more often than not blurred the lines of work and play. I was trying to find the balance between achieving my goals and enjoying the ride.

I became particularly close to three guys during my time at RMC; Sam, a skinny kid from Bundaberg with a brain the size of a small planet and a man who loved his rum. Sammy would go on to have a very successful career in the Army as an Armoured Corps officer; he deployed to Iraq before leaving the Army to pursue a career as a Doctor, a career more suited to his natural intelligence. Adrian, a physically strong and mentally tough individual who was also very good at rugby. Butch would go on to have a successful career as an Artillery Officer, deploying to Afghanistan, and even completing the extremely challenging SAS Selection course before eventually succumbing to the effects of PTSD. Butch now chooses to live a quieter life with his wife and kids outside of Defence. And last of all was a strange little fellow named Hugo.

Hugo was somewhat of an enigma, an ex-serving infantry soldier like myself, and with an incredibly high IQ yet, not always making what others would think to be common sense choices and an uncanny ability to land himself in trouble. He was also essentially an alcoholic and needed very little encouragement from the rest of us to spend a night at the pub.

I was competent in the basic military skills of weapons, infantry minor tactics and navigation and as a result breezed through my initial six months of training. This probably set me up with a little false confidence and I tapered my efforts off over the next six months of the course. As a result, I was challenged academically more than I had been challenged previously and came to the realisation that my lackadaisical approach to study through school and university would not get me through RMC. I would struggle in the areas of essay writing, military history and certain aspects of planning and I had to work hard to ensure I passed all subject areas. I had a natural ability to speak and a tactical mind to think my way around the problems and situations presented to me in tutorials; however, it took dedication and hard work to get through; there were no shortcuts or easy paths to take and fakers were quickly weeded out from the ranks and sent packing.

RMC was extremely effective at weeding out those less committed individuals and our class seemed to decrease in number on a daily basis throughout the 18 months. Every individual would stand or fall on his or her own merit. I played the part of a larrikin for much of my first 12 months avoiding positions of authority or prestige, preferring to make my own way quietly in the background and prove my worth independently as I viewed many of the positions of authority as self-serving. The reality is many of the people elected into these positions did a wonderful job and deserved to hold their posts.

The vast majority of trouble I would get into was certainly of my own making and was always associated with my extra-curricular activities whilst on leave and never in relation to my military work. I spent many cold Canberra mornings on the parade ground doing Extra Drills, punishment for my 'un-officerly' conduct, as I struggled with the strict conformity demanded of an Army Officer. In reality I was still a rough around the edges kid, keen to have fun with my friends, and we would often find ourselves in all sorts of trouble as a result of too much alcohol and testosterone. We would occasionally get involved in a fight in one of the bars in Canberra, or be late for a parade as a result of nursing a huge hangover or waking up on the other side of town.

One particular morning I was awoken by a friend saying we had approximately ten minutes to be on parade, having slept for a total of about one hour I jumped into a cold shower got dressed and ran outside to line up with the rest of my platoon. We marched down to the parade ground from up on the hill outside the Kokoda Barracks block and I felt terrible to say the least. I was trying my best not to pass out or throw up on the back of the uniform of the man in front of me and I was behind time in all my drills making the rank and file seem somewhat disorganised. We marched down to our parade position, halted, turned and conducted an open order for a formal dress inspection by the Commandant of RMC. My uniform although not perfect should pass; however, my heartbeat quickened at the thought I had forgotten something in my haste to get dressed. I stood at attention trying to listen to the Commander's address but failing in my fight to stay awake. My eyelids got heavier and heavier until I gave into the lure of closing them completely. I must have blacked out for some time as I was jerked awake by the sharp prod of the Regimental Sergeant Major's stick and standing directly in front of me was the Commanding Officer.

She looked at me and turned to my Company Commander questioning him as to whether "I was asleep". She muttered something to me and continued on in her inspection followed by the all too familiar words from the RSM that I was to report to his office at the completion of the parade for some more "re-training". I didn't know it was possible to fall asleep standing up; however, apparently I had pushed the limits of sleep deprivation and a tenacity to stay on my feet and had managed to achieve just that.

Drill was never my strong suit although I had significantly more practice than other Staff Cadets. On one occasion I was on the parade ground doing sword drill when, at the command salute, I jerked my sword holding hand up with such force that I projected the sword some ten meters to my front and directly towards the instructor who did her best not to break her position in fear. The sword clanged and bounced a few times, to which a number of muffled chuckles were heard, and I simply came to attention and swiftly marched out front using my best drill to collect my sword all this to the complete disbelief of the instructor. If there was a drill movement for such a task I believe I would have pulled it off flawlessly; I don't think the instructor knew exactly what to say and I simply re-joined the ranks and continued the class only to later receive even more Restrictions of Privileges (ROPs) and spend even more time on the drill square.

At the twelve month mark we were given Christmas leave and Hugo and I decided to travel to Europe in search of adventure and a break from the realities of RMC. We flew to Rome followed by New York, London and on to Wimbledon in the South of England to enjoy Christmas with his family. We then travelled through Wales and on to Ireland for New Year celebrations in Dublin and back through England before coming home. This entire trip could be best summed up as a giant pub crawl and Hugo's family expressed their concern on numerous occasions seeing how very wild and carefree we were enjoying our time overseas.

We returned to RMC and I placed myself on the dry for a month in order to recover from our misadventure and focus on the task at hand. Hugo unfortunately never stopped the party and soon became another statistic for flunking out of the College.

RMC was a melting pot of personalities placed in a confined and challenging environment and the pressures placed on individuals would prove all too much for many who started. I was certainly not amongst the academic elite of my class and for the first time did not stand out as the best at anything in particular, although I had my strengths in physical strength, endurance, quick thinking and the ability to talk my way out of any given situation. Amongst this elite group of selected individuals, I found it challenging on many levels simply to maintain my position in the middle of the pack. I was elected, for a leadership position as a Corporal within my Platoon, however, it did not take to long for me to lose my second stripe for misconduct and I would go through a period of regaining and losing my position over my final six months at the college navigating my way through trouble at almost every turn.

It was about this point that I realised I needed to shape up to the expectations of being an Officer in the Australian Army. I realised after 12 months I had forgotten why I was here, what had driven me to join and what I wanted to achieve as an Officer. My career was now on the line and I needed to take life a little more seriously. It was no longer just about having fun and I focused my desire to achieve and excel in my final term at RMC. I had a heap of potential that others had seen in me, including the selection panel, my previous commanders and my own family and friends.

I had opportunities to lead, yet previously, I chose to lead in the wrong areas. My personal qualities needed to come to the fore. The reality that one day soon I could be expected to lead men and women on a battlefield hit me like a ton of bricks and I did not want to be the guy people could not rely on. RMC to me was much bigger than an opportunity to have a good time with mates and chase a few skirts. It was about establishing a name for myself, identifying who I was as a man, and cementing a future career that I could be proud of as a leader, someone people could look up to and respect. I took a good hard look at myself and realised I did not like what I was seeing. I knuckled down, studied hard and excelled during my final six months at the College exceeding all grading requirements and assessments.

I continued to be challenged academically however I had time to show my true potential during the physically demanding field exercises. The harder the challenge the more I liked it, surprising even myself at the levels of discomfort I could operate in and still achieve. I was more capable than I had given myself credit for and I began to grow in confidence.

One of the most difficult exercises we conducted was Defensive Operations in the Puckapunyal Training Area. We were required to dig trenches, command posts and tunnels into hard ground and conduct defensive operations holding ground against an invading enemy force. I distinctly remember questioning the relevance of digging holes with an entrenching tool on the modern battlefield and thinking that this tactic was outdated but I got stuck in and dug my own pit as well as three others. A few short years later I would be reliving this experience on the battlefield of Afghanistan, digging a hole in the ground to protect me from enemy fire and rocket attack.

Over 60% of the people that started the eighteen-month course would not graduate either by self-removal, psychological or medical discharge. The odds were not in my favour; however, after 18 months I stood on the parade ground as part of the graduating class of 2001 and was assigned to the Royal Australian Corp of Engineers, a very highly sought after Corps and one I had worked hard to earn my position in. Unfortunately, of my close mates only Sam graduated with me as Butch was set back six months due to illness and Hugo was discharged due to continual misconduct.

My time spent at RMC is one I will always look back on with fond memories. It shaped the type of officer I would become and pushed me to new limits within myself forging a stronger, more resilient and courageous person willing to do whatever it took to achieve the mission. My mindset was one of servitude to the Army, something much more important than one individual.

Friendships were cemented through a bond only possible by pushing through trying circumstance together and my view of the world had changed. I respected the uniform and the Officers who wore the rank and I wanted nothing more than to serve my soldiers and do a job that I could be proud of.

I took more interest in global affairs, wars and politics and I began to educate myself in things that once meant very little to me. My world has expanded significantly and I was standing on my own two feet as a young man. I was happy to share my opinion on matters and would stand on my beliefs, often debating the intricacies of conflict and peace-keeping operations and how to achieve a mission within the Rules of Engagement without interfering with an individual's civil rights or crossing a moral line that should not be crossed. I had developed a new air of confidence and was ready for the next adventure.

At the point of graduation, I remember feeling a true sense of pride for my achievements and excitement for the career and opportunities that lay ahead. I was also very judgmental and critical of others at this time in my life and would view any form of weakness in an individual as a significant flaw in character. This judgmental attitude was forged on a lack of empathy for others and a desire to climb over people whenever required, without remorse, to get where I needed to be. It was a dog-eat-dog world as far as I was concerned and I would do whatever it took to win.

One of the key things I would learn during my time at RMC was that I needed to take command seriously and that the welfare and potentially the lives of the soldiers placed under my command were my responsibility. It was a great privilege to lead men and women within the Australian Defence Force and I viewed my position as one of great honour. From the day I graduated I vowed to do my best to look after the people under my authority and to do so with as much integrity and courage as I could muster. I would learn throughout my career as an officer that the burden of command was something that should never be taken lightly and something that would challenge my fortitude, moral courage and tenacity to the core.

3

True Love

After Graduation I decided to take a well-earned holiday with mates so we spent the next few weeks travelling up the NSW coast surfing and partying. It was on this trip that I was to meet my soul mate and future wife, Zoe. I was out with Mitch in Byron Bay enjoying the nightlife when I came across a beautiful and amazing young woman who would change my life forever. I knew she was special from the moment I met her and I was immediately infatuated with her. I distinctly remember Mitch giving me grief over my innate ability to pick up chicks and joking that he wanted to throw acid on my face to improve his chances. He dared me to dance with the hottest girl in the place and pointed at this young, tanned, skinny, brunette dancing in the middle of the dance floor like she was the bell of the ball surrounded by seedy guys all trying to impress her like a bunch of peacocks fluffing their feathers. I quickly responded to the challenge and jumped up out of my seat somehow knowing I could not miss this opportunity to meet this striking young lady, pushing past a few guys and with all the confidence in the world I walked up to her, introduced myself and asked her to dance with me!

"I just want to dance with you?" he shrugged as he said it. I could barely hear him over the 'Billy Jean' remix that was playing on the dance floor of 'Coco-Mangas' in Byron Bay. I usually just shrugged the requests off, enjoying a dance on my own or with friends, but there was something about this guy, nonthreatening, genuine even. He could move well with ease, a real bit of swagger about him and loads of confidence. Yep confidence, that was it, there was lots of confidence, that should have given me some indication of the player he was. "I like the way you dance; you dance like J-Lo". I laughed, he was definitely a charmer, I looked up at him in the darkness as he was quite a bit taller than me and thought 'he looks like Ricky Martin'.

I remember she looked stunning, a beautiful olive complexion on her flawless skin, with amazing almond-shaped deep brown eyes, a cheeky smile that dipped at the edge of her mouth. She was what I considered a real natural beauty. Looking at her I had a sense that we had met before; knowing I had not, yet there was a familiarity that I could not put my finger on. She looked me in the eyes and said: 'Sure', and we proceeded to dance to a few terrible 90s disco songs including, Michael Jacksons hit, Billy Jean, in a crowded little nightclub in the middle of Byron Bay.

At the end of the song he walked me over to a booth where a couple of his friends were sitting and introduced one of them as Mitchie. With a hint of jovial annoyance, Mitchie informed me that he had just bet Andy a beer that he couldn't walk over and get me to dance, he rolled his eyes conceding defeat and went to the bar to grab us all a drink. I suppose I should have been annoyed that I was the subject of a stupid bet but I just laughed. There was something refreshing and respectable about these guys, not at all like the guys I knew. Andy and I met when I was 24 in Byron Bay. Life felt a little off track after a few failed relationships. The idea was to be married by now and there were no hopeful prospects on the horizon. By this stage I was pretty unimpressed with the male breed, I thought they were all a bunch self-serving rat bags.
  "You have really nice teeth," Andy said. Okay now this was getting cheesy, but I felt utterly comfortable and special with this guy.

He had beautiful eyes I noticed, not quite green and not quite brown.
I was quite smitten, I was a good girl though so I recognised a pick up when I saw one, but I felt safe.

I always thought you could judge a lot by the way a person looks after their teeth, which to be honest was a little rich considering I had already lost a number of my own in fights due to an inability to duck a decent right hook. I think Mitch had the realisation he was now on his own and he headed to the bar in pursuit of the future Mrs. Mitchell with little success.

I asked Zoe if she was hungry and we left to get something to eat. We found a bakery on Main Street and I thought she was worth the splurge so purchased a couple of meat pies, I even got her a tomato sauce for the extra 20 cents!

He bought me a pie from the bakery and we walked up to main beach chatting and eating.

I asked her why she had agreed to dance with me considering all those guys were clearly interested in her in the club. She told me it was because I was the only guy who came up and introduced myself and asked her to dance! We walked to the beach and ate our pies in the rain, it took me all of about one minute to eat my pie at which point I stood there staring at Zoe eating hers and making her somewhat un-comfortable. In truth she probably felt like I was staring at her and, in part I was, although I was also staring at her pie still being a little hungry.

I don't know what prompted me and timing has never really been my strong suit and I leaned in for the first kiss, half squinting my eyes try-ing to catch her response to determine if my advance was wanted or not. Zoe pushed me away, kindly and said "wait till I've finished my pie"! Then after an awkward period, Zoe said, "Okay, now!" and we kissed.

At one point he swooped in to kiss me, but I had a mouthful, so I pushed him away. He looked rather crestfallen so I hastily said "just let me finish my mouthful, now you can kiss me". He gave me a sweet, gentle lingering kiss, and then it started to rain. He picked me up with a shout of laughter and spun me around. I thought to myself 'this guy is literally sweeping me off my feet'.

I thought wow this chick is awesome. She is beautiful, intelligent and I think she likes me.

It started to pour. Luckily my car was close so we ran over and hopped in. We chatted for what seemed like hours whilst I nervously drew stars on the fogged up windscreen. We both kept looking at each other with some bewilderment realising our common interests.

We spent hours talking and getting to know each other. We spoke about our dreams and aspirations, what we wanted to achieve in life and how we viewed the world, until my dream date was cut short when Zoe said she had to go home. I immediately asked the question, can I come? However, this was met by a swift reply of, "No way, you don't know my parents." Zoe confirmed my suspicions that she was in fact a good girl and would not allow herself to be some notch in a belt or a one-night stand. This just served to fuel my infatuation more and I could not get her out of my mind.

The question of how great we would be together hung in the air but this wasn't the time, he lived in Sydney after all. He explained to me he was on his way to Noosa to conclude his holiday celebrations having just completed his final year of Officers training with the Australian Army.

I was impressed. He spoke with passion and pride about his dreams to serve his country and I felt rather intrigued with the honourable man he was and the potential of whom he was to become. I mean, he was still a player and he tried to get me to take him home then and there, but I told him "I'm not that kind of girl, I live at home", to which he replied, "Parents love me." "Um, you haven't met my parents," I said. We exchanged numbers though. Although I didn't see a future meet up eventuating any time soon. I mentioned meeting this really nice army boy to Mum and Dad the next day. My infatuation with him must have been obvious, because Mum and Dad both gave me questioning looks.

Andy tried to call me later that day, but I was so nervous I didn't answer.

About three months later, I heard on the radio about some Aussie troops getting sent to Iraq and I thought of Andy with some concern. It wasn't until one night shortly thereafter when I was driving home from work in the rain that a bunch of stars reappeared on my windscreen. Memories of our night together came flooding back, so I rang him.

His voice was exactly like I remembered it and his laugh was contagious. I told him what I had heard and that I was worried about him, he assured me he wasn't going anywhere anytime soon.

I continued my trip North and we would not see each other for another four months although she consumed my thoughts. We spoke occasionally on the phone and started to developed a deeper friendship. After about four months I convinced her to come to Sydney where I was working and after spending the planned weekend together she decided to stay longer, much to the displeasure of her family and her work, as she effectively resigned in order to extend her stay with me.

Shortly after my birthday I flew down to Sydney with my sister and met up with Andy. He was just as charming as I remembered. We spent a few days together and when it was time to go home, he didn't want me to leave.

Our connection was undeniable, so I threw all caution to the wind and stayed. Much to my sister's dismay we drove her to the airport to board the plane alone. Andy couldn't believe I had stayed, I called my work and quit my job. I was at a point in my life where I wanted change, and that required action. I wasn't happy with the direction my life was going and the irrational decision to stay felt right, I was listening to my heart not my head.

Zoe stayed in my single room accommodation on base during the week we spent together. I would smuggle her in and out of the barracks block and our relationship grew rapidly.

I couldn't explain why, but I had fallen so quickly head over heels in love with this girl from a small town in Northern NSW and I knew then and there that this was the woman I wanted to spend the rest of my life with. We would sit and talk for hours on end about life, love, spirituality and family.

We decided to get serious and a long distance relationship was established. I focused on graduating from the School of Military Engineering and we spoke almost every day.

The week together was spent with our days on the beach and the nights on the town. When reality finally caught up with us and I felt it was time to go home, Andy said to me that he couldn't let me go without committing to a relationship with me, because 'there was something special about us'.

I agreed with him and the relationship we entered into was with maturity, not ignorance. We both knew a long distance relationship would be difficult, and we laid down some ground rules. I wasn't a push over, I told him. I knew my beliefs in life and I didn't want to compromise the person I wanted to be for any man and I told him as much.

Prior to this, I had discovered I was in Andy's phone as 'Byron Bay Zoe' and I had questioned how many Zoe's were there? Andy assured me that he would take this relationship seriously and would be 100% committed to 'us', his 'player' days were over. He also asked if I thought I could handle being with an officer? I light heartedly told him I'd give it 5 years, but didn't much fancy the idea of living a pseudo single life.

He agreed, as ultimately his goal was to own a property down in Byron somewhere, where we could work for ourselves and focus on lifestyle rather than money, truthfully he was a hippie at heart and I think the army was squashing his rebellious, adventurous spirit. I managed to save my job and we began our long term relationship.

We would talk for hours at night. Sometimes Andy called me in the early hours of the morning following a night out on the town, intoxicated, he would tell me how I made him want to be a better man, often falling asleep mid conversation.

Not long after Zoe left, I received the phone call from my life-long friend Scotty. He seemed quite sad and said he wanted to see me, I agreed to head over and visit him later that night once I had finished work and he hung up the phone. I was tired and I put off the visit telling myself I would drive out to see him after having a rest. A few short hours later and my best mate was dead. I knew he was struggling with a failed relationship and was using various drugs, but I didn't think for a moment he was suicidal. I went through a period of blaming myself for not being there for my friend in his time of need and failing in my role as a best friend.

He had reached out to me just hours before his decision to end his life and I had not understood the gravity of the situation. His death was a complete shock to me and I took it badly. Scotty's family requested I read the eulogy at the funeral and I agreed to do it.

The following few days after his death were extremely difficult for me as I went through the emotions of guilt and grief for my friend. Writing his eulogy was the most difficult task I had ever undertaken. How do you capture the brightness of a man's life, who commits suicide at the age of 25? My mate was gone and I needed support.

Zoe flew down to Sydney to be with me for the funeral and support me during this difficult time. In truth her being there was a huge support and laid the foundation for our relationship. I knew I could count on her to always be there for me during hard times and I was able to talk openly to her about my feelings and emotions.

Zoe acted as my emotional compass reassuring me that this horrific tragedy was not in any way my fault and that I had done nothing wrong. I remember speaking to the priest after the funeral and I asked if he had gone to heaven, to my complete surprise the priest stated point blank that as he had taken his own life he would not in fact go to heaven. I was shocked by this statement and struggled to comprehend what a relationship with God meant and tried to determine what my own beliefs were on this matter.

I spoke to Zoe about her understanding and she assured me that her understanding was that God could reach people at any time and no man can dictate or profess to know if an individual was going to heaven or not and that anything could have happened in those final moments of Scotty's life. Also that his sin was simply that, a sin, and that if he had a relationship with Jesus Christ and had accepted him, that he was forgiven of his sin and pure in the eyes of God. I took a lot of comfort in her words and remember thinking how Catholicism was such a legalistic religion, and made little sense to me, although this idea of Christianity as something other than Catholicism was so foreign to me. It was at this moment that I began to question my Catholic faith and upbringing.

On completion of my Initial Employment Training at the School of Military Engineering I was posted to Darwin in the Northern Territory. I knew now beyond all doubt that Zoe was the girl for me and I was nervous as to whether she would come with me, but to my absolute delight she agreed to leave her family home and employment and throw caution to the wind, joining me on my posting to Darwin all within eight months of us meeting.

I took him home to meet my parents, and they loved him. They even thought his tattoos were cool, well, Mum did anyway. Dad wasn't a fan of the tatts but I think they were more smitten than I was. He slotted so neatly into my vibrant crazy family, it was scary. A great friendship developed between him and Dad and I know Andy respected my father and was in awe of his great gentleness. My mother and Andy would sit up for hours at night debating about politics and religion. My mother's groundwork in those days is still appreciated because she had the confidence to debate what I wouldn't.

My conclusion was that my faith would be evident by my actions not by my words. I knew this to be true as Andy often questioned my ability to love and forgive people so easily.

The first time I walked into Zoe's family home was an incredible experience, a stunning mud brick post and beam home perched on a hill overlooking the volcanic sub-tropical basin of the Mullumbimby Valley.

I was amazed at the home and immediately fell in love with the place. It felt incredibly peaceful and was an absolute credit to Zoe's family who had built the home themselves over a number of years.

Zoe's parents accepted me into their daughter's life in the most loving way and I was awestruck by the incredible relationship she had with them. They openly showed affection and love for one another without discomfort and this seemed so foreign to me, not that I lacked love but simply that it was not displayed in a way I was used to.

A common phrase in the Briffa household was "I love you", one that was rarely said in my own childhood home. Zoe and her mother, Daphne, had cooked every Greek delicacy under the sun and lined them up on a table for my visit. Suffice it to say I was in heaven. I can attest to the saying 'the fastest way to a man's heart is through his stomach'.

Zoe's Dad, Peter, would prove to be one of the most gentle men I have ever met in my life and he was to become a great friend, confidant and mentor, providing support and inspiration to me throughout our marriage.

Daph is a fiery Greek woman with an intense love and passion for anything worth discussing. She would not let anything go unsaid ensuring she had a true understanding of my position on everything from my spiritual beliefs to philosophical views, values and intentions for her daughter. She pressed me on issues of faith, realising that I was a nominal Christian at best and challenged me to look at my relationship with Christ in a very different way than I had ever been challenged to do before. It made me nervous and defensive and I tried my best to deflect questions but I was left with a lingering question in my heart after each of our discussions. It's no surprise to me that the Greeks invented philosophy!

As you can see, it was clear to me that the way to Andy's heart was through his stomach. We spent many nights at my family home in the hills of Byron bay eating and drinking, everything I cooked, the true 'Wog' way. Andy embraced my family, and they embraced him, I knew this solidified our relationship.

We continued our long distance relationship, managing to see each other every second weekend or so. This gave me a taste of what it was like to be involved with a Military man when he would be off on training deployments and would be out of contact for weeks on end.

On one such occasion he had been out of contact for 8 weeks, so I spent my time working, exercising and sun-baking, counting down the days 'till I would see him.

One time I flew to Sydney where he met me at the airport. That night we went out on the town and after a few drinks too many. We thought it would be a great idea to go skateboarding and scootering.

When everyone else went up the hill, I decided to go down, preferring a little bit of speed and exhilaration. It ended poorly, as you can imagine. Coordination was not my strong suit and that certainly wasn't about to improve after a few drinks. I ended up face planting on the road with bloody grazes all the way from my chin to my knees and putting out my shoulder joint to boot. It was not a pretty sight!

The next morning, I was so stiff and in so much pain, I had to go to emergency where they dressed me like a bandaged bear and gave me a tetanus shot in my good arm. I was so depressed, I had waited so long to see him and now I looked horrible.

I completed some further training in Puckapunyal Victoria, and Zoe flew to Melbourne to meet me for what was to be a 5,273km road trip to Darwin, from Melbourne, via Sydney, Brisbane and onto the Northernmost city of the Australian continent. It was whilst we were in Sydney that I received a call from my long-time friend Johnny (who was still fighting his own demons, battling with a serious heroin addiction and suffering from anxiety and depression.)

After only recently going through the loss of our mate Scotty, I really didn't want to fail my other best friend and I felt I should do anything I could to support him. Zoe and I visited his parent's house and I decided we would take Johnny to Darwin with us, in an attempt to clean him up and give him a new start in life, away from the Sydney drug scene and his circle of junkie friends. In truth I didn't really give Zoe an option and looking back, I think it was an unrealistic expectation and burden to place on Zoe who was effectively giving up her entire life to join me. Yet, here I was about to take along one of my junkie mates for the ride. Zoe's commitment to me in moving away from her entire life was huge, yet now she was expected not only to live with me, but also with my drug addicted friend. To be honest my commitment to friendship was a little over the top and my priorities should have been with my soon to be fiancé; however, I was so over-whelmed by the recent death of my mate Scotty, that I had a burning desire to help another friend in need, and Zoe agreed to support me. Now the three of us continued on to Byron Bay to spend a few days with Zoe's parents. This is where I had planned to ask her father for her hand in marriage.

We camped at the famous Brunswick Heads caravan park where Johnny showed his lack of crab catching skills, almost losing the end of his thumb to an aggressive mud crab, and causing him to shake his hand so violently that he was left with nothing but a claw still attached to his thumb. Zoe and I were in stitches of laughter as this went on and we eventually filled our bellies with the crab.

There was no doubt in my mind that Zoe was the woman I wanted to spend the rest of my life with. She captured my spirit and saw in me the man I wanted to be. She made me accountable and gave me the desire to honour her, protect her and provide for her. She was very clear about her Christian faith but never pressed it upon me, al-though I was often intrigued by her constant willingness to forgive and help people. This was manifested one day at Byron when Zoe took me with her, for moral support, to forgive an individual who had hurt her very deeply in her life. The significance of this confrontation was a very difficult thing for Zoe to go through and I am still amazed by the level of forgiveness and acceptance she displayed on that day.

She continues to be my moral compass and keep my conscience to the fore during difficult times driven by her grace and love for others. This moment made me evaluate everything I knew about forgiveness and acceptance, as I had easily hated and hurt people for much less in my own life, in pursuit of my own sense of justice. The realisation that I was incredibly blessed to have her in my life was not lost on me.

Her father Peter said he could not be happier when I asked for his blessing in marrying his daughter. I kept the news to myself, as I wanted to get into Darwin before proposing to Zoe. I think she had a fairly good idea though as she had spent a day picking out a ring with her mother from a local antique store. So I purchased a second hand diamond ring from an antique jeweller in Lismore, blindly lead there by my soon to be wife and my plan was almost complete.

We continued on our journey north with all our belongings for our new life together tightly packed into a box trailer, wrapped in tarps and bound with rope. I thought the load would be okay for our journey; however, once again I was to be proven wrong. We took extra water, food and fuel, understanding the extreme distances and isolation we were to travel through. We continued our journey Northwest via Roma, Longreach and Mt Isa, stopping along the side of the road to sleep in swags under the desert sky. On one night we decided to sleep alongside a public toilet in the middle of nowhere as we thought the lure of a flushing toilet was too hard to pass up. Unfortunately, this concept of 'glamping' turned into a horror scene as I escorted Zoe into the toilet block and the walls appeared to move. Upon closer inspection the toilet block had been overrun by a swarm of locusts of Biblical plague proportions. We ran out of there, Zoe screaming and insisting she preferred to pee behind a bush rather than even contemplate entering the infested, isolated building again.

It was within a few short months that Andy asked me to move to Darwin with him. We discussed continuing our long-term arrangement as I had just been offered a great managerial job within the bank on the Gold Coast. He wasn't keen on the idea of us staying apart so I agreed to move to Darwin with him and consequently passed up the job offer. Much to my surprise when I met Andy for the big drive to Darwin he had brought his mate Johnny to come with us. I thought it strange that he hadn't told me or even given me a choice in the matter considering we were moving in together and it didn't sit well with me. I understood that Johnny was struggling at the time with drugs and Andy wanted to help him out, but had my reservations at not being asked considering it would affect me so greatly. This was soon to be a proven trend with Andy. The pecking order was mates, Military then me. I respected and understood his decision but had my trepidations about living with a guy I had only met briefly, who appeared to be a rather loose cannon. My gut instincts proved correct as Johnny became completely dependent on both of us. We worked long days to return home to find Johnny asleep in bed having lost yet another job due to his drinking and drug addiction. Removing him from his drug environment in Sydney did nothing to curtail his addictions as he had found new ways and means in Darwin. His presence became a strain on both of us and it seemed no matter what handout we gave him; we couldn't help someone who didn't want to be helped. Andy ended up asking him to leave as it was beginning to put a dark shadow over our relationship. I know this was hard for Andy as he had only just recently lost another mate to suicide and he blamed himself somewhat for not being there enough for him.

Sacrificing my position with the bank and arranging a transfer to a teller position was very unsatisfying and I absolutely hated it. I found it terribly monotonous, but the compromise was worth it to be with Andy. Compromise is what makes a relationship work, isn't it? I quickly realised that my career and my goals would take a serious backseat to his, and it did.

The landscape in the Australian Outback was surreal and at times it almost felt like we were on another planet passing kilometres of red barren land with dry scattered grass and occasional fencing, but soon all signs of human habitation had given way to extreme isolation. Not even another vehicle to be seen on the road for hours at a time. Only coming across the occasional abandoned 4x4 on the side of the road. I was awestruck by the sight of huge termite mounds that stretched two to three meters in the sky breaking up the otherwise completely flat desert landscape where you could see the curvature of the horizon in the distance. The landscape was like nothing I had ever seen before and it took my breath away.

Further into the harsh interior we would pass kilometres of red boulders scattered along the flat open desert like giant marbles across a carpet of red earth. We could have been driving across Mars for all we knew. As we hit the Three Ways and headed Due North the harsh red dust gave way to an ever increasing sea of tropical greenery getting denser and denser the further North we travelled. The journey itself was rather uneventful until Johnny was driving at around 140km/h. The roads had open speed limits and he ran directly over a large steel belt that must have come off a truck at some point and lay directly in our path. The impact tore out a large portion of the exhaust and damaged the fuel tank. Further down the road I heard something shift in the trailer and watched our newly purchased dinner set bounce out the back and down the highway, I pulled up and quickly realised we had lost a number of boxes out of the trailer, probably shaken loose by the previous impacts. We lost a number of household items Zoe had purchased for our new home together and I felt terrible about the entire situation. The stress of the trip was something quite new to Zoe. I could see the worry growing on her face as she probably questioned her decision to leave her comfortable life, to pursue a new life with some crazy Army guy and his junky friend, to the furthest reaches of the country.

Unfortunately, this was not our only accident as we decided to push our luck a little further, driving through dusk, the most dangerous period on the day. We had been warned repeatedly of the risk of driving at these times due to the vast number of big red kangaroos found along the roadside at that time of the day, the reason being that there was always a small stretch of green grass along the side of the roadway, due to the extra rain runoff from the road. This provided a lush feeding zone for the local fauna. We pushed our luck a little too far when we hit a big red roo at about 140km/h. Fortunately we hit the big fella on his upward bounce, his legs and tail smashing into the bonnet as his body flipped up bouncing off the windscreen and falling between the car and trailer. The trailer jerked violently and after regaining control of the car we pulled over to review the damage. The radiator was leaking badly as the front end of the car had taken a significant hit. Lucky for us we were able to limp into the next town to do some temporary repairs. My future wife was not the only one concerned at the beating that my car had taken, but whether we could get to Darwin and complete our journey unscathed. Once we finally arrived, I lost my car for repairs for over a month and scored a stinky, wet-dog-smelling bomb, courtesy of the garage. We settled into a rental property in the suburb of Durack.

Darwin was a blast, a city of extremes. We partied like never before and settled into the idea of living in this unique city. We felt more like we were in Southeast Asia at times rather than in Australia's Northernmost city. The nightlife was brilliant and the days were uniquely hot, humid and rainy. You could set your watch by the afternoon downpour, it was so predictable. We acclimatised quickly spending much of our time out and about in the elements.

I was certainly thrown into the deep end in Darwin with my first taste of what being an Officer's wife meant. It sounds glamorous doesn't it? You'd be forgiven if you thought so, I mean I did, but it's not all 'Officer and a Gentleman'-like. There were glimpses of that, but reality hit hard when early on in our move to Darwin, which may as well be in a different country, he was posted to 'Op Relex' which entailed three months away at sea.

So here I was. I had basically left my family, my friends and my promising career to move to a place in the middle of nowhere, alone! It was daunting to say the least and lonely! Yet, those feelings of abandonment, and loneliness would become and are commonplace for an Officer's wife. I pondered the fact that every time we'd move, I'd have to find a new position and new friends. The new friendship thing was exhausting and would prove to certainly add to the loneliness I felt. I would find people I could see myself getting along with and try to grow a friendship with them. All too often these friendships weren't that meaningful as I knew I would leave again. It's not surprising that my closest friends today are mostly from my youth. Luckily Mitchie, whom I'd met in Byron was also posted to Darwin and moved in. He proved to be a great house mate and drinking companion during Andy's absence. We spent many nights on the town over-indulging in Alcohol and seafood, and the days were spent water skiing and shooting. He just made Darwin fun and was a great 'partner in crime'. When Andy returned he saw the brother and sister relationship that had developed between Mitch and I, which he viewed with a degree of scepticism and quickly found his way back into the household. Those were good days but were abruptly cut short as Mitchie found himself serving a lengthy stint of guard duty following some orderly misconduct, courtesy of one of those nights on the town in which he was found conducting traffic in the early hours of the morning.

It was at this time that I decided to execute my formal proposal to ask Zoe to marry me, I heard of a place called Cullen Bay and found out that there was a well-known seafood restaurant on the bay. So my plan was complete. With a reservation confirmed and my pre-loved ring in my hand I took Zoe out for what was supposed to be an incredibly romantic night. However, when we arrived at the restaurant in our best clothing I quickly realised I had not done my reconnaissance as the locals, who were dressed in their Darwin best of thongs, stubbies and a singlet for men and women. I quickly realised this place was more like your local budget buffet rather than a romantic restaurant and my proposal plans seemed to be under attack. We sat down and tried to enjoy a meal amongst screaming kids and the constant onslaught of people attacking the self-serve, all-you-can-eat seafood buffet. I buried my head in my hands thinking it's not happening the way I had pictured it in my mind.

Not all was lost, as Zoe seemed to know something was happening and she tried to brighten my outlook on the evening. We finished our meal and headed down to the beach for a romantic stroll along the foreshore, although the well-known crocodile-inhabited beach put Zoe on edge and she refused to venture any further down to the water. Realising the environment was clearly not with me on this evening I decided 'bugger it' not wanting to admit defeat I dropped to one knee and asked the question: "Will you marry me!" Zoe with one eye on me and the other warily on the lookout for crocs in the background, excitedly and nervously said: "Yes!" Maybe more out of fear of being eaten and wanting to get out of a rather precarious situation than anything else. I leaned forward to place the ring on her finger and in true form dropped it into the bloody sand below! I started combing the sand for the ring as Zoe, now panicking, yelled at me not to comb for it and in her womanly way, with a diamond at risk, found it in an instant picking it up placing it on her finger. Grabbing my hand and dragging me off the beach. My job was done! A romantic meal, followed by a calming stroll along the beach and a heartfelt proposal in an area bearing the name my fiancé would take once we were married. Perfectly executed Andy! I thought to myself and the phrase, "time spent in reconnaissance is seldom wasted"! rang in my ears. No harm no foul, she had agreed to marry me, and we celebrated into the early hours of the morning.

Spiritual Attack

The next period of my life was rather tumultuous. I was settling into a new position as a Troop Commander, (my first command position leading soldiers) and enjoying my role. At home I was finding my way into a deeper relationship commitment, with Zoe and I was also helping out a friend in serious need. Johnny had found work and was living with us. At this time, although it was difficult, he was staying dry. One particular Sunday morning I was walking in our neighbourhood with Zoe and we passed a Baptist church; I felt an urge to go in and I asked Zoe if she would come with me. I don't know why, as I had not been thinking about religion. It was simply a spur-of-the-moment decision. I had absolutely no idea what to expect as I had never set foot in any church other than a Catholic church before, so all I knew of church was badly sung hymns, standing up, kneeling and sitting down on command.

Zoe looked at me, a little bemused by my request, but agreed to follow me in. I think the service must have been on for some time as everyone in there was already seated and listening to the pastor give a message. We found a seat near the back and sat down to hear what was being taught. For some reason, and I can't explain exactly why this occurred or when or how it did, but I heard this man preach a message of Jesus Christ as *my* Lord and Saviour that I had never heard preached before. It resonated so strongly in my heart that after about twenty minutes the pastor asked if anyone there wanted to know Jesus and did not know Him, to raise their hand.

I immediately shot my hand up in the air, confidant that he was speaking directly to me and that I wanted and needed to know Jesus. I felt an undeniable connection to the name of Jesus. I was not afraid to commit myself to him. Zoe looked at me with equal measure of shock and amazement. I then walked to the front of the church and the pastor prayed for me and asked me again if I wanted to commit my life to

Jesus Christ. I boldly said: "Yes, I do," not even really understanding the gravity of what I was doing.

At the completion of the service we were ushered into a side room and a few members of the church asked us for personal details like our home address and phone numbers etc. I looked at Zoe and said: "Let's go", suddenly feeling very uncomfortable. I no longer wanted anything to do with that church or anyone in it. We left and walked home the whole way talking about how crazy and spontaneous my decision was. Zoe was very happy for me as she was a Christian and had a very strong personal relationship with Christ. She has always held onto her faith, however, she had never pressed her beliefs on me. I would occasionally ask her questions more out of curiosity than anything else, but that was about the extent of it. I couldn't explain the desire that filled my soul to openly confess my belief in Jesus as my Saviour but it was so undeniable in that moment that I could not ignore it.

That night we went out for dinner returning home around nine. Dinner was nice and we enjoyed a normal evening out until, in the car on the way home. I became very agitated, angry and aggressive. I don't know why or even what set the change off but I started swearing and cursing at Zoe and felt very overcome with fear. We pulled up in the driveway and I remember feeling a heavy, cloudlike object pressing over me and I started fighting with it to get it off. All the while Zoe kept asking: "what's going on? Are you okay?"

I got out of the car in the front yard of our rental property and looked up at what I can only describe as a black shadow of a figure attacking me as if it were trying to enter into me and control my body. It had rootlike tentacles that would try and bind under my skin and I furiously tried to pull and shake it off. I realised how utterly crazy this was and tried to convince myself it was not happening; however, it was very real and very physical.

Johnny, hearing the commotion, came running outside asking what was going on, I immediately asked him to help me, trying to explain something was attacking me. He looked at me like I had lost my mind and to be perfectly honest I thought I had. I probably looked like someone trying to escape a swarm of bees. He asked Zoe if I had taken any drugs and I said I had had a few beers at dinner, certainly not enough to cause demonic hallucinations. I truly felt like I was losing my grasp on reality. I grabbed Zoe and begged her to help me all the while thinking, I'm going to be locked up in some mental asylum, lose my job. My life, as I knew it would be over, not to mention the terrifying fear that this thing, whatever it was, could come back and attack me again at any moment.

Zoe and Johnny ushered me inside the house and tried to calm me down but the attacks kept coming in waves. I grabbed for a phone book and looked up a local catholic church. Frantically dialling the number. A priest answered the phone. I tried to explain what was happening and reassured him that I was not on any drugs and did not have a mental condition. He asked me what I had done earlier that day and I remembered going into the church and accepting Jesus as my Saviour. I looked at Zoe as I said the words and a chill hit me, tingles flooding my entire body, I suddenly realised what I had done. The decision I had made earlier that day was much more significant than anything I could have comprehended and I had given it very little to no thought as soon as it was over. I was so very scared at that moment that I did not know what to do.

The sound of the priest's voice in my ear faded out and I heard Zoe saying: "Talk to my Dad." My rational brain kicked in and I said: "There is no way I'm talking to your Dad about this, he will think I'm crazy! He won't want you marrying me!" I pictured my life falling apart in that one moment.

She put the phone in my hand and looked me in the eyes, begging me to talk to her father. I saw the absolute fear in her eyes, she was panicked, tears flowing down her face, and I turned and looked at Johnny who at this point had retreated to a corner also looking at me with fear and disbelief. I lifted the phone to my ear and said: "hello." Peter answered as calm as anything and said 'mate, what's going on?' I frantically tried to explain and he calmly said: "It's easy mate, just call out in the name of Jesus." I almost couldn't comprehend what he was saying or how calm he was. I thought, 'did you not just hear what I said about the weird black fog attacking me.' He said it again, "Call out in the name of Jesus for this thing to go away." So I looked up and in the smallest voice with no confidence at all I called out, "In the name of Jesus, leave me alone!"

I was in tears at this point not knowing if this nightmare would ever end and in an instant all the chaos and anger and fear left me and left the house, I handed the phone to Zoe not even capable of talking and just sat on the floor in complete disbelief of what had just transpired. I thought to myself that what just happened defies belief. I'm an educated man with what I thought to have a fairly good grip on the world around me and yet I had no logical explanation for what had just occurred. Shortly after this experience Zoe embraced me and told me that I was fortunate to have experienced something so tangible as I could not deny the truth as a result.

Zoe's account of this event differs slightly from my own in that I seem to have lost moments and have no recollection of certain events. She would later tell me that during this attack she told me that it was a spiritual attack as a result of my actions in the church earlier that day. Apparently I grabbed her and looked at her with eyes that were not my own. Apparently they were black, restless and piercing. Zoe retreated to her room and locked the door calling her Dad for help.

I vowed never to speak of this event again and asked Johnny and Zoe to respect my decision as something had happened that I could not explain and that scared me to the core. This was my first real spiritual experience outside of praying in the plane ride and my experience with Ayahuasca in South America and it was all too real, too much to handle. I knew one thing at that point, there is a very real battle between good and evil going on around us and I wanted nothing to do with it. This experience scared me so much it would take a few years before I was to even consider spirituality again and it was over a decade before I was comfortable enough to discuss the events of that night. What I had felt and seen on that night was so real that I felt like I was in a fight to hang onto my very soul. I returned to work the following day doing my best to push the memory of the previous night behind me never wanting to recall it again.

Not long after this event Johnny began using heroin again resulting in him losing numerous jobs and not being able to support himself financially. He had found the same type of druggie crowd in

Darwin that he was running away from in Sydney. The financial and emotional toll became too much for us. We sent Johnny home on a flight back to Sydney. I felt bad that I was not able to help him break free from his addiction; however, we had tried and the reality was that he simply was not ready to leave his addiction and I needed to focus on my new fiancé and the idea of building a new life together. I still carried guilt for a time over the fact that things didn't work out.

4

First Deployment

A little later I was selected to lead a team of forty odd Army personnel made up of Engineers, Artilleryman, Military Police and Medics on Operation Relex II. An operation conducted in conjunction with the Royal Australian Navy, targeting illegal immigration, smuggling and illegal fishing of the Northernmost reaches of Australian National waters. Zoe was thrown into the deep end of being a Military spouse, now fending for herself for the next four months, in a new town and far from the support of family and friends.

Op Relex was my first real test of command, controlling the tactical and logistical aspects of the operation were relatively simple. It was the disciplinary and personnel issues that were to prove a challenge and took up much of my time. I enjoyed the role of boarding parties and even enjoyed our time at sea initially; however, three months of ship transfers at sea, residing in the nooks and crannies of a frigate as a relatively unwanted guest, did test my patience. I would invent requirements to get the team to land whenever possible, stating reasons such as Army training requirements or the need to conduct land-based operations such as Observation Posts (OP's) on Christmas Island. We enjoyed the opportunity to test our skills against our Navy friends and on one ship, HMAS Canberra, we established a Navy vs. Army Military style Olympics involving everything from shooting, navigation, pack marching, obstacle crossings and long distance running.

Most of my time at sea, I felt that I was missing Zoe. I was fortunate to have email contact and the occasional satellite phone call home. By far the most challenging aspect of this deployment was dealing with a young suicidal member of the unit who had openly discussed killing himself. I was deeply concerned for this individual's welfare and thought he needed support and 24hour care. After speaking with him it was clear to me his threats of self-harm were serious and I needed to act. There was some talk of this being a ploy to get back home and the mutterings of 'malingerer' and 'bludger' were heard throughout the troop. I was not willing to take the risk, being all too familiar with how final a momentary lapse in decision-making can be. I placed the member under 24 hour watch and informed the chain of command of the situation. This member was well cared for and evacuated within a day or two for further treatment and support back in Australia and I could get on with the day to day operation at hand. I was very impressed with how the Navy approached and handled the individual and was happy to hear that he recovered fully from this period of darkness in his life. I have seen the isolation of deployment eat away at individuals. Some people handle it better than others. Some people really struggle being away from loved ones, whilst others are simply able to concentrate on the task at hand and return home happy to see their loved ones. I was a bit like the latter group. Although I missed Zoe, and I found it comforting to bury myself in my work and concentrate on the task at hand. I did not want to allow myself to long for Zoe. I would actively try to stop myself from thinking about her too much as it was not helpful. It's not that I didn't care how she was coping, or missed her any less than other people missed their loved ones, it was simply a survival mechanism I employed to get through extended periods of absence.

The only other real issues we needed to deal with, were the occasional punch up between Army and Navy personnel. Tempers would flare on occasion, more as a result of us constantly being in their way. I did have one personal run-in with a young Navy Lieutenant who was the Liaison Officer based on Christmas Island and my contact for whenever my Troop was to stay on the island. We did not get on from our first meeting, as he tried to undermine my authority over my unit and attempted to order me about in front of my soldiers, on the docks. I asked this individual to follow me behind a few shipping containers out of sight and earshot of my Troop and began to tear verbal shreds off this clown, leaving him under no illusion that I was in command of my people and he was simply an administrative liaison for our transportation and accommodation arrangements, whilst we were on the island. The argument got a little heated and I did punch the fella in the face when he grabbed me as I turned to walk away.

I instructed my Troop Sergeant to take the Troop to their accommodation and requested my Military Police Sergeant to accompany me back to the ship. I informed him I had struck the Navy Officer and was required to report the incident that had occurred. I assumed the Navy Lieutenant may wish to press charges against me. On return to the ship I was taken to the Captain and addressed in his cabin. I quickly learned that the individual was a massive pain in the backside and that everyone on board was extremely delighted to hear that I had dealt with him in that manner. Charges were never laid and I was given a stern warning, along with a pat on the back and told to give the individual a wide berth during our time on the island. I was relieved that nothing came of the incident and continued with my duties.

The entire operation itself went without incident. People were cleaned, fed and quarantined and then transferred to Christmas Island detention centre for processing. There was no mistreatment of individuals and for the most part people complied with instruction, happy to receive a shower, clean clothes and food. We did come across some very smelly fishermen in what struck me as extremely small fishing craft in a very large ocean. The bottom of their small vessels were lined with shark fins and I wondered how many sharks were thrown into the ocean to die. It struck me as a huge waste of a vital resource. Some individuals would try to prevent boarding with machetes or spears, but were quickly overwhelmed and I never felt like we were in much danger. The biggest risk of injury or death was going overboard, particularly at night, as we were in areas of the ocean that were extremely remote, very deep and subjected to violent storms at short notice. We conducted the occasional ship transfer at night via Rigid Hulled Inflatable Boat (RHIB) and would climb up rope nets cast over the side of the vessels and lift the RHIBs into position via winch, a very exhilarating experience.

As the Army commander on board I was fortunate enough to go for a number of reconnaissance flights in the Navy's Sea King Helicopters and I enjoyed my time in the air immensely. I was always a little nervous on landing as the ship below would rise and fall with the swell, the pilot would need to judge his timing precisely to place the aircraft down on the landing pad at the rear of the vessel. I am reminded of the dangers of this manoeuvre, considering the fatal incident that occurred on 29 November 2006, when an Australian Army S-70A Black Hawk helicopter operating from HMAS Kanimbla crashed and fell overboard, while attempting to land on the aft helicopter deck. Of the ten Army personnel on board, eight were injured, one was killed, and the tenth was declared missing until his remains were found on 5 March 2007, trapped in the helicopter wreckage 3,000 meters below sea level.

On one particular morning I had an incredible encounter with a whale shark off the coast of Christmas Island. I was fortunate enough to swim next to the shark for a short period. The size of the animal was incredible and the patterns on its body just beautiful. I was amazed by the beauty of the ocean and everything that lived in it, fearing it at the same time. The last uncharted territory of our planet. It made me realise just how small we are when swimming over the coral reef to the continental shelf, where the land simply drops away into a deep dark abyss. One minute the ground was a few meters below clearly visible and then just darkness. I imagined giant sharks swimming below looking up at me like a wounded seal which made me quickly move back to the safety of the shelf.

Another experience I will never forget is the feeling of swimming in the open ocean. We had snipers posted on high points along the ship with the duty of 'shark watch" and tasked with shooting at any sharks that may wish to feed on the unfortunate swimmers below. Fortunately, no sharks attacked during our time in the water and we swam in an area of the Indian Ocean that was literally kilometres deep. I remember feeling incredibly small compared to the world around me. It was a very eerie feeling and as a result I did not spend a great deal of time in the water. I know from the months spent at sea that I am a land lover at heart. I did not get sea sick as a rule, although my stomach was certainly tested during one rough storm that saw me strapped to the chair on the bridge wing as the frigate powered towards Darwin on our final push home. The frigate would lurch over enormous swells as I watched the entire bow disappear into the deep blue-grey water and shooting enormous sprays of white water over the bridge, only to be violently pushed back to the surface once more. It was like a horrible rollercoaster ride that just would not end. During our time at sea we had spent time on HMAS ANZAC, HMAS Arunta, HMAS Canberra, HMAS Adelaide and various patrol boats. I was very glad to see the conclusion of this deployment and my short yet interesting stint with the Royal Australian Navy.

Newly married

During my absence Zoe was busy planning our wedding, with lots of assistance from my Mum and Dad, and I was back in Darwin for all of one night before flying to Sydney to meet her and do some final preparations for the big day. Zoe had even picked a suit without me and I tried it on the night before we were to be married. We were married in North Sydney in front of our family and friends and I was the happiest man alive. I had somehow managed to convince this incredible beautiful and loving woman to be my wife. She had looked past all of my misgivings and flaws and seen the man she wanted to spend the rest of her life with.

In 2004 Andy and I were married, I remember the day before as we discussed our future, I said to him, 'I would take first place now, it would be me before his mates and Military'. Looking back now, I recognise this as an ineffective and desperate attempt to address the growing foreboding feeling of the underlying issue.

The act of marriage was a sacred commitment to us both and we knew there would be good times and bad but we dedicated ourselves to the goal of always staying together no matter what. Over the years, circumstances would prove to test this commitment to the very edge, but Zoe's strength and belief in us, as a union, would never fail. Looking back, our wedding day is still one of my happiest memories of my life, as I felt like I had found everything I could ever want in another person and more.

We returned to Darwin to complete our posting and made the most of our love of the outdoors with regular camping, fishing and boating adventures in the croc-infested regions of the Northern Tropics.

Back to Sydney with a posting to Holsworthy we lived in Coogee, in Sydney's Eastern Suburbs. Life was great, I was enjoying my work and Zoe was working for a large company. We were finally earning good money and trying desperately to save for an overseas trip. We were making the most of Sydney and enjoying the opportunity to regularly see family and friends.

Having grown up in the hills of Byron Bay to second generation Greek and Maltese parents I was no stranger to culture, but we rarely ventured outside of the northern rivers aside from the occasional visit to family in Sydney, so by the time I met Andy I was ready to conquer the world. In the space of the first few years of our marriage I went from a relatively naive and sheltered young girl to a seasoned traveller and I loved it!

We finally took our delayed honeymoon that we had planned for some time, and as it was Zoe's first time overseas we wanted to ensure it would be a memorable holiday We packed up and headed off to Europe to visit Zoe's family origins in Greece and had an amazing adventure travelling throughout the Greek Isles and onto Turkey. Zoe shared my desire for travelling and adventure. She was fascinated by culture, food and music and we landed in Athens and made our way to a hostel I had found in a lonely planet guide. On arrival Zoe made it very clear, she did not want to stay in a shared room on our honeymoon so we left to find more suitable accommodation. We found a place with our own room and a rooftop balcony that overlooked the Pantheon. Very romantic. We did have to share a bathroom with other guests on the floor and the lack of hot water in winter was undesirable, to say the least, but we made the most of it buying some cheap local wine, a tub of olives and some bread. We were in heaven; a dream to see Greece was realised on a very tight budget. Situated right in the heart of Plaka, the old city centre, we spent the days walking through the streets, taking in the sights and sounds. Followed by dinners long into the night. We soon headed off on an island hopping trip with the main goal of getting to Simi, a small island off the coast of Turkey where Zoe's mother and grandparents came from.

Boarding a giant ferry, we set sail stopping off at a number of Islands before spending some unforgettable nights in Simi. We were amazed by the simple and slow life afforded to the locals. Eating incredible seafood, swimming in the Aegean Sea and riding mopeds around the island. We even visited a local church where Zoe's great grandfather was a priest. It was exactly what we wanted to do, to solidify memories of an otherwise unknown ancestry. It was our first overseas adventure together and we loved each other's company. After returning to Athens we hired a car and spent about two weeks driving the mainland across to Corinth and Sparta and stopping whenever we felt the need, at small fishing towns. The freedom was great, to do as we pleased. We met some lovely locals and had great moments exploring the countryside.

We decided to spend 6 weeks in Greece and Turkey for our honeymoon, where I got a bit of first-hand insight at the way Andy travelled. He sought authentic experiences in every encounter, where I was much more reserved and cautious. From my point of view it was a careless complacency, that more often than not found us in some rather precarious situations and questionable company. On one occasion an Australian girl, whom Andy had befriended on a ferry en route to Santorini, tried to manipulate us into spending the night in our hotel room, because she hadn't organised accommodation or something. That was her excuse, anyway. I remember her following us to our hotel room. Andy and I were looking at each other questioningly?

In the end Andy had to uncomfortably address the situation and say no. Andy might have felt a bit guilty for saying no, because he recognised a like-minded traveller, I on the other hand, was horrified! I had instantly disliked her and was suspicious of her motives which had proven opportunistic and inappropriate. Another individual we met up with on our travels, whom I also viewed with reservation and scepticism, that Andy failed to acknowledge; later revealed he had fled Australia on an allegation of rape!

We then headed to the ski village of Delphi and had what I would consider a very scary experience with a number of Albanian's who were living there. What started out as a fun night playing pool and dancing, ended with our drinks being spiked and my realisation that we were in real danger.

We were sitting in a nightclub in town enjoying a drink and speaking with a few guys who seemed harmless enough, however, after I left to go to the toilet, I realised Zoe was very upset. I asked her what had happened and she grabbed me and walked away from the table. She explained that the guy had made a pass at her and that she felt strange. I recall getting quite angry and looked back toward the table we were at. By now there were three guys talking and pointing at us.

Undoubtedly, this was a most dangerous circumstance and it saw me 'Rohypnoled' (date-rape-drugged) and nearly being kidnapped by some Albanians right in front of Andy's eyes! If it hadn't been for the assistance of some rather savvy Greeks that we had met earlier in the day on the Ski fields of Arachova, I shudder to think of the outcome. They managed to sneak us out of the night club with a complete protection party and transport us back to safety.

My skin crawled and I felt the effects of something more than alcohol in my system. My mind immediately went to the worst case scenario of me being overpowered and beaten and Zoe raped or worse. I looked around for a weapon or help and spotted a local Greek guy we had spoken to earlier in the day. He worked in the ski hire shop and I grabbed him explaining what was going on. At this point the effects of the spiked drinks were taking their toll on Zoe. She could barely stand or keep her eyes open. I asked this guy to help me get her home and was kicking myself for getting us into this situation. I should have been more cautious, what would I do if Zoe got hurt? Our new friend spoke to a number of his mates and told us the guys we were talking about were known to them as bad news. They were Albanian gang members and we were in trouble as there were more of them outside the club. He and his friends agreed to escort us home and we left. I carried Zoe in my arms and as we left the club the gang approached us. I kicked one guy on the way out and we were pushed clear onto the street. The Greeks started shouting at the Albanians and once the gang realised we were no longer alone, they decided to back off and we escaped to the safety of our hotel room. I put Zoe to bed, locked the doors, checked the windows and sat up, on guard half the night, too wired to sleep.

For the first time in our marriage I felt like I was in a situation that I could not control. One that could result in the serious injury or death to my wife. I had so much anger towards the guys that had threatened my wife, I wanted to kill each and every one of them for putting us in that position. The anger felt so strong, I thought it would burn a hole in my heart. I sat there imagining the ways I would execute my revenge. I hated the idea of failing in my duty as a protector and I promised myself not to let anything like that happen again.

The next day we packed our gear and headed out of town.

Looking back on the experience today I realise with horror how close I came to being another statistic or being introduced to the abhorrent world of sexual slavery! The whole experience certainly put a damp-ener on the trip, I remember feeling so sick the next day, courtesy of the Rohypnol no-doubt, as we drove back to Athens with frequent stops. I literally swung open the door and vomited down the cliff faces of the mountainous surrounds. This served as a real wake up call for Andy as he now realised he had the responsibility of my protection beyond just himself and his risky, care free attitude very nearly could have been devastating.

We continued our journey back to Athens. I could not get far enough away from that village and the fear it drove into my heart.

The next place we visited was Istanbul, Turkey, or as Zoe called it Constantinople. It was amazing. We were delighted by the sights and sounds of the ancient city. We visited the typical sites, and drank apple tea until we could drink no more. We fought off a constant barrage of carpet salesman and left with a feeling of gratitude for a nation of people that were friendly and accommodating to our visit. We continued our journey South to the city of Troy and let ourselves be swept away in the history of the land before travelling on to visit Gallipoli. Initially Zoe could not understand my desire to go, but once we got there it was an experience neither of us would ever forget.

We toured the graves of the first ANZACS and walked through the trenches and along the shoreline. The feeling on the ground was incredibly overwhelming; the atmosphere was filled with hidden secrets of mates lost and stories untold. We were overcome with a solemn feeling of the magnitude of sacrifice that had occurred on those shores. We were fortunate enough to have a guided tour from a local Turkish historian who did an incredible job at presenting both sides of the campaign from a very unbiased perspective and with great respect for the Australian, New Zealand and Turkish soldiers who fought and died during this campaign.

We travelled home, happy to see Australian shores, with six weeks of travel behind us and a lot of experience under our belts. We settled back into life in Sydney and before long, we were blessed with our first child, Joseph. The day my son was born was the second proudest day of my life. Second only to marrying the woman of my dreams.

On December 22, 2005 we welcomed the birth of our beautiful boy Joseph, I never saw such pride and love in Andy's eyes as at that first moment, when he looked into his son's eyes. The arrival of his little boy sent him on a quest for finding the man he needed to be as a father, questions of faith were commonplace as he sought to find all the answers he would need to raise this new life responsibly. The love and gentleness toward his son were no surprise to me as I always knew the man and father he would become. Fatherhood sat well with Andy but his partying habit didn't sit well with fatherhood. I had long since learned the value of sleep, but Andy, although less often, still had his long nights of drinking well into the early hours of the morning and would spend most of the day sleeping. It was not good that Andy lost so much precious time he could have spent with Joseph and I didn't take too well the fact that Andy didn't get up until noon on my very first Mother's Day. He still had a bit to learn.

We had a happy, healthy boy and life changed forever as we navigated the pitfalls of parenthood. Joseph was born on the hottest summer day in Sydney for over 40 years and the air conditioners in the hospital were failing under the extreme heat. He is a gentle soul and is an incredibly stabilising influence in our family. His nature is so loving, like no one I know, having a gentle heart and intense curiosity for life. I would spend many nights sitting by his cot holding his little hand as he went to sleep. The feeling of being a new father was incredible and overwhelming at times. I did not realise I had so much love within me to give to another person. I felt such a strong need to protect and care for my family that I prayed for protection over their lives.

We bought a block of land in Byron Bay. Not without some reservation on my part I might add. We went into the deal with another of Andy's mates. Now I was beginning to recognise that Andy saw a huge part of his life with his mates included, and the more the merrier it seemed. Funnily, I don't know if he would have considered buying in with some of my friends? The five-year plan was to build two houses on the land and live happily ever after, I guess, with an idea of leaving the military and starting up a landscaping business together.

Life within the military continued to present its challenges though, as Andy spent long periods away in training. I was at home with our baby, living in Sydney at this stage. So when the opportunity of going to Florida came up we seized it. This was one of the times where the army was definitely working for us as a family. Although they originally didn't support the idea of family on the posting preferring once again to send Andy off on his own. After a fair amount of determination, we were all going. So there we were with our six-month old son Joseph on the sunny sands and emerald coasts of the panhandle Florida.

What an amazing experience that was! Andy was not so inundated with work so he would be home by 10am on many days. We spent our time on boats in the Caribbean waters sipping Pina Coladas and eating freshly shucked oysters.

It was around this time that my ambition to be a bomb disposal expert really accelerated, I had studied various specialist military engineering courses and decided that this was something I wanted to focus my career towards. It started an incredibly challenging journey of endless study, practical examinations and assessments. Zoe was very supportive of my goal to be a qualified Explosive Ordinance Disposal (EOD) Technician and would spend late nights quizzing me about explosive materials, various guided missiles and chemical weapon characteristics. She probably knows more about military ordnance than 98% of the population. I was drawn to everything explosive, and saw the perfect fit for my talents and ambitions in the stream of specialist military engineering, so I focused all my efforts towards qualifying myself in all aspects of the trade including Chemical, Biological, Radiological and Nuclear studies which included Explosive Ordinance and working with Explosive Detection Dog teams. I worked my way into the position as second in Command of the Specialist Engineering Wing as my first posting as a captain. I completed my EOD training in Australia and was qualified prior to receiving a posting to the United States to further my studies in Explosive Ordinance Disposal; I spent the next six months studying at the US Navy School of Explosive Ordnance Disposal in Florida. Joseph was only five months old when we departed for Florida, and Zoe and I loved every moment of our US adventure making great friends and enjoying the beautiful emerald coast and everything it had to offer. The training was challenging and interesting and for the vast majority of it I was just so grateful to be there.

As a family we had so much fun in Florida, it was proving to be an amazing place that brought Zoe and I closer together. I was often so amazed at how incredible Zoe was as a mother, she had a natural ability to do everything in a loving and caring way for Joseph and I often found myself in awe of how gentle and loving she was.

Watching Zoe as a new mother gave me so much hope for our future together as a family because I felt confident in the fact that my wife was an amazing mother. I learned so much about how to be a Dad by watching and trying to replicate my wife's behaviour of patience, love and acceptance of our new son.

Towards the end of our posting we decided to travel to New Orleans with a mate's family who was also on the course with us. As we travelled into New Orleans the level of destruction amazed us as we approached the city. It was approximately one year since Hurricane Katrina had struck and turned New Orleans into a lawless city of destruction. There were cars piled four high, stacked under overpasses, homes and buildings left abandoned in what looked like a scene from WW3. The only area of the city left standing was the popular tourist area, the French district. It was the costliest natural disaster, caused by one of the five deadliest hurricanes, in the history of the United States. Overall, 1,245 people died in the hurricane and subsequent floods. Nearly every levee in metro New Orleans was breached as Hurricane Katrina passed just East of the city limits, which left approximately 80% of the city flooded.

We checked into a hotel and were provided a room across the street from the hotel lobby in a stand-alone building with four units. Our friends were staying in the main hotel and we decided to get together for a night out. As we both had young children, the boys stayed home and the girls went out on the town to explore the French district. Zoe returned to the unit without incident and reported a good night.

The following night I went out with my friend and his younger sister. We had a good night and met a number of ex-US defence personnel working for a company called Black Water. One of the major private security organisations brought in to regain control in the city, in a quasi-martial law scenario. These guys were cool and invited us back to their apartment where we drank beers, shared stories and chilled out. One of the guys took great pride in showing us his personal gun collection. At some point my mate started to get into an argument with one of the American guys, so we decided to get him home before the situation got out of control. My friend was drunker than ten men when we left and it took all my effort to guide / carry him back to our accommodation and get him to his room. I got home, kissed Zoe and went to sleep thinking my mate would be nursing the mother of all hangovers in the morning.

This was the only dark encounter that marred the trip worth mentioning, when Andy came back blind drunk to our hotel room in New Orleans, after a night on the town with his army mates. There was a loud banging on the door that woke us a few hours later. A quick look through the peep hole confirmed that a group of three guys with guns were at the door. Misguidedly on a quest to find a gun that had apparently been stolen from them earlier in the night. All in a blink of an eye, I looked at Joseph sleeping peacefully in the bed and realised we were trapped in this room. I envisioned the door being knocked down and myself flying over and rolling off the bed with my baby to shield him from the anticipated onslaught of bullets.

I was awakened by the phone ringing in the small hotel room, answering half asleep. A voice asked, "is this Andy?"

I said, "yea, who is this? Do you know what time it is?"

The man on the other end of the line became extremely aggressive, saying something about, 'give me back my gun!'

I sat up at that point realising this was serious.

He said he was coming up to my room with his friends to get his gun back. I immediately responded stating I didn't know what he was talking about, but he was not to come to my room because my wife and son were with me. The individual identified himself as one of the guys that had taken us to his apartment and displayed his guns for us to see. He insisted I had his gun and that he was coming to get it. Then he hung up the phone.

I looked at Zoe who was staring into my eyes with a worried look on her face and listening intently trying to understand what was happening. I heard the first door to the building break open violently and looked through the peephole down the long hallway as three men approached my door, pistols drawn.

I turned to Zoe, looking for any way to get out of the room, but we were trapped, the only window heavily barred and offering no way out. I told her to take Joseph into the bathroom and lock the door. As the men approached the door I yelled out ,"The first person that comes through that door is going to die!"

The three men stopped and spoke to each other in hushed tones before backing down the hallway the way they had come in. The phone rang again and the next two hours were spent trying to convince this individual that I did not have his gun and had no idea what he was talking about. He finally accepted that I may not have the weapon. He then focused his attention on my friend insisting if I didn't have it, my friend must.

I told him I would call my friend and find out. (*Zoe now standing next to me in disbelief.*)

I phoned the police to report what was happening and requested an officer attend as soon as possible. Then I called my friend's room and his wife answered. I explained the situation and she tried to wake her husband. Even after throwing a bucket of water on him she could not wake him enough to confirm if he had taken the weapon or not. She searched the room and found nothing.

So I called back to the guys at the front desk to speak to the drunk irrational lunatic holding us hostage. I insisted that neither of us had his gun and that he needed to leave as I had called the police. He then told me he owned the police and that he wasn't leaving without his gun.

We had a Mexican standoff for the next hour or so as I debated with Zoe about going down to talk to him face to face. Zoe in her wisdom insisted I did not leave the hotel room and at least we were safe in there, as they would not enter without fear of being shot.

I called the police every twenty minutes asking where the responding officer was. However, each time I rang, I was given some strange excuse as to my complaint being dealt with by an officer already on site. This guy's statement of owning the police was becoming more and more real.

Eventually my phone rang and a new voice asked to speak with Andy. This individual was very calm and rational and sober. A welcome change from the abusive lunatic I had been conversing with over the past few hours. He explained to me that the individual threatening me was his employee and he had searched his apartment and found the apparent missing gun in his room. He continued to apologise profusely and confirmed that he had left the area. I hung up the phone and charged out of my room for the lobby across the road.

A large black man approached me from the lobby asking if I was Andy. "Yes, I'm Andy, the one whose family has been hiding in fear for the past few hours, terrified that some lunatic was going to charge in and shoot everyone!", I replied.

I then grabbed the man behind the desk by the collar and asked him why he gave my room number to some lunatic? He replied that he thought he was a police officer as he had a gun. I proceeded to berate the concierge for placing my family at risk and then turned my attention to the other man.

He tried to calm me down, explaining how he had intervened with the police on each occasion I had called and that he had sent his employee home. He also assured me he would be losing his job as a result of the incident. I insisted on pressing charges, but he continued to try to convince me not to. He paid for our hotel accommodation and gave me some money in an attempt to appease my appetite for justice and revenge.

I insisted on speaking with the man that had terrorised my family and he got the individual on the phone. I berated him for a few minutes, then listened to his heartfelt apology crying into the phone, insisting he never meant me or my family any harm. He honestly believed I had stolen his weapon from his room earlier in the evening. I took a deep breath and told him that I forgave him and agreed not to press charges, leaving him with the warning, "Never threaten a man's family!"

I handed the phone back to the large man and walked back to my hotel room to tell Zoe it was over. I was so relieved at the end of this ordeal. I felt sick to my stomach at the thought of my baby and my wife being hurt or killed. Yet again, trouble had found me and my family was at risk. This made me furious and a little angry with my friend as well, although it was not his fault. It was simply annoying that he had slept through the entire ordeal.

Yet again we escaped unscathed. Suffice it to say a dark shadow was cast over our New Orleans trip and Zoe could not wait to get out of there.

Luckily they never came in and by some miracle we escaped unscathed. It turned out the whole thing was just some misunderstanding and the Black Water employee, responsible for gathering his posse for the re-trieval expedition, found the gun in his apartment. Needless to say, I was soon making irrational demands to be sent home to Australia, far away from what I now viewed as a God forsaken country. For the most of it though, Florida was so rewarding for us as a couple and a young family, we spent many hours in the emerald waters soaking up sun and living a life that seemed far from reality.

I find it hard to imagine how it would've been if we had of stayed home and not been a part, of that posting. For an organisation that suppos-edly held family in high regard, this was the first glimpse of how the Australian Army, in fact did the exact opposite. If Andy had been in Florida alone, it most likely would have torn us apart. He was already qualified in the field of training and much of his time was spent as downtime, which would have provided ample opportunity for promis-cuity for someone with lesser conviction, and for many it did.

After graduation from the US Navy EOD School we decided, before heading home to Australia, to take a trip through parts of Europe that we had not yet seen together.

We travelled to Rome, taking in all that the majestic city had to offer and then headed onto Malta, the traditional home of Zoe's father. Malta is a beautiful little island in the Mediterranean Sea with a deep history. More recently as a major player in both World Wars, and prior to that as the historic location used by The Order of the Knights of Saint John, the most famous of the Roman Catholic Military orders during the Middle Ages. After enjoying Malta's rabbit stew and pris-tine castles we headed for Spain.

We landed in Valencia and hired a car. Driving down the East coast to Alicante and then on to Mercia to stay with friends in a crowd-ed inner-city apartment. We were amazed at how so many people lived together in such a small area, yet there were extensive open expanses of countryside, just outside the city limits.

The architecture and lifestyle was so different from anything we had ever experienced back home. Large multi-story apartment blocks filled the horizon with green parks spotted between them in what seemed to be a maze of buildings. To be honest, it felt quite claustrophobic and I was happy to depart the city as we drove to our friend's holiday apartment on the beach, in an area called Cartagena. Cartagena is a quaint little fishing town with beautiful beaches. We were spoiled by our friends with local dining, wine and music. We tried goat for the first time. I was amazed by the flavour. It was truly delicious.

We left Spain to continue our journey on to Thailand to visit the busy city of Bangkok. I had been to Bangkok previously, during my deployment to Malaysia and I knew what to expect. Zoe however, was amazed at the busyness of this city, the various smells of the street-side cooking, all mixed with the open sewers. We caught a tuk-tuk to the famous Patpong night market, where we were constantly hounded as it seemed every person wanted to touch little Josephs head. They simply could not resist his blond hair and big eyes. We left again via tuk-tuk. This time fearing for our lives as the driver was hell bent on breaking a land speed record to get us back to our hotel. Zoe held onto Joseph and I held them both, as the little bike swerved in and out of traffic squeezing between vehicles and down alley ways. I was so relieved to arrive at the hotel I think I paid the guy a lot more than I should have.

5

WAR

Afghanistan 2008

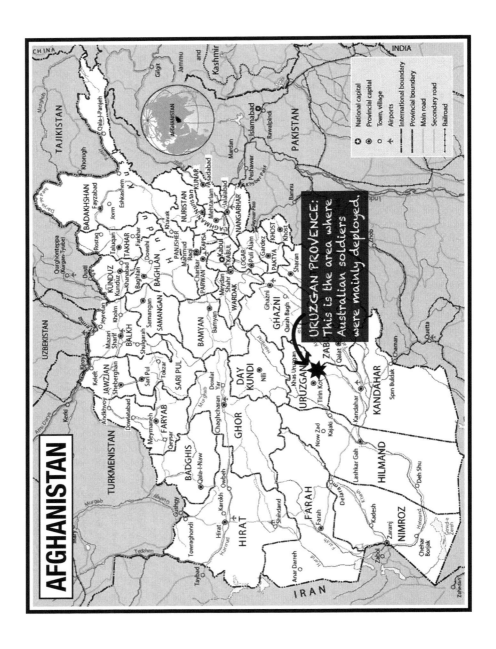

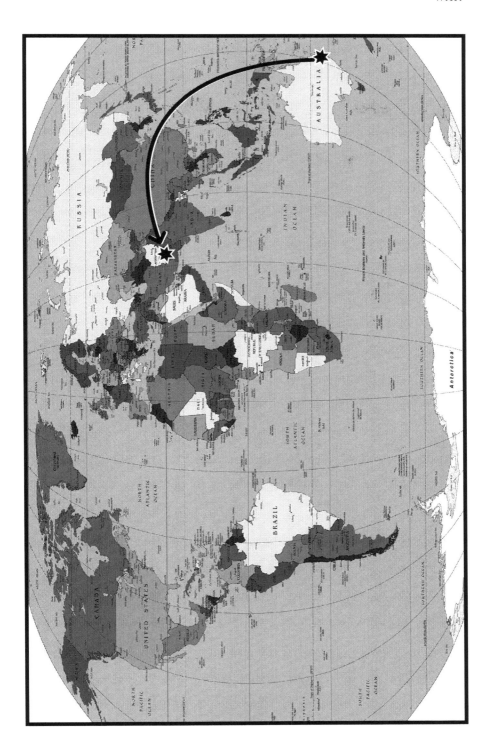

WAR

My next job was with the 6th Engineer Support Regiment in Brisbane working in a small unit attached to the Headquarters, The Army Explosive Hazards Centre (A-ExHC). The unit was formed in 2006 with the purpose of delivering Improvised Explosive Device (IED) specific training to deploying forces and was critical in the education of Australian troops in understanding and dealing with the biggest threat to Australian lives in the theatre of war. It was only a short posting as I was soon assigned to deploy to Afghanistan with the 4th Reconstruction Task Force, as the EOD Manager, under the command of Lieutenant Colonel Stuart Yeaman. The main role of the deployment was the reconstruction of local infrastructure in the Area of Operations with the goal of winning the hearts and minds of the local population. We would be involved in building bridges, schools and businesses, as well as military facilities for the Afghan National Army and Forward Operating Bases and Patrol Bases for Australian and Allied Forces to operate from.

Being selected for this position meant everything to me. It was what I trained for and it embraced everything I aspired to within the Military from the day I joined almost 12 years earlier. If you liken it to a sportsman it was like being chosen for the Olympic team. It did; however, raise a few big questions in my mind, like:

What did I think about the War in Afghanistan and should Australia even be involved? The short truth to that question, from my perspective, was that we absolutely needed to be involved and I knew without a shadow of a doubt that we were going over there for a justified cause: To free a people from being subjected to atrocities and horrors at the hands of the Taliban, a ruthless murderous cult responsible for enforcing a strict form of Sharia law onto a population that did not want it and essentially forcing half the population into virtual house arrest; stripping them of their civil liberties and rights to such things as education, health care and employment.

The war had been raging in Afghanistan since 2001, and ever since the September 11 attacks in New York and Washington

DC, Afghanistan had been a major focus. As far as I was concerned we were there at the request of the Afghan Government helping the civilian population regain peace and stability, in an otherwise hostile and horrific environment. I was reading military reports daily on the atrocities being committed by the Taliban and I felt I had a very good understanding of the purpose of our mission, and I had no doubt that I agreed with it.

Over the next few months I would study Afghan history, learn about the various ethnic tribal groups that make up their nation and the cultural beliefs that might affect our mission. I would also try to learn some key phrases in Pashto and Dari such as "Stop or I will shoot". As a part of the Reconstruction Task Force we were sent to make a practical difference to the stability of Afghanistan. The unit consisted predominantly of a Headquarters, an Engineer Squadron, an Infantry Company and various supporting assets, including medical, logistics and construction teams.

Zoe didn't share my enthusiasm for the deployment, nor did she really understand my commitment above all else, to want to go. I guess, as a wife and parent she simply saw this as me choosing the Army over being with her, Joseph and our unborn son.

In some ways she was right, as far as an ultimate decision to leave from a black and white viewpoint. However, for me it was not a matter of choosing to deploy over family. To me it was a willingness to deploy, to protect my family, my country and our rights to freedom.

Someone had to step up and I had made that commitment and pledged my allegiance to my country a long time ago and I intended to fulfil that commitment no matter what the cost. I could not explain it, but in my heart it was because I loved her that I was deploying. Life is not black and white and I was in a position to fight against a fundamentalist Islamic group responsible for ongoing atrocities around the globe that threatened to destroy everything we believed in as a nation. Our freedoms, our peace and our way of life. I was willing to die to do my part in ensuring this terror did not reach our own shores. It may sound a little exaggerated or melodramatic, but this was the reality of the world I was living in and I had made my decision.

Was I afraid of being killed? And the answer to that question was no, not really. I thought if I was killed in the service to my nation I would be proud to have had the opportunity to die in that way. My family would be looked after with a pension and it would be better than dying in some random way and not to be remembered for doing anything of any real importance. At least this way my family and friends would remember me in a positive way.

I'm not speaking for everyone but I imagine it would be similar for many soldiers as it is something you must consider prior to even enlisting in the Army. Death as a result of service is a very real possibility. So if you're not prepared to die in the service of your country, then don't join up.

Was I afraid of losing someone under my command? I was genuinely afraid of being responsible for the death or injury of a soldier under my command. This is something I would think about often. This thought would drive me to ensure training was thorough and no short cuts were taken. The way I figured it, it was my job to do everything I could possibly do as a commander, to ensure the odds of injury and death were reduced as much as humanly possible, before we even stepped foot on the battle ground. The thought of Michael Lyddiard, an Australian EOD Tech who suffered significant injuries in November of 2007. These include the loss of his right arm, most of his left hand, his right eye, significant damage to his left eye and severe muscle damage. This would serve as a constant reminder of the dangers of the job we were about to encounter and would drive me to stay on task. The significance of Michael's injuries was due to the fact that he was an EOD Technician who was blown up attempting a render- safe procedure on a land mine in Afghanistan only months prior to our deployment. He was doing the very job we would be expected to do each and every day whilst deployed. The risk of injury and death was very real. To date, there had been five Australian Soldiers killed in action since 2002 and over 35 wounded in action.

Pre-Deployment training was conducted for the most part in Brisbane and made it a lot easier on my small family as I was able to return home most days. Zoe was moving along in her pregnancy and we had worked out the baby was due to be born around the time I was to deploy.

This made her increasingly nervous as we neared the deployment date. The vast number of briefs and medical checks were slowly completed as we edged closer to deployment. It was my privilege to command the first duel service EOD Team deployed into Afghanistan, consisting of both Army and Navy EOD personnel. The reason was simple enough. The Army didn't have enough EOD assets to continue to support the operational requirements alone. We needed to engage the support of our Navy brethren to help fill the gap.

The individual Navy personnel provided were at the top of their game and a credit to the Navy. Both individuals became good friends of mine during and after our deployment and both served to keep me sane with their hilarious behaviour. I could not be happier with the team overall. There was the Senior Army Tech, Warrant Officer Finny, Chief Petty Officer Shirles as another senior tech, Petty Officer Stiffy EOD Tech and Corporal Barto as the Explosive Ordnance Reconnaissance (EOR) Tech. The team gelled fairly well after some expected initial teething issues as we worked out the kinks between our services. It felt like we had developed a bond and trust before we deployed and I could not wait to get on the ground.

The EOD chain of command is an interesting beast in a theatre of war. Technically it resides as a direct asset to the highest level of command. This is due to its specialist role and small number of assets, therefore allowing the asset to be dispersed as effectively as possible throughout the battlefield, supporting all elements on the ground. Essentially, this meant I answered directly to the CO but for all intents and purposes I came under the supervision of one, MAJ Mick the Operations Officer (OPSO). This was fine by me as Mick was a switched on guy who's no-bull approach to operations I both respected and admired. Mick would become the lubricant that would allow me to operate my assets effectively in theatre and without the need for me to be involved in any macho competitions between combat team commanders, over who owned and could command my team. He would also push me to my physical limits as far as achieving my EOD Manager role, as well as stepping up in the role of watch keeper, whenever required within the Tactical Operations Centre, (TOC). As a result of picking up this rather unexpected and unwelcome second position, my six month deployment would be incredibly busy and challenging.

Before I left, I would have a short break to spend time with my family. Zoe was now heavily pregnant with our second child and due to give birth any day. She was anxious to ensure I was going to be around for the birth and I was given a slight extension to my departure date in order to allow me to be there for the birth of my son. We were starting to get concerned he may not come in time even with my delayed departure; however, we were blessed with the arrival of Charlie Cullen on the 17 April 2008, a few days prior to my departure.

We welcomed the arrival of our second son Charlie, with a 6 month posting to Afghanistan looming on the horizon. I was so anxious to give birth with my husband by my side, I fought with the doctor to allow an early induction. It was granted under the circumstances but ironically I went into labour naturally the morning of the induction. I experienced firsthand the power of the mind and the affects anxiety can have on the body. I was so anxious and simply couldn't fathom the idea of Andy not being there for the birth, I went into labour early! Charlie was the smallest of all my babies at birth. He had a thick mop of dark hair that fell out, not to be replaced until he was a full year old. Then he grew a head of the whitest blonde hair I could imagine. He looked like a little pixie, rather appropriate, given he was born in the birthing clinic of Mullumbimby hospital, which according to folk law, was a place where women went to give birth naturally.

From the moment Charlie was born I loved him so very much. I remember being a little surprised that only hours earlier I had no real emotional connection with this person, but only the idea of who he might be. However, as soon as he arrived into this world, it was as if my heart expanded just enough to fit this little boy into a place that had always been there just waiting for him. The moment Charlie was born he looked at me and I looked at him thinking he was the most incredible, beautiful boy, I held him in my arms and told him I was his Dad and that I would always love him.

My biggest fear for the deployment was that something would happen to Zoe or the boys whilst I was away. I trusted Zoe implicitly as she was an extremely capable mother and it was her strength that made it easier for me to leave as I knew she would hold the family together. I also knew I would never forgive myself if something happened in my absence while I was not able to help. Zoe was so strong during those final days before I left and she held the family together as I packed my bags, hugged Joseph and little Charlie and said my goodbyes.

I tried to explain to Joseph that I would not be around for a while and that he needed to be a good boy for his Mum. At two years of age he was visibly saddened at my departure. I looked at Zoe and I knew she had already started to build up walls between us as a survival mechanism. The gentle, loving and kind girl I married, was starting to harden and I prayed that I would return in time to break down the walls and continue with our life, as a family before it simply became all-too- hard for her as a single mother and she decided to leave me.

I really felt for Zoe at this time and although my heart wanted nothing more than to be with her and the kids, my burning patriotic desire was to serve my country on operations and nothing was going to stop me. To be blunt, the Army was my first priority in life at this time.

It was hard enough with me going away all the time on exercise and training but now, going to war, it all became very real to Zoe that I may not come home. She could be responsible for raising two boys without their father. I remember thinking deployment is harder for the spouse left at home, as they are expected to pick up and keep life moving along without their partner, with little to no contact and constant worry.

For deploying members, it was relatively easy, at least in my experience. We had a job to focus on, to keep us busy and a reason to come home. I thank God every day for Zoe's strength, she was and is the glue that holds my family together; without her unique tenacity and dedication to our marriage and family we would have separated on numerous occasions over the years. A great number of marriages simply don't survive the rigours of Army life and deployment.

Zoe drove me to the airport with the boys and we said our goodbyes. The kids were great. Joseph just wanted to hug me and didn't want to let go and Charlie looked up at me from his seat, his big blue eyes staring back at me. I felt a tear welling up in my eye which I quickly wiped away so as not to get too emotional. Zoe seemed to close up to protect herself and avoid the tears. I could see she was sad, but I also saw fear and pain in her eyes. Zoe told me much later that as she drove away she had to pull over to have a good cry before continuing on to an empty home. I should have said more clearly how much I loved Zoe and the boys, and felt that I didn't explain well enough how much they meant to me. I was kicking myself for not finding the words to express my love for them sufficiently.

*****

The purpose of our mission in Afghanistan was to progress the Afghan population towards a future that they wanted by improving security and governance. My personal mission was to save as many Australian and Afghan lives as possible through the safe detection and clearance of IEDs and to bring my team home in one piece to their families.

We flew out of Brisbane Airport on a charted civilian plane, which I thought was a strange way to go to war and not one I had imagined as a boy growing up. I was anxious to meet up with my team who were already in theatre as they had departed a bit over a week before me. We eventually landed in Ali Al Salem Airbase, a military airbase situated in Kuwait, approximately 23 miles from the Iraqi border. The airfield is owned by the Government of Kuwait, and was used extensively by coalition forces fighting in Iraq and Afghanistan. It housed around 17,000 people when we came through. In the 1990s, the base was overrun during the Iraqi invasion of Kuwait and still bore many of the scars from that battle.

The heat hit me as we landed when the cabin doors were opened. The wave of dry heat was unlike anything I had experienced before. Average temperatures were around 45 degrees Celsius and the air was so dry with no relative humidity to speak of and a constant hot wind blowing in my face like a hairdryer on full blast. The heat shocked me at first and I found it difficult to do the simplest of tasks.

We shuffled onto buses for a short journey to a United States Military (monster) base just outside the airfield. In this base Australia had a small corner for staging its logistic and command operations for forces deployed in the Middle East. We collected the rest of our personal belongings including our weapons and ammunition and were shown to our tent accommodation in "tent city".

The tents were enormous air conditioned canvas tents, housing around fifty personnel. Each tent had airlocks to shield the inner tent from the heat and dust outside. The base had everything from McDonalds and Starbucks to KFC. It had a huge military kitchen and civilian staff everywhere. The civilian staff also provided much of the security within the base which I found strange, the idea of civilians protecting defence personnel inside a defence base in a conflict zone just didn't seem right.

The next few days consisted of final lectures, weapons drills, live fire exercises and intelligence briefings before our final leg into Afghanistan. Before we left Kuwait we were to experience something I had never even dreamed of. A siren sounded on the base and people started running in all directions. I had no idea what the siren was and asked one of the yanks running past, he sreamed, "It's a sand storm man!" in a southern accent and I looked up in time to see a hundred foot wall of brown-red earth moving towards us at an incredible speed. I ran towards my tent and as I got within twenty meters of the door the front of the storm hit. My face was wiped with sand and I shut my eyes removing my shirt and tying it around my head like a mask. As I looked up, now able to breath under the shirt, I could see the light fading to black as the red dust engulfed everything in its path. I staggered the last few meters to the Velcro door of the tent and threw myself inside the outer chamber falling to the floor and catching my breath in the relative safety of the tent. The sound of the wind was incredible and I wondered how people would survive if caught in the open in one of these storms.

The next day we loaded up into an Australian C-130 Hercules aircraft and departed Kuwait for Tarin Kowt (TK), Afghanistan. The flight in was fairly relaxed but I was filled with a sense of excitement and fear. My stomach flickered with pangs of anticipation as the pilot announced we were now flying over Afghanistan and everyone was to don helmets. We were all strapped in shoulder to shoulder in full combat attire, helmet and body armour. I did not let go of my rifle for an instant and constantly checked that my 9mm Browning was still in its holster on my hip, constantly getting the idea that it was missing, like when you lose your wallet and then remember where you put it. This constant checking behaviour would stay with me for the duration of most of my first tour.

As we approached our final decent the plane banked heavily and we all grabbed for our harnesses, we had been warned to expect this as the aircraft would undertake a tactical approach when landing, in order to limit exposure to enemy fire on final approach. We landed on the dirt airstrip of Tarin Kowt airfield as the smell of vomit filled the cabin, apparently the landing was too much for some.

Located in south-eastern Afghanistan 2km south of Tarin Kowt, the capital city of the province of Uruzgan, is what was known as Regional Command South (RC-S). It is 97 km north of Kandahar, and 330km south-southwest of the Afghan capital of Kabul.

Camp Holland is located next to Tarin Kowt Airstrip and would be my new home for the next six months. As I exited the rear ramp and my feet touched the dry dusty landscape of Afghanistan for the first time, I looked out to the surrounding mountain ranges in the far distance. We sat nestled in a dry dust bowl at the foot hills of the Hindu Kush, the Zhar Ghar and Kuran Ghar mountains.

The Australian Special Forces had made their home in Camp Russell since 2005 and it sat directly next to Camp Holland off the air field. A little further down the airfield was the American Special Forces compound FOB Ripley. The air was hot and dry, sucking any moisture out of my lips as the wind hit my face. This place had an eerie feel about it and I felt like an unwelcome visitor in a foreign land. So far from home and anything that resembled my country of birth.

The place was buzzing with activity, vehicles and soldiers moving in every direction, helicopters taking off and landing across the far side of the Airstrip, and for a moment I was like a deer in the headlights, not able to get by bearings on my immediate surroundings.

Australian forces came under the regional command of a Dutch commander. The Dutch forces established Task Force Uruzgan (TFU) as a provincial reconstruction team aimed at not only utilising military force to establish control of the region, but to rebuild the region and introduce diplomacy with the assistance of political advisors and constant engagement with the Afghan people. The overall goal was to make the Taliban irrelevant. The Dutch forces in Afghanistan were often characterised as bringing a soft approach to warfare. However, in my opinion, they made a lasting and impacting difference to the rebuilding and establishment of governance in the region through well thought out and planned approaches to insurgent warfare.

Our initial port of call was the hanger, CPL Glen Barton, (Barto) met me, grabbed my gear, threw it in a Rover, and waited for us to complete our ground safety brief. The main point of the brief was to familiarise personnel with the layout of the base and the various sirens indicating everything from ground attack to incoming indirect fire. This particular siren would become very familiar to all personnel based in Tarin Kowt.

Barto drove me to my accommodation, effectively a large series of shipping containers joined together, half buried underground and covered with sandbags and tin to protect us from the constant threat of rocket and mortar fire. I was acquainted with my bunk, dropped off my personal items and headed across the base to the EOD compound to see the rest of the team.

After that we headed over to meet the Dutch Engineer route clearance guys who told me they were hit by 4 separate IED's in the past week and one of their guys had lost both his legs. As we were talking I heard in the background the big Dutch 155mm Howitzer fire into some enemy positions, that's when the reality, that I was now in a war zone, really sunk in.

The first few days in the country were a blur, I attended planning groups, received orders and got the lay of the land before heading out on my first patrol. Anywhere outside of the relative safety of Camp Holland was known as 'Outside the wire' and effectively meant you were now at serious risk of attack from the enemy through Ambush, IED attack or suicide bomber.

Placed in one of the search team command vehicles, I experienced a rush of adrenalin as we left the base driving through the small city of Tarin Kowt and out into the desert. Tarin Kowt was a busy city now thriving with people and commerce, largely due to the impact the Australian and Dutch forces had over the past four years working hard to stabilise the region and free it from Taliban control.

For much of the patrol I was standing in the rear hatch on the Machine Gun as I wanted to get a feel for the environment and the people. I was startled at how close vehicles would come to our own bushmasters and at how seemingly relaxed they looked when I pointed a machine gun in their general direction ushering them to stop or back up. I quickly discovered that a pistol was a much more effective means of instilling a little fear and gaining the instant cooperation of the Afghan people. I was told they associated fear with a pistol due to the number of executions committed with this weapon during the Soviet – Afghan War. I'm not sure how accurate this statement is but, the pistol did have an immediate impact.

Tarin Kowt was not like any city I had seen in my travels around the world. It would more appropriately be described as a shanty town with only a handful of buildings over a single story. Parts of the city had paved roads and the main road into town was connected with a large roundabout. To the left of the roundabout as we drove into town was a hotel known as the Taliban Hotel. It was a place from which we would occasionally receive the odd harassing fire from as we drove past. To the right was a market where local traders sold their products and a significant amount of the towns commerce would take place. This area was particularly popular with suicide bombers and gunman wishing to inflict large tolls on innocent civilians. People freely walked the streets trading and talking. Children ran out onto the road to wait for soldiers to throw lollies to them.

Blue utilities with armed men in pale blue uniforms were on every corner, the Afghan National Police, made up from local people in order to limit issues with tribal law and disputes. The Afghan National Army personnel, unlike the police came from far and wide and were typically never posted to their home locations. The fact that they were not close to home often attributed to soldiers going AWOL or running away and deserting their duties.

Our first mission through the city and out to one of the forward patrol bases went off without incident and I took the opportunity to watch the searchers complete their drills on the ground. These brave individuals risked their lives daily, walking out in front of convoys, along dirt roads and tracks, searching for explosive devices buried beneath the sand. Looking for any sign of recent digging, markers or anything that looked slightly out of place, all the while keeping one eye on their surroundings in the event a suicide bomber might approach from a flank, or someone who might open fire from a covered position.

The High Risk Search Engineers are the bravest of the brave, day in and day out walking the path to ensure the mobility of our ground forces. I was constantly amazed by the confidence and professionalism displayed by these individuals, often searching and concentrating so hard for hours on end, remaining vigilant so as not to lose focus and potentially miss a device. I would often dismount and walk behind the searchers or take up an F3 mine detector and clear a particularly vulnerable point to allow the Sappers to rest and keep my own skills up.

I found being on the ground, walking through this incredible landscape, strangely calming and a great way to get a feel for the environment. There is only so much you can take in bouncing around in the back of an armoured vehicle and I wanted to know intimately how and where our enemy was targeting us so effectively with IEDs.

The terrain in Uruzgan Province Afghanistan is a sight to behold with vast expanses of open desert that give way to narrow stretches of lush green foliage, known as "the green zone". A vegetation belt of farmland and a series of aqueducts that feed crops ranging from wheat, barley, maze and vegetables to extensive marijuana and poppy crops. This green belt meanders along the main rivers leading to the base of the steep rocky mountains that looked like giant shark teeth erupting from the earth. The climate is extremely dry and hot in summer with very little rainfall and often gives way to sand storms. Winter brings with it bitter cold and extensive snowfalls. There is so little rain in this region that I can only remember it raining on three specific occasions in my six-month tour.

As I looked around while walking along a dirt track I noticed colourful flags on many of the bald hills just outside the villages, these were the cemeteries and were a stark reminder to the harsh environment we were now living in.

The average lifespan for an Afghan male in the region was around 40 years, eventhough they looked much older, beaten by the harsh sun and driving wind.

Occasionally, I saw a tough old-looking bloke walking or riding on horseback and think they probably spent much of their lives fighting the Russians with the Mujahedeen in the 80's.

The occasional ute would drive past our positions carrying a handful of fighting-age males. They would stare at us with a darkness that is difficult to explain. I had no doubt they were Taliban but because they had no visible weapons we could do little but search them and let them go. The extreme difficulty of fighting an insurgent war in a place like Afghanistan became clear to me in that moment. There is no way of identifying the enemy other than when he is shooting at you, in effect giving him all the advantage. Knowing full well that any difference we made here during our time would quickly be eroded after Coalition forces withdrew and the people would go back to their "natural" state. All the Taliban had to do to defeat us was wait us out.

Summer is also known as the fighting season as historically the Taliban would be more active in their kinetic attacks whereas in winter the fighting would decrease. Fighters would return to their homes or to Pakistan for training. We were now entering the hottest time which was the peak of the fighting season.

As we arrived back at Camp Holland we received word that two Dutch soldiers were killed earlier in the day when their vehicle drove over an IED. Life gone in a flash! The mood around base was quite sombre and people walked past as if in a world of their own, contemplating the deaths of their mates.

The frustration felt by everyone at the difficulty in finding IEDs was intense. Thoughts of how we could better detect these devices and how we might adapt the techniques and procedures to improve our survivability, were constantly on my mind. The fact remained that even when we did change them to keep up with the constant changing threat, there was no silver bullet for defeating this insidious threat.

Before I left home I assured Zoe that I would be in a command position and not on the ground conducting patrols and defusing devices. I knew this was a lie but I did not want to upset her unnecessarily and figured I could live with the lie if I knew it would bring her some level of peace.

The truth was, over the next six months, I would take every opportunity to place myself at the very point of the spear constantly seeking missions to employ my skills and lead my team from the front. I was not one to sit back and let those under my command "have all the fun", or take all the risk. A common phrase around the Tactical Operations Command (TOC), was "where is Captain Cullen?" As I would avoid the TOC as much as possible during my tour and spend a significant portion of my deployment outside the wire as it was the only place I felt like I was making a difference and where I felt free.

The freedom I was afforded to run my team somewhat autonomously was due to the command relationship I had formed with the OPSO, my immediate superior. He, through his good management and understanding of my role, allowed me to be out on the ground as much as humanly possible. I only needed to be in the TOC filling in when necessary.

I only had one EOD team and as far as I was concerned I could best command them by being on the ground with them. I would complete my other responsibilities from the field and no one seemed to mind, except the CO on occasion. The truth is I was addicted to the adrenalin rush that was associated with being on task. It was embedded within my every fibre and I found it very difficult at times to control. I had to remind myself that I had other responsibilities to focus on whatever task was at hand. Never really considering the additional risks I was taking or danger I was seeking.

There was no consideration for my family when I constantly embedded myself on missions. I just loved my job and wanted to do it every chance I got. There was no thought about dying or the real risk of injury to myself as I had a general feeling that I would be okay. I was careful to a point and methodical about my procedures and confident in my own ability to do what needed to be done to protect myself.

Looking back I would think almost every Tech injured or killed on operations probably felt the same way and thought they would be okay too. I was, however, in constant fear of something happening to one of my guys. I was confident in their abilities and trusted them to do their job but felt burdened with the responsibility of bringing them home in one piece and wanted to do everything I could to ensure that that happened. To that end, I worked my arse off liaising with: The Dutch EOD Teams and command elements; Intelligence staff; the newly formed Australian Weapons Technical Intelligence Team; the US Task Force Paladin support elements; and our Task Force 66 Special Forces personnel, to ensure we had up-to-date, reliable information available for every mission relating specifically to the IED threat. I also worked very hard to ensure we had the right equipment for the job.

Unfortunately, it wasn't long before we took casualties of our own. Jason Marks, 27, a lance corporal in the 4th Battalion, Royal Australian Regiment (Commando), was killed after an intense fire fight with Taliban insurgents on 27 April 2008. When a RPG landed near the patrol vehicle he was taking cover behind whilst reloading his weapon. The attack occurred 25km south of the Australian base at Tarin Kowt in Oruzgan Province. Four other Australian soldiers were wounded in the attack. All five were flown to a nearby US military hospital, where the wounded were expected to fully recover.

A bit of an odd thing happened the very next day, one of the 3 RAR Paratroopers shot himself in the foot whilst on patrol in TK. This was a bit of a wakeup call to the Para members who, as a whole, were quite embarrassed by the incident as it reflected badly on them as a unit.

Whenever I was not on a mission outside the wire I was sitting in the TOC completing the duties of a watch keeper and running low on sleep. I would do an eight to twelve-hour shift and then complete my EOD Manager duties for the next four hours prior to crawling into bed at around midday to try and sleep a few hours during the heat of the day before getting up to do it all again. On average I was sleeping 3 – 4 hours a night and after a few weeks my body simply adjusted to the cycle. So I took every opportunity that I could to get outside the wire and when the CO planned a significant movement to the North of the Area of Operations (AO), taking key staff, I was quick to ensure I got a spot on the mission.

Baluchi

We secured a position on a prominent hillside overlooking the region and were surrounded by what seemed like impassable rocky mountains on either side of the valley. It was an ideal defensive position and we dug into the hard ground completing trenches and fighting pits to protect ourselves from enemy fire. Digging in 60 degree heat in helmet and body armour thinking this is crazy, but we all chipped in and soon had ourselves a very defensible position to stage operations from in a region known to be dominated by the Taliban.

If we were looking for a fight, we had come to the perfect location. We had secured the local area to construct a ford crossing across the Baluchi River. This would allow the locals to travel to Tarin Kowt without the need to go via a much longer route on the Western side of the river. This would increase trade and commerce and increase stability in the region. Patrol Base (PB) Baluchi was a dry, hot dust bowl.

Australian Forces Push into Taliban Territory,
Press Release, Department of Defence, 19 May 2008
'Australian soldiers have begun a major push into the Taliban heartland of Uruzgan Province in Southern Afghanistan with the intent of pushing out the Taliban, restoring vital infrastructure and creating a safe environment for the Afghan people. The Australian push is being spearheaded by engineers, infantry, cavalry and support troops of the 4th Reconstruction Task Force (RTF 4) who are drawn mainly from the Sydney and Brisbane areas. RTF 4 Commanding Officer, Lieutenant Colonel Stuart Yeaman, said the Task Force has moved into the

Baluchi region, North of its base at Tarin Kowt as part of a joint Dutch and Coalition operation.

"This is an area of huge tactical and strategic significance for the Taliban extremists," Lieutenant Colonel Yeaman said. "This is the Taliban's back yard and we are right on their main supply route between Helmand Province and their supply bases to the North. The aim of this series of operations is to clear out the Taliban, and then build the physical infrastructure – patrol bases particularly – which will allow the Afghan National Army (ANA) and police, with support from the International Security Assistance Force, to dominate these areas."

On one of our first dismounted patrols in the area we saw a strange sight, we ran into a giant of a man, over 8 feet tall. He was a real life Giant! I had never seen anything like it. His shoes were enormous and his hands were easily twice the size of my own. He looked very awkward when he stood and seemed to be in pain as he would crouch over. Obviously fascinated we got a few photos with the big fella, like he was a rock star, before continuing on through the medieval village. The story of David and Goliath popped into my head and I figured they must be distant relatives.

We would build the base all day and take turns on picket-duty at night, staring out into the darkness, waiting for an attack or observing the occasional gun fire in the distance. The biggest threat would again come from above in the form of 107mm rockets fired rather haphazardly into the patrol base from the green zone. This generally prompted a dismounted patrol going out to search the point of origin, noting the enemy was long gone by the time we would arrive. However, they often left a buried IED for us to find. We could not return fire into the green zone due to the civilian population and the Taliban took full advantage of this fact.

I remember on one occasion we were receiving indirect fire and Shirls had the shits so he jumped up on the HESCO walls took his shirt off, waved it around, calling out "here I am you bastards, hit me if you can," effectively taunting the aptly named Rocket man to adjust his rounds onto

Shirls. Fortunately, their aim was often so poor they couldn't hit the side of a barn door relying more on luck than technical ability.

We had been recovering a number of hoax devices in and around the Baluchi area and saw this as the enemy watching us and testing our procedures. Whilst en route down the Western bank of the Terri Rud (main river), we came across an IED at a typically vulnerable point. Shirls was the number one for the job. We conducted a handover with the search team and pulled our vehicle up next to theirs to get eyes onto the target location.

The left hand searcher had identified a metallic device buried in the dirt road, at a small water crossing, where the dirt was softer and easier to dig. The team had marked the find, conducted an isolation of the area. Infantry had been dismounted to provide flanking protection to drive off any ground threat or potential triggerman, who could initiate the device remotely from a distance.

The trouble was the cordon was spread very thin and could not effectively cover all of the surrounding terrain. We prepared our equipment and Shirls conducted an initial reconnaissance, utilising the robot to approach a device. We located the device and a power pack through some isolation techniques and decided to place a charge and attempt to separate the main explosive charge from the power source and trigger. Unfortunately, the remote placement of the charge failed for various reasons and Shirls was required to don the EOD 9 bomb suit and conduct a manual approach to complete the job.

We dressed him in the heavy suit in the 55-degree heat and he made his approach. As he got to about a metre from the device he just stopped. We watched from the relative safety of the bush master window and noticed some movement to the high ground approximately 100m from our position. It was a fighting age male. Shirls was completely exposed to enemy fire and also vulnerable to someone initiating a device remotely. He was effectively right in the kill zone with enemy watching his every move. If there was a command type device, now was the perfect time to initiate. We informed our security elements who dispatched personnel to drive back the spotters. As we were organising this, Shirls, knowing he was in a dangerous position, was busy trying to identify any possible command wires coming into the target area.

He knew he was in a very bad spot. He identified a wire running off towards a small group of buildings, known as Qallas, 20 metres to the left hand side of the road. This discovery was quickly identified as the real threat as the device was still live and the possibility of it being initiated by remote means was now very high. Shirls jumped to his feet and ran the 50m back to the vehicle in his bomb suit in a time that would have impressed Carl Lewis.

We removed the heavy suit as quickly as we could, he was shattered by the heat and energy he had expended as well as being overcome with fear at the realisation he was lucky to still be alive. We conducted our drills to complete the task without incident however, we were unable to catch the spotters before they fled. After speaking to Shirls later he revealed how he had thought of his wife and children when he identified the danger he was in and completely expected to die in that moment.

The potential triggerman had been driven off by infantry elements and the rest of the job was completed without incident with us recovering a switch, power source and destroying a 20kg explosive main charge that would have the potential to completely obliterate any life at close proximity, even in a bomb suit.

We were all excited that as a team we had cleared another IED and no one had been injured or killed, although we came too close for comfort. Exactly how close was revealed when we investigated the location where the triggerman was seen and we identified a Remote Control transmitter that would have been used to fire the device. It is very likely that the triggerman was preparing to fire the device whilst Shirls was over the top of it. We were all very pleased to walk away that day with the team intact.

The only thing that really upset me about this day was the fact that the commander did not allow us to pursue and detain the spotters or search the compounds they were observed in, more thoroughly. I believe decisions like this really cost us in Afghanistan, as we were simply not taking the fight to the enemy in an effective way. We were just reacting to being targeted. It was a frustration that was shared by many amongst the patrol and one that would plague much of RTF 4 operations throughout the deployment.

The completion of this job gave us a lot to consider and ensured our drills were tighter and set a standard for the remainder of the deployment. It also gave us the collective confidence to continue with our job and focus on the task at hand. I would often reflect back on the events of this day as a reason not to wear a bomb suit on task in Afghanistan. A 20kg charge would kill you instantly, regardless of the fact you were wearing a bomb suit, so from that day on, I never completed a task wearing the cumbersome and awkward suit, opting for the increased awareness and mobility provided by going down range in flak jacket and helmet.

There had been an element of luck on our side that day and the idea that a "force-field" of protection was surrounding Australian Troops in Afghanistan was cemented in my mind. This idea was not new as many soldiers had walked away from contacts with the enemy with little to no understanding as to how. It was a strange phenomenon, Australian soldiers in combat would not receive significant casualties when around us coalition and Afghan forces were being killed in much higher numbers in the same area and often in the same engagements. It was odd to the point of amazement at times and we would often talk about the bizarre reality that it presented. Coalition forces would ask why Australian soldier casualties were so low compared with their own and although we did operate differently than many of our coalition partners, we were in the same fight and sometimes 'luck' or this "force-field" of protection just sat over us. Unfortunately, this protection would not last forever.

I remember my first IED task and the fear and uncertainty it raised up in me. I had completed a number of standard EOD tasks by now, dealing with unexploded ordnance, cache clearance, search and recovery operations, post blast clearance and other clearance tasks. However, all this experience did little to calm my nerves. I remember feeling petrified that I would do something wrong and I took a few moments to steady my nerves before starting the job trying not to reveal my true emotions to anyone around me.

In reality my first task was a fairly simple one with a suspect device located on a route near the main town of Tarin Kowt. Targeting coalition forces who had been using the route to access a work site in town over the past week. A high metal content device was identified on the route and approximately 20kg of Home Made Explosive (HME) was in it. The searchers had done a great job in identifying the components and marking a clear route into the device, which lay on the road on an approach to a small water crossing known as a Wadi. I felt incredibly nervous the first time I walked down on an IED. Trying to remember all the training and preparation I had completed for this very moment. I was still not confident and the nerves continued to build in my stomach. I muttered a few prayers like a mantra in my mind in an attempt to focus my mind and not allow myself to be carried away with fear. Thankfully it worked. My mind stopped racing and I began to focus on the task at hand.

I was very aware that there may be a secondary device or another threat and that I was out the front of the patrol and completely exposed to the enemy. I could feel my heart beating in my chest and the sound echoed through my ears as I fixated on the ground in-front of me. All of the ground looked the same, hard dusty and rocky.

I walked down the safe lane marked with spray paint, this lane is typically about one-meter-wide and was marked by the Engineer searcher who had discovered the device. I knew it was clear, but slowly swung my mine detector in front of my feet anyway. I stopped occasionally, swinging the detector over the metal islets on my boots, just to reassure myself that it was working, and as I heard the familiar tone of the detector reacting to metal, I felt a great sense of relief.

The equipment was good and I trusted it with my life but I constantly checked for peace of mind. As I got closer to the IED site the ground softened, it was obvious why the insurgents had chosen this location as it funnelled our vehicles onto a narrow part of the road where water crossed over the road making the ground much easier to dig and therefore conceal a device.

I imagined the person emplacing the device, calculating his probability of hitting a coalition vehicle verses a civilian vehicle and wondered how they justified taking the risk of killing innocent civilians with such an insidious weapon that does not discriminate against its victims.

Our enemy was smart and cunning. They took time to emplace their devices in a way that would give them the best chance of success. They did not have an infinite number of resources to target us with and they wanted every device to count. They were trying their very best to kill me and I was trying my very best to stay alive. There is a lot of pressure to complete an IED task as quickly as possible to keep friendly forces moving, routes open and reduce the amount of time we are a static target on the ground. There is no time to muck around.

In the end I dealt with the device without incident taking the easier option to dispose of the device rather than attempt recovery. I positioned an explosive charge over the main explosive component. I thought about attempting a recovery of the components however, understanding the threat from secondary devices and anti-handling devices, I didn't want to take any chances and just wanted to get one successful job under my belt without pushing my luck. After destroying the main explosive component, I remotely pulled the remaining components out of the ground mitigating any further threat.

On my final approach I was focused on clearing for secondary devices, gathering evidence and opening the route for mobility forces to continue through. There were remnants of a yellow palm oil container all over the road as a result of the blast that set off approximately 20kg of explosive. There was not much else to recover, save some wires and a battery pack. Much of the pressure plate which would have triggered the device was destroyed, due to its close proximity to the main explosive charge.

There was a decent hole in the ground and I methodically and slowly cleared the site, marking my movements, and being careful not to place a foot outside of my cleared area. I searched with my mine detector and visually, looking for any sign of another device or mine and occasionally stopping to lay down and investigate with my mine prodder.

One of the most essential pieces of equipment for an EOD Tech working in Afghanistan was a prodder, that equates to a chopstick on the end of a handle used to poke and prod the ground in a way that hopefully won't kill you if you hit a mine. For all our reliance on technology its interesting how your life can come to rely on something so simple. I probably took longer than I should have to complete this task but that did not matter. I just wanted to get it done and get home safely. I handed the site back to the manoeuvre commander as there were no other devices on this particular day and returned to the back of the vehicle to smoke a cigarette and calm my nerves.

Fighting an enemy, you see daily and can do little about is excruciatingly frustrating. We would search and detain suspected Taliban or fighting-age males on an almost daily basis; however, they knew how to remain free. They would never openly carry weapons or explosives, preferring to use a sophisticated network of caches, and allowing them to travel between areas without fear of being arrested or prosecuted. They would access weapons, explosives and bomb making material only when they were going to use it and as quickly as the task was done everything would go back underground.

We found it very difficult to detain and arrest individuals based on gathered intelligence at this time and relied heavily on explosive swab testing to detain suspected bomb makers. The Taliban had the advantage and they knew it. They would look at us with utter distain and mutter under their breath as we searched them. All we wanted was a face to face fight with an enemy that would not run behind the safety of women and children in the villages after taking a few pot shots at us.

The locals were under constant threat from the Taliban and murders were a regular occurrence as the Taliban would simply cut the throats of anyone thought to be assisting Coalition Forces. Regular night letters were dropped door to door, threatening death to anyone assisting the infidels or accepting work, or trading with us in any way. It was a constant battle for the hearts and minds of the local Afghan people to have them rise up over the fear and oppression the Taliban were imposing upon them. We would do our best through holding *Shuras* (a term for an important meeting) to involve the locals as much as possible in improving their community, safety and freedom.

We could not shower for weeks at a time and resorted to baby wipes and the occasional wade through the river whilst on patrol to try to keep clean. The dust would get into everything and we had no way of preventing it. The days were averaging over 40 degrees now and life in the Baluchi Valley was tough. No fresh rations received and not enough rations to keep going. People began to lose weight and gastro spread through the forward operating base quickly and uncontrollably, due to the poor living conditions. People were regularly being evacuated due to poor health and dehydration.

Defecating in the field was always an experience and you could not afford to be shy about doing your business. I remember a period where everyone seemed to get the squirts at once. Patrols still went on and work needed to be completed. The guys would come back in from a patrol with brown stains running down the legs of their cams. There was nothing you could really do other than pick up a hand full of sand, throw it down your pants to soak up the mess and keep on walking. Showers and toilets were brought in towards the end of our time at Baluchi, just as we were ready to hand it over to the Afghan National Army.

On one occasion we were on patrol, stopping a series of trucks on the road, and searching them for explosives and weapons. This was an unfortunate task bestowed on us because an officer in Tarin Kowt had unwisely released all the civilian "Jingle Trucks" out of the base prior to their movement forward to Baluchi. Essentially this provided an ideal opportunity for the Taliban to repack one or more of the supply trucks with high explosives and drive it straight into the forward patrol base and kill a large portion of the people inside, because the convoy was now unmonitored for more than a 24 hour period.

Fortunately, the error was identified and we set out to meet the huge convoy in the desert and manually search and clear each and every truck prior to them being allowed access into the base. While we were conducting the clearance operation Shirls decided he needed a dump and headed off over to a small creek and proceeded to do his business. About an hour later we looked up at the sound of an Afghan male screaming and jumping up and down after he had stepped directly into the poo mine Shirls had laid earlier; we were in stitches with laughter watching this man hop around on one foot swearing and carrying on.

Humour was a critical part to our survival in a war zone and was my personal pressure release valve. I often got frustrated with command decision that were adversely affecting us on the ground and with operational decisions that simply did not make a whole lot of sense to me at the time. It was humour that got me through on those occasions.

Communications back home were extremely limited and we were allowed a 5-minute satellite phone call once every few weeks, that we had to pay for! I called Zoe once during my time at Baluchi.

Fortunately, I was traveling back and forth from TK providing EOD support to supply convoys running up and down the AO. Some individuals remained in Baluchi for months on end which was pretty hard on them. On one particular operation the opportunity to improve our diet arose when Barto spoke with one of the truck drivers and bartered with him so we could purchase watermelons, cucumbers and coke. We ate like kings that night, the fresh food filling our bellies and we laughed at how the Afghans were feeding us better than our own command.

On Tuesday the 8th of July 2008 a radio message came in that an Australian SF patrol had struck an IED a few kilometres North of our position and that they required EOD and recovery support from RTF ground elements. We moved out after a short planning session and married up with the Special Forces elements on the ground. When we arrived it was clear the damage from the blast was significant and the CASEVAC had just been completed taking Signaller Sean McCarthy and three other injured Australians and one Afghan National interpreter to Tarin Kowt for treatment.

Sean was standing in the centre cupola of a Long Range Patrol Vehicle (LRPV) when a large device initiated directly under his feet. It tore through the belly armour of the vehicle creating horrific blast injuries and blowing him out of the vehicle. The driver, passenger as well as an interpreter in the rear of the vehicle were ejected and suffered significant injuries.

Sean was treated and awaiting medical evacuation. He had been lying on the ground drifting in and out of consciouness, but for Sean and the men in those terrible circumstances the evacuation seemed to take forever. Unfortunately, Sean reportedly died on route to the medical facility.

The time the medical evacuation helicopter took to get on site that day eroded the men's confidence in the supporting elements they relied upon to get them back to treatment inside of the critical hour of an incident occurring. This timeframe is known as the 'Golden Hour' and is widely understood as the critical time in which your odds of survival significantly diminish if you are not at a medical facility within this period. Sean was the second SF soldier killed in the province since our tour began.

Finny and I moved into the blast site to hand over from the EOD Tech supporting the SF ground movement. The SF operator was physically shaken by the day's events. It was his job to identify and clear these devices and on this, his first patrol, he had failed to identify a device and it had a catastrophic result. The truth is his job was an extremely difficult and demanding one. Circumstances on the day added to mission failure and the fact that it was his first mission did not fare well for his confidence. He was unable to assist with the vehicle clearance due to shock. To his credit this man would continue on with his deployment, serving with distinction and would be involved in a number of significant conflicts in later months, bringing great credit to himself, his unit, his trade, and the Corp of Engineers.

The LRPV was a mess and remained just outside a small wadi on the track. Petrol was draining all over the dirt and various weapons and explosive charges were scattered around the site, thrown from the blast. These included RPG's, grenades, small arms ammunition, claymore anti-personnel weapons etc. Leaving a relative arsenal of damaged explosive hazards around the site. The smell of explosive residue sat heavy over the blast site filling my nostrils. We conducted an isolation of the vehicle with a search team, recovering whatever we could of our fallen comrade to be returned with his remains.

We searched for secondary devices before trying to recover components from the blast site, so we could better understand the cause of the incident and how best to avoid similar incidents in the future. The clearance was very difficult due to the huge metallic contamination of the site from the vehicle debris scattered everywhere. The hole from the explosive was large but there was no sign of any bomb components. No switch or power source, indicating the device was likely a low metal content Anti-Tank mine, explaining why the EOD and search personal had missed it on their clearance of the vulnerable point.

We completed the clearance of the site, handing over to a vehicle recovery team. Just before departing the area we conducted a controlled demolition of the damaged explosive components at the site, which sent a large explosion echoing through the valley at dusk. We returned to FOB Baluchi and examined the physical evidence we had and ascertained that there was no trace of components or fragmentation embedded in Sean's severed legs and boots. I later returned the remains to the RSM of TF66 in Tarin Kowt. A grim delivery to a visibly upset individual. The details of this incident would live in my memory for a long time. The smell of blood in the air, the pools of blood on the ground along with soaked bandages and medical equipment used to treat the injured. The extent of body fragments scattered around the blast site and the memory of a fallen Elite Australian Soldier.

Release of the Inquiry Officer's Report into the Death of Signaller Sean McCarthy, Media Release, Department of Defence, 9 October 2008.

"The Inquiry Officer's Report found that Signaller McCarthy died from massive wounds sustained when an improvised explosive device detonated under the Long Range Patrol Vehicle he was travelling in. The Inquiry Officer found that the Aero-Medical Evacuation process was conducted within timings specified by the International Security Assistance Force (ISAF) and agreed to by Australia. The Inquiry Officer also found that no equipment, personnel or process contributed to Signaller McCarthy's death."

*****

The after effects of the death of Sig Sean McCarthy are still a part of our lives today.

Looking back at this event, I distinctly remember looking at Barto and seeing an immense sadness and pain in his eyes. This huge man suddenly looked like a small child as he tried to come to terms with what was happening in-front of him. I recognised his mental struggle and simply told him to crack-on and do his job. I knew that at that moment we could not stop to process what was going on emotionally and we needed to focus on the task at hand. I have no regrets in telling him this at the time as I believe it was the right thing to do.

Unfortunately, I never followed up with Barto after this incident and many others, to see how they were processing the events of the day. I had simply removed myself to think about them and I had an expectation that others would somehow do the same.

I ran into Barto years later, at Mates4mates in Brisbane, and he expressed to me his wish that we had spoken about this and other events in the years following the 2008 deployment. I realised I had failed in my duty of care as a commander and the weight of so many of my soldiers who I know were struggling, fell on my shoulders. I had failed to respond to people whom it was my duty to protect, who were in need of help and it haunted me.

The reality is that I was not equipped to manage my own struggle let alone be in a position to help others. I feel like all my training in leadership and personnel management had not prepared me to help people suffering from the mentally traumatic effects of war. This personal observation is one of the many facets of why I have chosen to tell my story. The Army had not prepared me to help others with mental illness and I feel that it is an ongoing problem within the Australian Defence Force. One that needs to be reviewed. The culture at the time was denial and avoidance rather than acknowledgement and treatment.

Barto is still recovering from his experiences in Afghanistan and I know and believe that if we were able to simply talk events through, post incident, it would have allowed us to process things better. It might have reduced some of the pain that avoidance has let to.

*****

Since our arrival in 2006, Australian Soldiers had formed a reputation with the Taliban as hard fighting soldiers that would pursue any attacker and would not fall back in a fight. As a result, the enemy would refer to us as the 'Red Rat' on account of the Red Kangaroo painted on the side of all of our vehicles. We would often intercept enemy communications from the Taliban waiting in ambush positions, hearing them say something to the tune of: 'Do not engage, it is the Red Rat soldiers, do not fire.' As a result, many of our contacts would be short-lived as Taliban soldiers would prefer to take opportunity shots at us, or target us with IEDs through night emplacement, rather than fight face to face in direct combat.

*****

Every few weeks a care package would arrive from friends and family back home. But none made me feel as loved and appreciated as I did when I opened the ones from Zoe. She had lovingly boxed up a bunch of my favourite things like Tim Tams, Shapes and canned oysters along with DVDs of the kids growing up and living life back in Australia. The cartons would also contain pictures and drawings and short notes. These care packages really lifted my spirits and made me feel so loved when I needed it most. I felt Zoe's heart when I opened these boxes and I felt closer to the boys although it did make me miss them all terribly. I also really enjoyed reading the short letters from my parents catching up on what my brothers were doing back home and hearing their voices through the words on the page.

*****

As we spent so much time in Baluchi building the crossing site we set a lot of patterns with our daily movements and therefor made ourselves vulnerable to IED attack. On one particular day our team was called to the crossing site late in the day after a PMV struck an IED on departure from their overwatch position.

This vehicle had been using the same overwatch position to provide security to dismounted troops working on the crossing for a number of weeks and complacency had crept into the daily routine. Rather than conducting a thorough search of the area prior to occupying the position the vehicle simply drove in with a cursory visual clearance and remained on site since first light. As the day's work drew to a close the vehicle reversed out and drove over an IED it had essentially been parked next to all day. In addition, dismounted personnel had been walking around the device all day without knowing how very close they were to a deadly end.

Complacency is the number one killer of soldiers in a war like Afghanistan. When soldiers get tired or comfortable, they let their guard down and miss things or slacken in their drills. Many deaths in Afghanistan were simply as a result of tired soldiers being pushed to their limits and losing focus if only for an instant.

Fortunately, when the PMV tire rolled over the pressure plate initiating the device the main charge deflagrated, meaning it did not function as an explosion and simply blew itself apart without the normal force of a high explosive. Again Australian forces seemed to walk away unharmed from a potentially deadly situation.

The size of the charge was approximately 40kg, enough to cause significant and even catastrophic damage, even to an armoured military vehicle, and the occupants inside.

*****

The days started to fly past as we spent time between Dihrawud, Shahidi Hassas, Chora and Tarin Kowt, on clearance patrol or aggressively conducting search operations targeting caches and enemy supply lines.

We would occasionally come into contact with the Taliban who would typically shoot and scoot in order to draw us into an ambush, in an area of their choosing and where they had placed IEDs to target our troops. If they didn't do this, they would simply just take an opportune shot at us before disappearing into the community of huts and fields.

Each day was generally made up of a few short rushes of excitement followed by hours of boredom sitting around waiting, walking kilometres, or sitting in the back of a vehicle for hours.

I enjoyed my time on the ground in the villages the most as we would interact with the local people. Mainly the men and children as the women would keep their distance unless they had a complaint or grievance to discuss and would not generally share information about the Taliban for fear of reprisal attacks on their families.

The kids however, would come up and shout and play. I would carry lollies and small gifts like tooth brushes to give to the kids in the rural villages, needing to show them what they were and how to use them. Most of these villages appeared to be built in the 17th century and had next to no modern amenities. Often the only modern item you would see was a pressure cooker that would be placed on an open fire to prepare meals.

We became a reactionary force in a lot of ways and would mainly respond to incidents. This was due to the type of stationary construction operations being conducted.

Some days were spent clearing rocket launch sites or searching for them, others were spent destroying old ordnance or digging unexploded rockets out of local back yards.

One day whilst attending orders for a significant cordon and search operation to clear a known Taliban stronghold, a PMV Bushmaster caught alight on the hill behind us.

All of a sudden there were small explosions, followed by larger and larger explosions, as the vehicle was completely engulfed in flames and all the explosive stores cooked off. The fire was started when a soldier was cooking a brew next to the tire and kicked his burner over. The vehicle quickly caught alight and a soldier inside was dragged out through the cupola after being overcome by the fumes.

Fortunately, only one individual suffered injury and we proceeded to put the vehicle fire out and then sift through the remains in order to remove all the ordnance and make the vehicle safe for transportation.

On July 9, I went with a small team of searchers, including an Explosive Detection Dog and Handler were flown out from Tarin Kowt to the North via Black Hawk helicopter. We were to assist the Dutch with a vehicle recovery operation of an IED strike that resulted in the death of a Dutch Soldier and the wounding of several others.

The soldiers were travelling in a flat bottom M113, on the top of a ridge-line north of FOB Baluchi. The Dutch were forced to leave the vehicle on site and withdraw to the safety of the FOB for the night, rather than be caught out on an exposed ridge and open to enemy attack. The Taliban had been observed, emplacing IEDs around the stranded vehicle and the Dutch requested Australian Search and EOD assets to assist with the rapid clearance and recovery of the vehicle.

We set out early on the 10th and made our way up the steep ridge-lines towards the vehicle. As we got closer, we continued on foot, me with a F3 Mine detector out front and an Explosive Detection Dog Team behind.

The dog would shoot forward and clear the ridge as I marked a safe lane towards the vehicle. We conducted an isolation and started a clearance of the site to allow the recovery vehicle in to hook up the vehicle and remove it from the site.

As I lay on my belly, clearing a suspect device we started to take Indirect Fire (IDF) from enemy mortars onto our position. The Taliban had us dialled in on the exposed ridge-line as they knew we would be back to recover the vehicle. So, they had time to plan a deliberate attack on our location.

The Dutch, immediately returned fire with direct and indirect weapons including a small but effective portable mortar. I was amazed at how quickly the team got rounds back down range. I looked towards my vehicle approximately 50m in front and thought I have two choices, stay on the ground and hope I don't get hit by the accurate mortar fire or get up and run to the safety of the Bushmaster. The only problem being the likelihood of stepping on a mine or IED between my position and the safety of my armoured vehicle. I decided to make a run for it. So, I took a deep breath, jumped up and ran as fast as I could, towards the vehicle. As I ran I tried to place my feet on rocks and not onto any obvious patches of open dirt. I jumped from one pad to another like a crazy person playing hopscotch in the desert. Calling out as I approached the vehicle to open the back door and dove inside as rounds continued to land around our open position on the ridge line. We returned fire and drove the enemy back from their firing positions, eventually regaining control of the area before continuing on with the clearance and recovery operation.

After we got back to the FOB we all laughed as we replayed the day's events. This was the closest I had personally come to being injured or killed in action to date and the reality of that didn't really sink in until later. I was buzzing with adrenaline, loving the excitement and the rush. Later, replaying the incident in my head, I remembered a number of steps I had taken, where there was no hard ground or flat rocks to land on. In those moments I thought, 'prepare for a bang,' and was somewhat surprised when it did not come as I took another bound, closer to the safety of the Bushmaster.

We knew there were a number of anti-personnel mines and IEDs on the site surrounding the vehicle that day, because the Dutch had observed the Taliban emplace the items during the night. That is why I was out front looking for them, to identify and clear them. I had my head over a device when the attack started and I was fortunate to walk away. That night, I said a prayer of thanks as I lay in my sleeping bag and thought of being reunited with my wife and sons.

As the first Army commander to take Navy EOD personnel into theatre I had an expectation that there would be a few teething issues as the "pussers", a term of endearment, got used to doing things 'the Army way'. We had plenty of laughs throughout the tour as Shirls and Stiffy were constantly baffled at the Army way of doing things. Although, I should mention their field skills, weapon handling and basic soldiering were certainly up to speed, in fact, as both sailors had passed the gruelling SAS selection course, there was no question about their abilities. On one occasion a member from 3 RAR decided to give Stiffy a little lip about being a Navy wanker, at which point Stiff- quickly adjusted this member's attitude on addressing a senior sailor who had more military experience in his big toe than this over eager beaver who considered himself "Elite". The conversation ended with the young soldier exiting the area with his tail between his legs and apologising profusely.

The boss asked me to tell the men to shave on various occasions to which I had to politely direct him to Navy standing orders, which clearly states Navy men are allowed to wear beards. This one fact pissed off a number of the Infantry Officers immensely, giving me incredible joy of refusing their direction to tell my men to shave, whilst our team was attached to them, for various missions. Some stating it was becoming a problem of morale for their men to witness some people being allowed to grow beards whilst others could not.

It never ceases to amaze me how much bullshit little issues give rise to in the Defence Force. Even in a war zone, where you might think people could just get on and do their job, without worrying about the little things others may be allowed to do.

It became a bit of a running joke at times as polite requests would come down the chain of command: "Please inform your personnel that they are in the Army now and need to abide by Army standing orders and shave in accordance with the CO's direction". To which I would reply they are in the NAVY, get it. Not ARMY. Shaving, who bloody cares?!

Working with these Navy guys mixed in amongst the team turned out to be a real blessing in the end. They injected a level of trade professionalism unique to their background and training. In a trade like EOD, where there is no single solution to a problem and the ability to see things from different perspectives really mattered, I saw them as a real asset. Their training and background was different to ours and it proved to be a real advantage in dealing with counter IED operations, Cordon and Search operations and counter insurgency warfare. Nothing could be templated and new methods of defeating the enemy were required on an almost daily basis. They also brought in a great deal of comedy, a commodity that is absolutely essential in war and one that I would welcome over many others.

*****

After the crossing in Baluchi was complete we focused our construction efforts back in TK and I spent more time back in the dreaded TOC. I would make the most of my time there deploying on Post Indirect Fire (IDF) Attack exploitation missions and disposing of foreign ordnance on the range.

One person that aided in my sanity throughout this period of my deployment was Captain Andy Bridge, "Bridgy", the Battle Captain for the deployment and one of the most professional, capable and respected officers I know. People like Bridgy keep the Army running, an incredible organiser of people and assets, who could juggle seemingly infinite tasks while looking as confident and poised as an acrobat on a tight rope. I would try to improve his mundane existence in the TOC with offers to come on mission in my vehicle or take him to a blast site, but for the most part he was stuck in a building without windows 18 hours a day, a victim to his own success and competence. To his credit, he never let it get him down.

One of the most rewarding tasks my team was involved in with, was building a Hospital for the local people. We were based out of a small Patrol Base, PB Lydiard, named after my friend Michael Lydiard who was severely wounded by an IED in November 2007.

We worked during the day, in the heat and dust, as labourers laying bricks and mixing cement alongside local Afghan contractors, to improve the facilities and way of life, for the people living in and around the Sork Morgab area.

One of the things I loved about being a Combat Engineer was the fact that we just got stuck into every task we could. Enjoying the constant change to daily routine. It also did wonders for making the time go by.

On one particular day whilst laying bricks at the new hospital we heard a very large explosion and saw a billowing pillar of smoke rise off the hill approximately 1km to the West of our position. We jumped in our PMV and departed with the Quick Reaction Force (QRF) to the site. On arrival we secured some high ground approximately 100m to the South of the incident site, revealing a chaotic scene.

There was a dirt road leading down to a creek crossing. Up on the other side of it was a red Toyota Hilux; parked to the right hand side of the road in a position often used by coalition forces to provide overwatch and covering fire to the valley below. There were fields to the left and right of the road and a large hill further on that was the location of a local cemetery; easily identifiable due to the large array of coloured flags on sticks on the hill.

The scene below was horrific and revealed numerous casualties in urgent need of medical attention. We needed to secure the area and provide assistance as quickly as possible. We searched down a road, crossing a small river and approached the site. We were moving as quickly as possible to get to the injured children and apply first aid. However, we could not simply rush in and put ourselves in danger of being killed by an ambush or secondary IED strike. I felt torn by my want to render assistance and my tactical brain telling me to wait, secure the area and get protection in place.

There were local nationals running everywhere by the time we arrived on site. Pools of blood soaking into the dust and individuals staggering and being carried off with various blast injuries. I could taste the heavy metallic aftermath of vaporised blood in the air and the smell of death filled my nostrils.

We immediately secured the site conducting an isolation of the area in an effort to mitigate any further attacks and threats and established a causality treatment area. Infantry elements were positioned in overwatch securing any possible areas of attack to allow us to work in the incident site without the threat of being shot at while in the open. As we were completing the isolation of the IED site, one of the Explosive Detection Dogs (EDDs) was off the lead and searching for secondary explosive devices, when his handler and I witnessed him take a few bites of a number of bits of flesh scattered on the ground. A little shocked and disturbed, I indicated to the Handler to put the dog on lead and we carried on.

The carnage from the attack was everywhere. I looked up and witnessed a man walking around looking on the ground and then watched him pick up his own severed arm before staggering off to the river; a child screamed in agony with severe blast injuries and burns over a large portion of her body; a man lay dying on the ground next to the vehicle; people were screaming in agony as others were calmly carrying bodies off to be buried on the cemetery behind our position.

Afghans strive to bury the deceased as soon as possible after death, avoiding the need for embalming or otherwise disturbing the body of the deceased. All of these things seemed to be happening in a strange dream like state as I blocked out the screams and confusion and concentrated on my task at hand. I found it almost easy to ignore the severity of what was happening around me because I had an important and dangerous job to do. My mind simply compartmentalised the events of that day to allow me to perform my duty without issue.

My main job was getting to the blast site and ensuring there were no more devices in the immediate vicinity that could injure additional personnel, including clearing the casualty evacuation point. After the scene was safe, my role switched to post blast analysis. Gathering evidence and information about what had happened, who was involved and how the attack was conducted. This was all done in an effort to learn more about the enemy and help catch and convict the perpetrators. This included the gathering of physical evidence, chemical explosive testing, gathering biometric evidence such as fingerprints and DNA and photography.

In my approach to the Red Hilux, I passed under the body of a small child impaled in a tree. The top half of his little body hanging lifeless and contorted in the tree above, I put the image out of my mind and then began to see additional body parts strewn all over the ground. As I searched in and cleared the site, it became apparent that the vehicle had pulled over in a location often used by Australian forces as an overwatch, to provide security to dismounted soldiers patrolling the green zone below.

This civilian vehicle had a flat tire and as the man was changing the tire his family stood around him, watching. A child had then stepped on a pressure plate, initiating a large Home Made Explosive charge that detonated under the entire family.

Bodies were torn apart in the violence of the explosion and thrown twenty feet, in all directions. Those that survived the initial blast were severely injured. Those that could, crawled away into the creek below, a strange phenomenon I had witnessed as dying people seem to be attracted to bodies of water. I imagine the idea of getting into the water to lessen the pain?

As I cleared the remainder of the site, picking up evidence and bomb components, I stared into the face of a man in his mid-thirties. He was the man changing the tyre at the time of the blast and was thrown into the car causing a significant dent in the side panel of the car. His body was cut in half by the force of the explosion, his legs missing, he lay on the ground facing up, looking at the sky and bleeding out. There was nothing anyone could do for this man his injuries obviously too severe to allow any chance of survival. His lifeless eyes now staring back into mine. His eyes had lost their shine and had dulled, a haze or cloud formed across his corneas. Where there was life only moments ago, now there was nothing. I photographed his face and body for documentation and continued on task. In total five civilians were killed and four more wounded in this event. A tragic by-product of a war waged amongst a civilian population.

One thing that stuck in my mind from that day's events was the professionalism of the Australian soldiers involved. Every soldier on site that day, got stuck into doing their job, professionally and quickly in order to treat and care for the wounded. Without the quick and decisive actions of many that day, the wounded would have surely died.

We turned to black humour to help our minds remain focused on the task at hand and tried not to get drawn into a world of death, despair and horror. I noticed on a few occasions the blank stares of men looking at the bodies on the ground, fixating on the horror of the incident. We used one another to pull ourselves out of those moments and to compartmentalise what was happening. For me, it took almost dehumanising the dead to allow myself to concentrate on the living and focus on my job at hand. I was not impartial to their demise but simply viewed it as though I could do nothing for the dead, so needed to ignore them and focus on the living.

It was not until later that night in the relative safety of the Patrol Base that I allowed my mind to process some of the graphic events of the day. As I lay in my sleeping bag on the dirt looking up at the stars above in the Afghan night sky, I allowed myself a moment to imagine the despair and pain the family was going through, losing so many loved ones in one horrific incident.

When I closed my eyes I just saw the cold dead eyes of mutilated bodies staring back at me. I opened my eyes, shook my head and said no! I did not want to give these thoughts or images any traction in my mind and made a concerted effort to push the day's events to the very back of my consciousness.

That night I slept uneasily and awoke with a fright seeing what I thought was a Taliban fighter standing over me and the sleeping soldiers around me. I grabbed my pistol and pointed it at the shape squinting my eyes to get a better look at him and understand what was going on. As I blinked my eyes trying to focus on the threat infront of me I realised I was pointing my weapon at nothing. Where I had seen someone with a weapon, now there was nothing. It scared me that night, when I realised how dangerous the situation was as I was very close to firing my weapon inside a patrol base at nothing more than a ghost! I never spoke about this incident to anyone and didn't want to acknowledge that it even happened. However, the memory and the fear of that moment stayed with me for a long time. I didn't dream for the remainder of my deployment after that night.

I started to see cracks appearing in some of the soldiers around me. The tough exteriors giving way to quiet contemplation and sadness. I spoke with a number of the men encouraging them not to think about the details of the day's events and to concentrate on keeping busy and doing their jobs. Again we resorted to the use of humour to get us through each day.

From a tactical perspective, the day's events were a complete success for Australian forces operating in the region. We were seen to provide care and support to those Afghan nationals in need after they fell victim to a Taliban attack. The Taliban tried to spin a story about a coalition force helicopter firing a rocket into the civilian vehicle but, the locals knew exactly what had occurred on the day. As a result the local people came to us with information about the location of the Taliban involved in the attack as well as locations of cached weapons, explosives and other intelligence to help us target the Taliban in the area. As a result, we conducted a series of successful cordon and search operations in the area over the following days, resulting in the capture and subsequent trial and imprisonment of a number of Taliban individuals as well as the ceasing of weapons and equipment.

In early September we visited the Role Two medical facility in TK, where a room full of wounded soldiers lay on beds recovering from the latest contact with Taliban forces. It was a sobering experience walking into a room with so many Australians injured. Amongst the wounded were two engineers I knew, who were supporting SAS operations in the Khas Oruzgan area. The EOD Tech had been shot in the hand and leg, the 7.62mm round drilling a neat hole through his femur, and a Sapper received significant secondary fragmentation wounds and burns to one side of his body including his face, from an RPG that exploded next to him. Both men recovered from their wounds and continued to serve with honour. It was also during this incident that Mark Donaldson was awarded the Victoria Cross. A news report of the incident read:

Nine elite troops ambushed in southern Afghanistan, Brendan Nicholson, Age, 3 September 2008

"Australia has suffered one of its worst battlefield incidents since the Vietnam War. The Australians, all elite special forces soldiers, were driving through rugged mountain country in southern Afghanistan on Monday evening when they were surprised by a barrage of rockets and machine-gun fire.

The attack occurred in fading light as the Australians were returning to their base at Tarin Kowt after a mission to hunt Taliban leaders and bomb-making factories in the heat and dust of Oruzgan province.

ADF spokesman Brigadier Brian Dawson said the Australians were in vehicles when they were ambushed. He said that as the northern winter approached, the Taliban were stepping up their activities before severe weather and snow limited their operations."

Towards the completion of my tour I was fortunate enough to travel to Kandahar for a period and onto Bagram Airfield in the North to spend time with our personnel deployed there. I was constantly amazed at the magnitude of the US led bases in these locations. They were literally like small cities and as such attracted all the typical social problems of a small city including theft, rape, murder and suicide.

I managed to go on a few missions with the US and Canadian EOD teams based out of these locations and enjoyed the experience. They seemed to take a lot more risks than we did which may have accounted for the larger number of injuries and deaths they seemed to endure. I drove through the streets of Bagram in an up-armoured land cruiser, dodging traffic, animals and people as we did our best not to stop or allow ourselves to become an easy target for suicide IED attacks. While in Bagram, there was a large Vehicle born IED that killed a large number of civilians and a number of US Army personnel. Even though war never really stopped and incidents were only a matter of hours apart, I never really felt as if I was in significant danger and simply felt like a tourist in a strange and foreign land at times.

The pace of life was fast, making me feel like I was a part of something significant. My team and I were making a difference to the people of Afghanistan.

During our tour, we had successfully recovered or destroyed numerous IED's and weapons, uncovered and exploited caches and hides, destroyed Taliban strongholds and resources and assisted in the arrests and prosecution of Taliban fighters.

We had also ensured the safety of our people and improved the safety for the Afghan people in the region. In total there were 27 Australian Defence Force personnel wounded in Afghanistan during 2008 and three killed.

In comparison the Dutch had six KIA during the same period. Of note, the Afghan National Army and Police casualties would be innumerable and horrendous by comparison. Rarely a day would go by without the report of an Afghan soldier being killed.

The microcosm of Afghan society that I witnessed through my khaki lenses, was probably quite different to the everyday reality these people were living. My interactions were limited and were conducted with me holding a rifle or pistol at the very least. There was little trust between us, and for good reason. Even so, I never felt overly threatened or endangered during our exchanges. I learned a lot during my tour about the various peoples and customs of this tribal land and felt enriched as a result of the experience.

When all was said and done, my fellow soldiers and sailors had made a significant contribution to the physical and economic stability of the region through the provision of roads, bridges, schools, hospitals and more. As well as providing opportunities of employment, training and experience to the local people.

One of the most succesul programs I witnessed from a human connection perspective, was the Trade Training School that involved the training of Afghan nationals in various trades, by Australian Army personnel. Resulting in the provision of tools and a trained individual returning to their local area to employ their trade and improve their own community.

When I stepped foot on the C-130 to depart TK and start my journey home I felt so relieved. I left Afghanistan proud of what we had achieved, proud of my country and my team. My personal goal was achieved when my entire team returned to Australia unharmed.

I landed back in Australia on my birthday with Zoe, Joseph and Charlie waiting to greet me with open arms. I missed them so very much throughout my deployment even if I tried not to think about it too much. It all hit home when I saw their smiling faces and I cried as I held my baby boys.

Joseph wouldn't let me go and Charlie, now seven months old seemed unsure of who I was. I had spent less than a week with him since his birth. It was time to get to know my son.

6

Zoe

Aftermath of War

Andy left for Afghanistan shortly after Charlie's birth. Leaving me with a one-week old baby and a 2 year old boy.

So there I was, in survival mode, practically a single mum. There was nothing left to do, but move back with my folks in the hills of Byron bay. I was blessed by the fact that my mum was running family day care from home, so I was able to focus my attentions on Charlie, comforted by the fact that Joseph was getting some attention at least.

My boys were so like Andy in their fairness. My heart would ache every time I looked at them. My little family unit was missing a big chunk with his absence. My time was filled with my newborn and toddler and I would constantly film them, making DVDs to send in the care packages that I lovingly prepared for Andy. The packages, filled with DVDs, accompanied with baby wipes, smoked oysters and Tim Tams. I knew he looked forward to these updates and gifts from home.

Six months later Andy came back, with hints of being a different man. You'd expect nothing less with the things they were exposed to.

He began drinking more than usual, and although I wasn't a stranger to a drink or two myself (Darwin will do that you), I recall many nights spent on the town with the army boys drinking Rum and Coke like it was water. His consumption of alcohol had gone beyond even military standards as it was evident it had taken an almost medicinal role.

The drinking didn't help the anger that was always just beneath the surface either. The man I knew who had always been patient, now showed little restraint or tolerance to others.

One such occasion involved him being thrown out of a pub in Byron on New Year's. Returning with a torn shirt and black eye. Even without alcohol he was angry. I recall a road rage incident when both boys were in the back of the car and Andy actively pursued and aggravated a fellow driver who had cut him off, ignoring my cries to calm down and cut it out!

The security of a protective husband was fast diminishing to fear of a hothead with a lack of self-control.

The anxiety I began to feel because of his drinking turned into a watchful eye, easily interpreted as a nagging wife. I was watching myself change rapidly from the fun loving, often impulsive girl to the nagging, over responsible, anxious wife, causing a lot of arguments and beginning to resent Andy for what I viewed as selfish choices, blaming him for who I had now become.

The disconnect he was experiencing, became evident in such arguments, as the once quick to apologise man, now became unyielding and unreachable.

I also worried about the apparent lack of connection between him and Charlie and this new toughness that he began to manifest toward both young boys.

When Joseph fell over or hurt himself, Andy would tell him to stop crying and barely show any concern.

I would watch in bewilderment as the father who was once so protective now appeared so removed and unaffected. I knew he loved them, but this new lack of compassion and affection toward them, was to be a trend in their future relationship.

Andy was having vivid nightmares too. This has happened before, but never like this.

On one occasion he actually picked Charlie up and began shak-

ing him and yelling and shushing him at the same time.

Horrified I grabbed my baby who was now screaming and tried to calm him, yelling at Andy to wake up.

When Andy was finally convinced it wasn't real and was awake, he revealed to me that he thought Charlie was a child in Afghanistan that had his arms severed from an explosion and he was trying to bandage him to stop the bleeding.

I couldn't understand how a dream could be so vivid that Andy would literally act it out without waking up.

This incident left me questioning his frame of mind from that point on, with a degree of anxiety. I slept on guard fearful he might actually hurt the boys or myself.

Andy felt that fear too and was somewhat confused, unable to explain what was happening, but yet, almost unwilling to acknowledge something might be wrong.

Life continued though, and for most part we settled into the new, barely functioning normality, accepting the battle scars as a fair trade for having him home in one piece.

We bought a house to renovate in Ipswich and in the leave period following his deployment Andy tried his hand at renovating and restoring the old home. It was with some reservation on his part, but he actually found he enjoyed the project.

He began to toy with the idea of leaving the military at this point and that wasn't without plenty of pressure from me. With half arsed effort he inquired about a few job opportunities in his field, but they all saw him doing the same role in Afghanistan or the like, only in the private sector as opposed to military and these would have seen him away for even longer.

This wasn't an option, I had decided that I was done with the military life as in my eyes I had done my bit. He had his opportunity to see his training to fruition and prove himself in the field.

But by then it was already too late, he had become that much more indoctrinated by the army, and that level of camaraderie and conviction to be there for his team was deeply ingrained. The responsibility for his men had begun to outshine his responsibility as a father and husband. We had become second place, I had become the mistress and the army held pride of place in Andy's heart.

I blame my strength as a woman and mother partly for this as Andy saw I could apparently cope and seized the opportunity to go further in his field. I often wonder what would have happened at that point if our relationship had been in jeopardy or my mental health in question, would things have been different?

He acknowledged my strength and commitment with gratitude, singling out a few comrades that hadn't been so lucky, suffering marriage break downs during their rotation, but rather than proceed with caution, this seemed to give him permission to keep doing what he did.

Somewhere amongst the turmoil we had decided to try and have a baby girl and add to our little family. It never took much in the past to get us pregnant, usually a thought or a look across the room, and this time was no exception. I soon confirmed the pregnancy and felt the usual trepidation as I looked ahead to a future that was still uncertain and a little overwhelming, knowing another trip away was on the cards if Andy stayed in the military.

This pregnancy felt different than the pregnancies with the boys, and the scans confirmed my suspicions. We were having a little girl! The usual mix of anxiety and excitement accompanied the entire pregnancy. The anxiety was amplified though, as Andy continued to become so highly qualified and valuable in his field that long stints to South Australia for training became commonplace, even when he was home, he wasn't.

I calculated at this point that he had spent half of our marriage away. Questions began to loom in my mind whether we were going to make it? Could I cope living like a single mum much longer? I knew it wasn't a situation I could ever be happy with. Some women relished the independent lifestyle, I didn't. I wanted to do life with my team mate, not catch ups. It wasn't strange to me that the more he committed himself to the military the more I closed down to it.

*****

In 2010, we welcomed our little princess Eden into the world. There was an immediate bond between Andy and his little girl, that looked so much like an Eskimo baby, with her intense black eyes, mop of black hair and beautiful dark skin. Andy told me she was the exact image of the daughter he always wanted, and with her arrival there was a dawning of hope that everything would be okay.

The fragile peace was soon shattered however, as he was notified of another posting to Afghanistan.

To say I fought against the concept tooth and nail was an understatement. I dug in my heels at every opportunity, begging him to decline. Telling him outright I didn't support the idea and he would go without my blessing.

He may not have had much of a choice but in my mind he had put himself in this position, he had made the career choices that he knew would lead down this path without consulting me. He was seeking purpose and adrenalin that he failed to find as a husband or father.

He argued that he was going for our family first and foremost and then our country. For financial stability and in his mind he thought it was righteous (and it was), but I failed to reconcile the relative meagre financial gain as a fair trade for the very real possibility of his death.

His misguided loyalties became alarmingly obvious however when the possibility of him not being able to take out a life insurance policy due to the specifics of his job did nothing to caution his decision to go. For the first time his disregard for our wellbeing became blatantly obvious.

7

Coming Home

After returning home from Afghanistan in late 2008, I was just happy to be back with my family. Afghanistan seemed like a lifetime away as we settled back into Australian life and bought our first family home, a very run down cheap old Queenslander in Ipswich.

It was not long after coming home that I started to consider how fortunate I was to return home from Afghanistan unharmed. My mind was often consumed with thoughts of how delicate life is and how it can be snuffed out in an instant. My mind would try to come to terms with my own mortality and my beliefs and faith. The truth is, in a lot of ways I missed Afghanistan, the rush of adrenalin, the mateship and the satisfaction that comes with doing a job you love.

My experiences in war had opened my mind to understanding life in a new way. I was much more open to thinking about and hearing about God and I believed in the existence of God; I just didn't really understand how my belief in the teachings of a man from over 2000 years ago fitted into my life or how I was to implement them in any real or tangible way. What I did know was that my heart's desire was to know Jesus, to have a personal relationship with my creator and I started to seek him more. Initially, I would seek him through talking to people and asking questions about Christianity, I started reading historical information about who Jesus was and what he did. For some reason it all started to make sense and I felt like a mental block had been removed and I was finally able to see without condemning the idea of faith as a crutch or weakness. The more I opened up to the idea of Jesus being sent from God the father for my salvation, the more I felt peace and understanding of my own purpose in life.

Zoe reminded me of how many people had been praying for me whilst I was deployed and I decided to attend church with her. After some deep consideration and long nights of contemplation we decided to get baptised together in a small ceremony in Byron Bay. The actual physical act of baptism was not that big a deal, although I did feel challenged in that I was confessing my new beliefs in a public forum, but as far as feeling born again, I didn't really experience anything overly spiritual. This event was however a catalyst to starting a much deeper change within my soul and turned the tide of a battle that was raging within me. I had reawakened the stirring of faith that smouldered away deep in my bones until it would eventually burst into a raging fire of faith for God.

When I wasn't considering my new found faith, I focused all my efforts on renovating and being a father and cared little for the day to day work of the Army.

My nights however, were a different story. I no longer slept well and would often wake up with nightmares and night terrors. Nothing too intense I thought, just part of settling back into society. On top of this and probably as a result of not sleeping well, I became more irritable and aggressive, particularly snappy at Zoe and the children. I started to withdraw from Zoe and resent her for things I was not even sure existed. I just felt unsettled and angry with the world.

Over the next year I had numerous incidents of extreme road rage and aggression and on occasion even put Zoe and the children at risk due to my behaviour. Zoe challenged me on my behaviour and for a while it kept me in check. I started drinking more regularly and looked forward to spending time away from my family. I started noticing things like my stress levels increasing and the rapid onset of fatigue that I had not felt before. Things that I once did easily, now seemed challenging or even difficult. Everything became a burden.

I didn't really discuss my symptoms with anyone other than Zoe and that was only when she would take the time to pry answers out of me. I felt like going to the Army for help would only destroy my career, so I continued to function on the outside like everything was fine and tried to focus my efforts on work but everything felt hollow and unfulfilling.

I even put in my discharge whilst in my position at the 2nd Combat Engineer Regiment (2 CER). I had no desire to be there and just wanted out. Work seemed mundane and unimportant and I felt like I was doing nothing, going nowhere, fast.

Home life was a mess, I was travelling two to three hours a day to get to work and I was tired. I thought, getting out of the Army would solve my problems and I started pursuing work opportunities back overseas.

Zoe supported the idea of me leaving the Army 100% and seemed truly excited by the prospect until I mentioned I had a job offer back in Afghanistan as a private contractor. I thought it would be ideal, an exciting career, away from the Army and away from family. Earning great money, providing for my family without any of the day-to-day drama. I soon found out that Zoe did not approve of my plan. She preferred me to be home rather than back overseas. She pointed out my responsibilities to her and our two children and we discussed other less dangerous and more inclusive career options.

In the end, the idea of needing to provide for my family weighed to heavily on me, so I decided to withdraw my discharge and stay in the Army, much to Zoe's dismay. At least this way I had a secure income and stability.

My decision to stay proved to be a good one as I received a posting back to the Army Explosive Hazards Centre (ExHC). The next three years were amongst the most rewarding in my military career as I was privileged to work alongside some of the most dedicated and professional soldiers I had ever met.

My focus and drive returned and I was in my element training soldiers for war and saving lives; I had found my purpose again and my troubled mind quietened. My demons silenced by the busyness of my daily work.

Even home life returned to normal as I found focus at work. I was sleeping better and was less angry. I had more time with Zoe and the kids and our lives began to improve. We moved back to Brisbane and my long travel days became short runs to work. Life was good again as I had found renewed purpose.

Under the command of Major Madina 'Chico' and then Major Brenton (Ben) White, the unit became pivotal in Australia's fight against Improvised Explosive Devices (IEDs) in Iraq and Afghanistan, as well as working closely with the Counter IED Task Force in Canberra.

The individuals in this unit set new benchmarks of commitment to Australia's fight against the ever increasing threat and I dedicated the next three years of my life to the training of Australian forces towards saving lives and decreasing injury and death from IEDs.

We ran pre-deployment training designed to better prepare our forces for the ever increasing threat of IED's in Iraq and Afghanistan and we travelled constantly, from State to State, preparing the next unit for deployment. We would go on to train thousands of soldiers, deploying to the theatre of war.

The unit was later recognised with a Chief of Defence Force Unit Commendation, for the work completed during the period 2006 – 2011. During which time, I served as 2IC and for a time, as the Office Commanding of the unit. We were also responsible for the establishment of an EOD and Search Specific Mission Readiness Exercise, the need which was highlighted, with the numerous deaths and injuries being inflicted on our frontline soldiers in these critical positions.

Much of my time was spent in the South Australian desert, training personnel out in the Woomera restricted area, a place not many Australians even know exists, let alone the historic events that have occurred in the area. It is a bit like Australia's version of Area 51. In its heyday, it was a bustling town with people from US, the United Kingdom and various other nations working on classified military projects and the like. These days, it is a ghost town, a shadow of its former glory and a simple bombing range that also happens to be the best realistic training ground in Australia for operations in the Middle East. It's hot, dry, full of sand and not much else.

I placed my own personal psychological issues to the very back of the recesses of my mind and focused on my work. I felt fulfilled and important in the world as I completed a very challenging and difficult role. In the final year of my position, we raised a new unit 20 EOD Sqn. I personally invested hundreds of hours into the establishment of this unit. The first EOD troop of which, I would have the privilege to take into Afghanistan.

Since 2008, the fight in Afghanistan had changed. Our focus towards reconstruction and development had shifted to stability operations focused towards supporting the elected government, and legitimising the new Afghan Government. As such, military operations were more focused on war fighting and kinetic battles aimed at driving out Taliban forces from the region. As a result, the Australian Defence Force required more EOD assets to support manoeuvre assets on the ground, as more war fighters meant more IEDs and a need for more EOD support to deal with them. So we formed a new unit, aimed at growing the ADF EOD capability and answering the operational requirements of war.

*****

I remember knowing that I was up for deployment some time before raising it with Zoe, possibly months. I was extremely motivated to return to Afghanistan and lead the first EOD Troop asset into theatre. Nothing was going to prevent me from deploying and I was extremely driven to ensure my Troop was up to the task.

When I did finally approach Zoe with the news of my pending deployment she expressed her disappointment and frustration. She was actually scared of losing me and raising three kids on her own. She was also scared of raising the kids on her own during my absence. Who can blame her really. I know the thought of raising kids without my wife for any period of time is terrifying to me. Our personal life was going okay leading up to the deployment, although I was more married to the military than my wife and kids.

Our third child, Eden, was born in August 2010. Our first daughter and an incredible blessing to our lives. I felt an immediate connection to Eden, one that is difficult to explain.

It was different with the boys, perhaps because she is a girl, however, it just felt like we had a very close bond from the instant she was born. I will never forget the feeling of holding her for the very first time, in hospital and looking into her eyes, it was as if our souls were somehow connected. She is a gift from God. This is not to say that I love my boys any less, it is just different. I didn't know it at the time, but Eden would play a pivotal role in saving my life later and reveal how important this bond truly is.

From a worldly perspective I was still somewhat absent, as a husband and father from my life and theirs. My priority was to my work and the Army was the most important thing in my life. This statement may sound quite confronting to people reading this as I was a married man and a father of three beautiful children. So clearly, my priority should have been with my family.

However, the truth was they came second to my work and the Army received my full attention and commitment, as I thought what I was doing was important and necessary for the survival of Australian soldiers. I was willing to sacrifice my own relationships to ensure that I gave this job its required devotion.

Joseph was a smart young boy and had developed the sweetest most caring nature of the siblings. Even from the age of four he was truly a caring kid and just wanted to please his Mum and Dad. Charlie was completely different to his brother and what Joseph lacked in temper Charlie made up for in spades. He was all emotion, a complete hot head of a child and still is today. He reminds me so much of myself as a kid that it is sometimes difficult for us to communicate because we are so alike. His hot headed approach to life often lands him in trouble, but I know from experience, his dogged determination will also carry him a long way in life.

Zoe was amazing during this time as it must have been incredibly tough to know she was not the priority in her husband's life yet, she stayed with me. She showed such resilience and commitment to our family and I will forever be in her debt.

Thank you Zoe,

For having the strength to stand by me
even in the toughest of times.
You saw in me the man I could be, a
man I did not even know existed.

You raised our children in a fatherless
home for many years and blessed them
with abundant love and support.
They are a complete credit to you.

Love
Andy.

8

The Call of Duty Returns

Much to my disappointment and reluctance, he went. With promises of a short 3 month stint and that would be it. Reluctant, reserved, tear-filled goodbyes were said and within days after his departure, three months became a daunting six, then nine and finally, a staggering 11-month rotation. I felt like Andy had completely deceived me. I was so angry, feeling completely abandoned and disregarded. I had been given no choice, but to accept the very real possibility of a future without a husband and father for my children. I resented him and the Army for it. Every day for 11 months, I waited with baited breath for news of the worst kind. I stopped watching the TV, hating every vague report on the overseas deployment. I even had the unfortunate experience of some insensitive parent at school telling me, we had no right as a country to be there. The ignorance and lack of compassion or understanding of the majority did nothing to help ease my own questions regarding the actual value and purpose behind this sacrifice. Five years I'd said, and yet here I was 7 years on and I was still an Officer's wife. We had moved 9 times in 7 years, but that didn't bother me. I loved the change and had an adventurous spirit.

This was different though, because every time he went away it was like he had died and we had to mourn him and then learn to get along without him.

My first tendency was to cut him out of our lives completely (that was my retaliatory way of coping), refusing to be the dependant wife at home, dutifully sitting there twiddling her thumbs, waiting for her husband to return.

For the sake of the kids I tried to keep him alive in our daily routine, putting photos next to the boys' beds and at night, we would blow daddy big kisses and say goodnight to him. Watching as my boys began to view daddy's work in a very negative light, as they only associated it with his long absences. My concern was that the only real male role model they had was away and I worried about how they might turn out.

I struggled playing the roles of both Mum and Dad, not an ideal situation in any way and I hold the highest respect for single parents as a result. My loving role was compromised by the need to be the sole disciplinarian and I struggled with constantly feeling guilty for having shortcomings and worrying that the entire experience was scarring my beautiful children.

I developed some great supportive friendships during this time and found that socialising provided somewhat of a reprieve. The absence of my husband from the setting was always noticeable though and I continued to feel the full burden of sole parenthood.

It was with reservation that I watched Joseph hug every man he came across, with alarming abandonment and began to recognise the toll his father's absence was taking on him and the need for male influence in his life. I began to rally my brothers and father for their support and was thankful for the role they played in influencing his young life.

My beautiful blue eyed Charlie became an anxious child, not too surprising as he had never really had the opportunity to bond with his father and his mother was now overstretched with her sole care of three children under the age of five. He had bouts of screaming and tantrums, which resulted in a rather traumatic incident with DOCS and a humiliating full scale investigation into my role as a mother, which I was completely exonerated of I might add.

Nevertheless, I already felt like I was failing as a mother and now, I was being called out on it. The scarring of this was long reaching. I still struggle with the memories of this and familiar feelings of inadequacy today.

A neighbour had heard Charlie's screams and assumed the worst, I remember asking the DOCS officer in tears if my husband's service to his country and resulting absence was viewed as a positive or negative implication in the circumstances. They didn't know how to answer that. Again the angry questions of how worth it, it all was, came to the forefront of my mind.

Thankfully, Eden was my easiest baby to-date. She self-pacified with her little thumb and would put herself to sleep. She blossomed into a beautiful baby girl. I watched her take her first steps and heard her first words without her daddy there. Her first birthday came and went. He missed it. I know this pained him greatly. He missed the majority of Joseph's first year at school. His absence was painstakingly obvious during Father's Day events at school. Thankfully he had the community around him that supported him under these circumstances.

I believe the whole experience created the resilient, compassionate, if somewhat overcautious, bright young man he is today. When talking to him, you see an 'other-worldly' wisdom and understanding in his eyes. I recognise that it was unfair to put so much weight and such a burden on those little shoulders, but he was my rock at many times. At the age of five he would get up and make breakfast for himself and his brother before school. The mess often wasn't worth it, but his heart's desire and effort was compensation enough.

I began to question how much more of this I could take, or rather how much more my children could take. The toll on my little family was too great, but I seemed to be the only one who was considering the damage. I began to ask myself when was enough, enough. The messed up priorities were continuing well on into this established marriage. Andy continued to put mates and work before me, and even the children weren't enough to change that. I was the only one making any compromises. I had thrown away my education and my career prospects so he could pursue his. He seemed to be pursuing it regardless of the outcome. I felt that Andy was actively choosing the military over us and in so doing was abandoning his children. He had lost all sense of responsibility to them. He didn't give us a choice in the matter, this wasn't a negotiation, this was a dictatorship and Andy was the dictator. He was making the big decisions for all of us regardless of our circumstances. Was I supposed to just stand aside and let the damage continue?

I started to separate in my heart from Andy, building up walls for self-protection and survival. I remember telling Andy that I didn't know if I'd be able to pull the walls down again. My fears were very real that this rotation would scar me and the children beyond repair. My anger and disconnect was growing and the situation was becoming completely hopeless.

When Andy returned briefly for a few days at ROCL I remember taking him to the school to pick up Joseph. Joseph saw us waiting outside and recognised his dad before running into his arms for a teary embrace.

The tears were expressed by all around us including Josephs amazing teacher who had proven to be such a wonderful support during this time. She will always have a special place in our hearts for being part of such a significant time in our lives.

The brief family holiday that followed brought with it illusions of peace and euphoria, but the reality and struggles would swiftly set in, as soon as he left again. I had gained some insight into the horrific experiences Andy was subject to during candlelit dinners, but still failed to see the full extent of what was to come.

Ten months dragged by and for the first time I began to notice the toll the rotation was taking on Andy. He hurt his back at one point and was now suffering kidney stones. All I wanted was to have him home to help and look after him. The reminder of my love for him shattered through my removed numbness.

I began to hear his pain above my own as he struggled with poor health and this was amplified by the senseless loss of comrades and friends on the battlefield. I heard his desperate need to make sense of it all as he finally began to audibly question the purpose of the sacrifice. For the first time I had a glimmer of hope that he was starting to see the reality and consequences of the path we were on. He didn't want to lose our family; he didn't want to lose me. For the first time he spoke of leaving the army with real conviction, recognising it was no longer a career for a family man. We began to hatch plans for his discharge upon his return in a few short weeks. We discussed and I researched in vain for a house that we could renovate and call our own, the first step in the right direction of our new life.

He returned home in February 2012. We met him at the airport. Joseph embraced him tightly, whilst Charlie, nearly four now, at this stage very cautiously took a few reluctant steps toward his dad before clinging onto him and not letting go. Eden was only too happy to cuddle her dad and there we were, all huddled together at the airport, unashamedly crying and for the first time in a long time eagerly anticipating what the future might hold.

- My photo journal -

Meeting Prime Minister Tony Abbott

Awarded the Commendation for Distinguished Service

The best girl in the world!

The Family

Zoe and me and the kids

...Smiling again

WAR

Life in the
Ghan!

WAR again!

Australian Light Armoured
Vehicle (ASLAV)

Culvert Clearence

RTF 4 EOD Team

Casualty Evacuation (CASEVAC)
post IED strike

Mortar Platoon
in action

The reality of war...

1 EOD Troop - Combined Team Uruzgan

BANG!!!

On the job!

Another day
at the office!

Still alive - just!

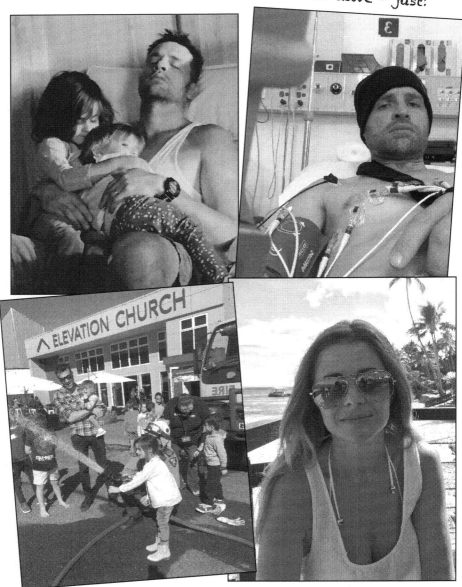

Home is where the heart is...

9

Diary from the Frontline

The next part of this book contains many excerpts from my personal diary, of my time in Afghanistan from May 2011 - January 2012. It is a raw account of life on the frontline of a modern war in which I am blunt, honest and confronting. There is no hiding the truth of my accounts and there is no removing of the uncomfortable facts. It is simply a diary I decided to keep for myself as both a coping mechanism and a way of remembering my deployment.

Details of incidents in this diary are not included to provide a shock factor, but are included to provide a detailed account of incidents and with the hope of clearly portraying the accuracy of modern warfare and the ongoing effect it has on the soldiers who fight and have to deal with the consequences of their involvement.

I apologise for the language and for the fact that I call out many people in this diary on what I viewed as shortcomings or failures. However, when we are in stressful environments, emotions can run hot and mine certainly did at times. I have no malice or ill will towards any person or organisation I served with and I feel extremely honoured to have had the opportunity to serve with every person I did, thank you all for your service.

Deployed - A Journal of Afghanistan

Captain Andy Cullen

3 May 2011 – 14 Jan 2012

My hope is to keep this journal as a record of my second deployment to Afghanistan as I kept nothing from my first deployment and I would like to have something to show the kids and explain why I had to leave them for such a long period of time.

3rd May 2011 – Day 1 – Today is the day to say goodbye,

Dropped the kids at school. Charlie, 3 years old, was quite sad, both Charlie and Joseph, 5 years, gave me wonderful cuddles and kisses. Zoe, my beautiful wife of 6 years, drove me to the airport with Eden, my gorgeous daughter of 9 months, and there were a few tears when it was time to go. I am feeling very sad about leaving them this time as the kids are at an age where they really notice when I am not around and it makes life very difficult for Zoe who becomes more authoritarian with the kids in order to keep them in line. She loses some of that beautiful soft mothering side as a survival mechanism for being a single parent and I pray it will return to normal when I come home.

I feel as though I will return home unharmed from this trip and I am not anxious about my deployment.

I find I am more anxious about leaving my family as I would never forgive myself if something were to happen to one of them whilst I was deployed. Zoe said that every time I go away it is as though I have died and the kids and her go through a grieving process until they come to terms with my absence. That concept is very hard for me to understand and it makes my leaving all the more difficult.

It must be very hard for a child to comprehend why a parent can't be at home when they see all the other parents at home with their kids. I feel like I will be repaying this debt for a lifetime.

My father also in the military all his working life spent a great deal of time away and I don't want that for my children. I believe it left a lasting scar on my mother and my brothers. Although I love the military and my country and feel I am serving for an important cause, the fire inside me is burning out as my desire to be with my family is exceeding my desire to serve. I have always been very patriotic and felt a strong desire to serve in the Army and follow my fathers and grandfather's footsteps. I guess it was in my blood. I believe all military people face this decision one day, family or defence? Either way the choice must be made eventually. It is little wonder why so many military marriages fail. Why would anyone want to be married to a partner that is never around?

At what point have you done your bit? The question I try to answer quite often these days. The call of duty is a difficult call to ignore especially when you have been indoctrinated in the military your entire life. I guess I will know at the completion of this tour!

I am deploying for the second time as the Explosive Ordnance Disposal (EOD) Manager, first in 2008 for Reconstruction Task Force 4 (RTF 4) and now for Combined Taskforce Uruzgan 2 (CTU 2) a truly joint coalition unit commanded by a US Colonel and an Australian Colonel as Deputy Commander (DCOM). I will command and control all Australian conventional EOD Teams and facilitate the employment of the US EOD Teams within Urzagan Province, Afghanistan. A hostile Area of Operations (AO), responsible for the deaths and injuries of many Australian, and Allied soldiers at the hands of the very capable and fierce enemy, the Taliban.

4th May 2011 – 1st Day of Leave

Landed in at the main Australian logistic base in the Middle East after spending some 26 consecutive hours aboard a plane to roll straight into our first day of final preparation training, which will take a total of four days prior to deploying forward into Afghanistan. I am feeling very tired and looking forward to having a good sleep.

The accommodation is fantastic and to think the people serving here are receiving an additional $175 a day deployment allowance. I really think the war fighters end up with the raw end of the stick. Good Internet coverage, movie facilities, shops and freedom to do as you please without the fear of being shot at or blown up. It surprises me that the conditions of service for these individuals whom are performing an important and necessary role are so similar to those serving on the front line of a war zone.

5th May 2011 – 2nd Day of RSO&I

Today was fairly relaxed, a late start around 0600h followed by a phone call to Zoe, which I appreciated very much as she sounded very positive and happy. I only hope the positivity lasts although I know she will have many ups and downs, as will I throughout this deployment.

I had my additional Psychological Training

tonight, "Operational Fatigue Workshop", designed for individuals identified with high stress and fatiguing jobs. Only a combat medic and myself where required to attend from the current group. The Medic SGT was a Pommy lateral, a former UK soldier who left the British Army to join ours, of which there are many these days, a nice guy who has had extensive operational experience in Bosnia, Somalia and Iraq and was heading back to Bagdad. He and I shared some of our more challenging and memorable operational experiences with a young female Captain who seemed a little shocked at the stories we told.

I am very pleased that the overall defence attitude to Psychological support these days seems to be improving. The negative stigma attached to seeing a Psych or talking about experiences of war is slowly being broken down. Veterans from past deployments and wars have often been left to their own devices and not engaged once they returned home and I think it was this approach that contributed significantly to the large number of PTSD cases that emerged in veterans back home. I believe as an organisation we are on the right track to reduce the number of people suffering in silence if we provide people with the opportunity and culture to discuss their thoughts and deal with the events in the open.

I have seen a number of soldiers who suffer from mental illness as a result of doing my trade and I worry about how it may effect me later in life given my experiences during my deployment in 2008. The reality is, when the brain sees things that are terrible it must deal with and process that information in order to file it away and continue to function as normal. We need our soldiers to be able to deal with combat stress and process it in a rapid manner to get back on the job as quickly and effectively as possible.

From my own experiences I know that during operations you do not have the time to deal with these incidents in detail as it will effect your ability to do your job and you simply put it to the back of your mind to deal with it once you are in a relaxed and safe environment. To attempt to deal with the psychological effects of a traumatic incident then and there is to be 'combat ineffective' and a danger to yourself and others. Focus on the job at hand and get it done the detailed processing will occurr back in Australia post deployment and that's when it gets ugly.

Night terrors and visions, inability to sleep, loss of appetite and general anger issues come to the fore. I know and Zoe knows this will occur again, however, I feel better prepared mentally for this tour as I have been through it before and I know that these symptoms of mental stress are completely normal and that is a relief as the first time I went through it I was unprepared mentally and thought I was going crazy.

8th of May 2011 – Travel to Tarin Kowt

Travel day was ok typical rough C-17 flight into TK. First impression was it has changed a lot - the runway is now sealed and the mountain to the North of the runway is gone to make way for the US Striker Bn Rotary Wing Assets Task Force Attack. The Forward Operating Base (FOB) is littered with Yanks and local contractor's a big change to the days of the Dutch.

Matt Murphy was there to meet me at the bag drop and has sorted an accommodation space for me so life is good. Said hi to a few old friend's typical run in to guys you haven't seen in years. And dropped into the Weapons Intelligence Team (WIT) and EOD branches to say hi. All in all, a good day and looking forward to getting into the fight. There will be lots of changes to come, however, I will sit back for the first few weeks as a professional courtesy to Matt and the others to get a handle on how they have run things prior to taking command and making changes.

9th of May 2011 – One week down – Tarin Kout

Spent some time in the Afghani National Army (ANA) Command Post (CP) and received a brief by the local ANA commander on his operations and force composition, which I found very interesting and informative. It really drove home the change in operational focus to mentoring as the primary effort.

I also met up with Murph and Budda Harmon the current MTF EOD Manager and discussed a number of the current issues and plans that need to be actioned prior to my team coming in. I am feeling comfortable in my role and keen to start enacting some significant changes, however, I am acutely aware that I don't wish to rock the boat with the current MTF due to previous tensions. I don't want them to close ranks and attempt to block the changes we have in motion. This really is a political juggling act at times and your ability to communicate and good interpersonal skills are critical in getting things done. Hopefully I won't piss too many people off!

The key goals I am aiming to achieve throughout this tour are:

1. Bring my entire troop home safe from a challenging and successful tour;
2. Provide valuable C-IED support to the CTU, MTF and coalition forces including ANSF to ensure all personnel are forewarned and armed to succeed in this difficult environment and reduce the number of fatalities and injuries caused by IEDs;
3. Move the Australian EOD asset under command CTU for improved Command and control, support, tactical and strategic benefits within the AO;
4. Establish the EODCC for the AO out of the CTU TOC
5. Continue to train and mentor the ANA Explosive Hazard Reconnaissance Course (EHRC) and develop

a ANA EOD / Search capability in preparation for a successful exit strategy;

6. Bring the US EOD teams under direct support to CTU or at least tie in the support relationships which currently don't exist and qualify the US EOD as ISAF Trainers to support the mentoring of ANSF EHRT and EOD personnel;

7. Review all current EOD specific TTP's, SOP's and policy documents for theatre, and

8. Provide 20 EOD SQN with current up to date info to better prepare the follow on forces for a successful tour.

10th of May 2011 –Tarin Kout

Today I went to see the Explosive Hazards Reduction Course, (EHRC). This is an awesome advance in the preparation of handover to the ANA and establishing a suitable exit strategy for Uruzgan. I am very keen to develop this concept further and ensure it is given as much publicity as possible to gain support and funding from ISAF and ANSF to establish and grow the C-IED capability within the province.

I have a feeling this aspect of my job will be very rewarding as we develop the ANA and ANP soldiers and eventually certify and mentor the ANA EOD Teams to conduct independent operations.

I am thinking of Zoe and the kids a lot and missing them terribly so immersing myself in work seems the right thing to do to get over the initial separation anxiety. I am really happy that Zoe is sinking her teeth into her business, as it will keep her busy and hopefully reduce the pain of parenting on her own and missing me. I know the kids are being difficult at the moment after talking with her and I hope this will ease as they become used to me not being around.

11th to 13th of May 2011 – Tarin Kout

A good couple of days handing over with Murph. We took the ANA and ANP out to the demolitions range and I must admit I was surprised at the skill level the students had reached over the duration of the course. They showed a willingness to learn did not seem nervous around explosives and followed direction well. I hold strong hopes for the individuals in the course. I wonder how many of them will be dead before the year is out! I imagine it will be around half due to the role they will be performing. Explosive Hazard Reduction Technician (EHRT) is not the easiest position to fulfil safely in a place like Afghanistan.

One or two of the best students will be identified to go to Kandahar Air Field (KAF) to complete the ISAF ANA EOD course and return as a qualified Technician.

Zoe and the kids seem ok but I am concerned that Zoe maybe over doing it with her new business and burning herself out a bit. It's hard to know what to say to her as she is doing it all by herself and I don't want to sound like an ass, telling her to take it easy all the time.

14th of May 2011 – Tarin Kout

I received my posting order to 6 ESR as the OPSO next year. Im not looking forward to picking up such a high tempo job after this deployment and I think I will ask for Long Service Leave of up to 6mths

The other option is discharge and I would be lying if I said I wasn't nervous about the prospect of getting out. I am terrified at the idea of not having a steady income with three mortgages and a family to support. Zoe seems a lot more open to the idea of just moving to the land and making a go of it.

15th – 16th of May 2011 – Two weeks down – Tarin Kout

Getting bored already! not a good sign for a lengthy deployment, although I know my role is about to expand significantly so all hope is not lost. I am looking forward to my troop arriving so I can take command and get stuck into the job.

Zoe seemed very distant on the phone today I am not sure if it was just a bad day or something more. I know the kids have been sick and that always adds pressure and stress. They seem to understand the fact that I am not coming back for a while. I hope Zoe is ok and it's just a bad day. I feel like I have started mentally withdrawing from home as a survival mechanism to dealing with being away for such a long time.

17th of May 2011 – Tarin Kout

Started in the IED training lanes teaching the Afghan Explosive Hazard Reconnaissance Technician (EHRT) course followed up with some exploitation of a cache that came into the Weapons Technical Intelligence (WTI) branch, The OIC is a good mate of mine and we served together for a period over here in 2008, a big trunk of weapons and explosives not a bad find from a corrupt ANP officer who has been helping the Taliban.

18th of May 2011 – Tarin Kout

Well 2 weeks in theatre and War boredom 'Woredom' is setting in. Had to babysit a Dutch Col from Regional Command South Counter IED and some Dutch Navy EOD Tech from CEXC KAF. Not a great day.

Spoke to Zoe and she was really struggling today. I upset Joseph on Skype and felt really bad I didn't realise how much my absence is affecting him and Charlie. They are both playing up, not sleeping well and having bad dreams. I hope things settle down soon because Zoe is not getting any rest and that will come to a crunch very soon if things don't change. I sent Zoe an email and offering support but not sure how it will go down.

19th of May 2011 - Tarin Kout Not a good day for morale

What am I doing here? It's 10:30 at night on a Thursday; I should be at home in bed next to my beautiful wife my children sleeping in the next room. Instead I am literally half way across the planet in a foreign country that does not necessarily want me here risking my life and everything I hold precious to me. My beautiful soft hearted wife is losing her mind at the thought of being alone for the next 9 months, my sons are driving their Mum crazy and they both just need some emotional stability in their lives. My beautiful daughter will not even remember me in a few weeks and why? Some sense of honour, some stupid idea of patriotism, I owe something to my nation to the nation of Afghanistan. I have had enough of this nonsense! Just stop this! I have to go home now!

That's what I want to say but I can't, this inner belief that I could not stand to be a deserter, a quitter, a failure. My sense of right and wrong and my conscience tells me I have to be here. I pray for God to tell me what to do and I come up with the same answer. I can't go!

I can make a difference here, I can limit the deaths and keep my men, my soldiers, alive and help bring them back to their families and loved ones. What makes my family any more deserving then theirs? My soldiers need me and I need them. We are all in this terrible fight together and if one link in the chain breaks all the links below fall, and I won't let that happen.

So, sorry my love, my beautiful children, my reasons for living, as difficult as this sacrifice is to make I have to stay. It is not a choice of them over you it is a choice to accept the pain I will cause through my absence IOT achieve a greater good and I pray and hold on to the hope that everything will be ok at the end and that one day you will forgive me.

20th – 22nd of May 2011 – Tarin Kout

Feeling good today I decided not to write over the past few days due to my low morale mainly and also very busy period. The first EHRT course was very successful. I have established links with all the major players in Paladin EOD, WIT and C-IED world now so I should be able to get a lot of my initiatives through.

Had some good conversations with Zoe who has become a lot more positive about things. Thanks mainly to Eleni, my niece who has been visiting and helping with the kids which is a huge blessing to our family. Just having the support and a little assistance plus someone for Zoe to talk to and hang out with makes an incredible difference.

I visited the TK Chapel today my first ever visit. The Chapel was there in 08 but I never went in, I did not spend a great deal of time in TK either. I took the opportunity to pray in quiet and reflect on family and life and felt better for the experience. I also looked through the honour roll and remembered a few lost mates.

I had my first IED call out today on a suspected VBIED at the front gate. The Explosive Detection Dog (EDD) indicated on numerous areas of the Petrol tanker so they called EOD. After we conducted a detailed search it turned out to be nothing but threw in a bit of excitement for the morning.

My main role is the command and control of Australian EOD Assets around the Area of Operations (AO), coordinate with other Counter IED assets and provide training and mentoring to Afghan National Security Forces (ANSF) C-IED assets, and to provide direct EOD support to local incidents in and around TK so I am finding I am very busy day to day.

23rd of May 2011 – KAF.

I just heard about an old friend of mine who was killed today whilst serving with the Special Operations Task Group. He was tragically killed by an Improvised Explosive Device. He and I joined the Army at the same time completing basic training and being posted to the 6th Battalion Royal Australian Regiment together.

He went on to pass selection in 1998 and served in Boganville, East Timor and Iraq and was currently serving on his third tour of Afghanistan.

A tragic loss of a great Australian soldier and husband.

27th of May 2011 – Tarin Kout

Just returned from a trip to Kandahar Air Field (KAF) a three-day visit with Task Force Paladin RC-S and the CEXC RC-S. A good few days meeting all the key players in the exploitation world and the EOD fight tying in with the US and Canadian EOD Training piece for the ANA.

The day we flew out an Aussie Commando who was killed in a fire fight and five of his mates wounded. We ran into a few of the wounded in KAF of whom I knew one EOD Tech Matt Tanner a big tough character who was going back to work in a few days. Not much keeps these guys down and none of them want to let down their mates so getting back into the fight is their #1 priority.

Whilst at Paladin 6 US pers where killed in an incident of which 2 where US EOD Techs and 2 Pathfinders. An unfortunate incident and it just goes to show the fighting season has kicked off again with a bang. I met one of the techs that died just 24 hours prior, seemed like a great guy.

28th of May 2011 – Tarin Kout

Got rocketed last night 7 x 107mm rockets in total a very unnerving feeling when you wake up to explosions all around your bed and hope the next one doesn't come tearing through your accommodation. Started the clearance at 1am so a very long day with no rest. 6 detonated on or around the base and we found 1 down at the point of origin that failed to launch.

Been very busy here, the fighting season has really kicked off with a number of casualties lately and the jobs are heavy but I am keeping my sense of humour. Can't wait to leave already. I spent a bit of time on the ground with some kids today clearing a rocket that was fired into their compound. Great kids I take photos of them and show them the pics on the digital camera, they love it. Then I hand out toothbrushes and show them how to brush their teeth. Something I got into on my last trip rather than just give them lollies. They crack up laughing when I show them what to do. I took a few pics to show the family when I get back.

29th of May 2011 – Tarin Kout

Well today was a good day. Started by completing a few reports followed by a meeting with the Special Operations Task Force (SOTF) South East (SE) EOD Technicians two US Navy EOD guys who are good value and keen to work in with us for support, reporting and exploitation so that's good. Also locked in to do a few operations with them in coming weeks.

I spoke to Zoe and she was concerned that she had not heard from me for a while we were so busy doing all the post blast with the recent rocket attacks and IED call outs I had no time. I don't want her to worry so I don't tell her much about the incidents and things going on. Better to say everything is fine because

I would prefer she think that and concentrate on looking after the kids and not wasting time and energy stressing about me.

30th of May 2011 — Tarin Kout

A horrible day for us today, 2 Australian KIA in separate incidents takes us to three in a week. The first young bloke, 25 years old, Lance Corporal Andrew Gordon Jones was a cook from out at one of the Patrol Bases was shot 3 times in the chest by and Afghan National Army (Taliban Infiltrator) whilst on guard together at his post. Bugger! The kid died on return to the Role 2 med facility here at TK. This is a really worrying trend as we cant trust the people we are fighting alongside and it means you cant switch off even for a moment inside our own bases. The enemy is everywhere over here. The Afghan National Army soldier who fired his weapon fled the scene of the incident. Another Afghan National Army soldier who had discovered what had happened, but was not in the area during the incident fired upon the offending ANA soldier as he was fleeing. A security operation was launched in an effort to capture the suspected gunman. Like the death of all our soldiers in Afghanistan, the death of this soldier is both sad and tragic; however the circumstances of this incident erode relations between Australians and Afghans given that the perpetrator was thought to be our partner and was the recipient of our mentoring and training.

The second soldier, 27 year old, a Lieutenant died due to a hard landing in an Australian Chinook helicopter. I had come into Afghanistan with him and we spoke often during our final training. He was an intelligent, happy young guy excited to be on his first deployment to Afghanistan as a Unmanned Areal Vehicle (UAV) operator. I was saddened to hear of his death.

The deaths have not had a massive impact on me

yet and I think I am just too focused on my job to dwell on the severity of it all we just have to get on with the fight. I spoke to a few of their close mates today in passing and they are shaken up by it all but again focusing on looking forward.

We also had one of our recent EHRC graduates deal with his first IED today, which was a notable accomplishment.

On a lighter note I received 2 packages from Zoe and the kids, which really brightened my day. Both Joseph and Charlie had drawn me some pictures, beautiful, and Zoe placed some goodies in the box for me, the niceties' she knows I like. That really cheered me up after quite a difficult day. Every time I think of them I smile and nearly cry at the same time. I miss them all terribly. I hope they don't forget about me.

31st of May 2011 – Tarin Kout

Other than a number of Troops in Contact (TIC's) today was fairly quiet. The SOTF EOD guys came to see me to get support for an Op on tomorrow.

I finally managed to call Zoe and although I woke her up at around 11pm her time she was very happy to hear from me and I managed to put her mind at rest. I told her about how excited I was to receive the kids' drawings and the gifts.

1st of June 2011 – Tarin Kout

A new month and the day started well, however; finished fairly bad. I had a run in with the biggest obstructionist in the ADF, MAJ B. This clown" attempted to block my operational equipment request on account of he had apparently submitted a request 10 months earlier that was not successful and he was upset that my request was approved in a matter of weeks of landing in country.

I am really looking forward to Gav and the boys arriving and I feel like I have paved the way to make it as smooth as possible for them ensuring they have the equipment and logistical support in place to allow them to do their jobs effectively. I know MTF 2 are going to continue to be a pain in the butt but I don't want it to detract from the handover in best preparing my men for the difficult job ahead. I hope to shield them from a lot of the nonsense.

8th of June 2011 – Tarin Kout

The past few days have been extremely busy with the arrival of Gav and the lads, about half the troop. I have been working very long hours to ensure they are prepared and equipped for war. My first team will depart TK for one of the forward Patrol Bases tomorrow and I have done everything I can do to prepare them. The men are eager to get into the fight and prove themselves. They have trained long and hard for this opportunity and now they are ready to do it.

I gave my final speech to the lads today speaking about mateship and looking after each other, the length of the deployment, discipline and safety. Often people on operations take greater risks and don't think the rules and precautions taken back home in training apply; however, they apply even more so. I reinforced my main goal is to bring each and every one of them home safely and that in the end is the most important mission.

We lost another mate the day before yesterday, 23 year old, Sapper Rowan Jaie Robinson, working with Special Operations Task Group (SOTG) as a searcher in a Mobility Team. I know the lead Tech well and he was shaken by the loss of one of his guys. He was shot through the neck after a successful cache clearance during an Op in Helmand Provence. A tragic loss and a wakeup call to my team stepping out to perform a similar operational role.

10th of June 2011 – Tarin Kout

The past few days have been rather insane, I feel like I have been going backwards in some ways and all my motivation just left me. Things were going very well with work and the home front was looking up, Zoe was settling into a routine and then bang! Everything just turned to custard.

Zoe is going through a really difficult time at home after being required to answer an unfounded complaint to the Department Of Child Services (DOCS) and I thank God Zoe is as strong as she is because I don't think I would have handled the situation as well. The saving grace to this situation is the DOCS people praised Zoe for being a great Mum who obviously cares for her children appropriately and ensures they are clean, fed, rested and attend school. What a terrible experience to go through on her own. This has really shaken me up and I am so disappointed she had to go through this and to deal with it alone. I am stuck in Afghanistan and my wife is dragged over the coals undeservedly. I am so sorry I was not there to support you my love and you are amazing to be able to look at this issue embrace your faith and move on. You are the strongest person I know and I love you so incredibly much.

I truly believe God is in my life and he will continue to bless my family and me. I ask he guides me to make the right decisions in my life and blesses us with happiness and health. Money is not the goal, happiness and love are what is important in life and to live a life in love is to live a truly blessed life. That's me getting spiritual and deep for one day.

11th of June 2011 – Tarin Kout

Today was a good day. Ty and Cam and the team came in today. We received 2 rounds of 107mm in-direct fire that I went and conducted post blast clearance and returned to the team to continue lessons. Welcome to TK boys! One of the lads said to me 'we just arrived and within 2 hours we are under attack'.

12th of June 2011 – Tarin Kout

Today was a good day. I finalised the majority of the troop admin and Duty Statements. We prepared Wallaby 1 to deploy forward tomorrow and conducted the exploitation of the Rocket Point of Origin from yesterday's attack.

I spoke with DCOMD about the EOD Command arrangement and he assured me all systems are go. This is a huge win for me and will allow me to do my job without being hindered by the minor call signs trying to task my assets without my authority. I am extremely happy that this has occurred and can now concentrate on best employing the asset across the entire battle space to support all organisations, improve response times to incidents and improve mobility across the a Area of Operations.

I spoke to Zoe and the majority of the conversation was regarding little Charlie. He is still going through a really difficult time and my biggest concern is that he is now getting aggressive with Zoe and Joseph and has started playing quite rough with Eden. I really feel for the kid I just dont know what to do to help the situation. Not that I can do a lot from here.

I am due to go out on mission again in a few days and I am looking forward to the change in routine. I can't seem to find time for myself at the moment. Most days I am working till midnight and rising at 6 am so the days are long but not as long as my last deployment. Having the Weapons Technical Intelligence Team (WIT) here helps as I don't feel like I am doing it all on my own and they are producing some great actionable intelligence from their reporting of incidents.

14th of June 2011 - Tarin Kout

Another IDF attack today 2 x 107mm Rockets landed inside the base again. The sound of an incoming rocket is something I don't think I will ever get used to. I am immediately struck with a fear trying to work out how close it is going to land to me, whether I have enough time to get to cover or simply hit the ground and pray, is it passing overhead or going to land short? There is an eerie feeling about the impending impact of 1.5kg of high explosive war head detonating around you sending large shards of red hot steel for up to 1000m in every direction. leaving a trailing barrel of rocket fuel, igniting everything it comes into contact with. Ah rockets, not my favourite thing in the world.

Prepared another group of searchers prior to sending them forward and sent W1 out to start operating. I'm confident the men in this team will do well and stay tight as a group. Thy Rodda is in my mind the most proficient technician in the Troop and capable of meeting any challenge the enemy can throw at him, and it is for that reason that I have sent his team to the most historically dangerous location in the AO.

I went through a few photos of the kids and nearly cried when I looked at how they have grown. I feel as though I am missing out on so much of their lives and may never fill the gap. It scares the hell out of me to think that they are suffering due to my absence.

17th of June 2011 - Tarin Kout

The past few days have been eventful with the arrival of my final team into TK and their subsequent training. I have secured beyond line of sight comms for the EOD teams to ensure quicker, safer and more effective conduct of C-IED/EOD tasks across the battle space and the arrival of the new US EOD Teams into TK.

Tonight I went to dinner at Camp Coal the US base in TK and had Copenhagen ice cream and lots of unhealthy although delicious dinner options. The new US EOD team seem good and enthusiastic to get involved.

I spoke to Zoe and told her she would not hear from me for a while as I am going on an extended mission and she did not sound pleased. It is part of the job and I have to go so maybe I just won't tell her in the future. No point making her worry any more than she already is.

20th of June 2011 - Tarin Kout

Did a stint in Chora, Baluchi and the Dorafshan. The lads are settling in well although there are the usual teething problems. I know the OC up there very well and he is a top bloke and will look after my lads.

I dealt with an IED on my way back today consisting of a 20kg main charge of Ammonium Nitrate Aluminium (ANAL), a pressure plate and power source, nothing out of the ordinary on the device for the area and all went well as far as recovering the components. Im keen to see if we can get any actionable intelligence from the components as everything was recovered without damage so there is a good chance of getting some finger prints or something we can use to link to a cell or a particular individual. My confidence is increasing with each job I do; however, i still get a strong sense of fear before approaching an IED and I think it helps me focus reminding me not to take any stupid risks and do everything methodically and considered as I only get one chance. "Initial success or total failure".

On my way back we stopped by a small patrol base housing around 30 Aussie diggers and one of the young searchers came very close to killing himself and his team through a sheer act of stupidity. He decided to manually open a main charge he had recovered from a cache with a knife to confirm it did not have a Trojan device in it. WTF! Thats a great way of getting yourself killed, I thought we had trained these guys better than that. This is one of my biggest fears, guys going rogue, cowboys deciding to go outside there lane because they are isolated and feel like they can get away with anything. I counselled the young bloke and although I felt like tearing his head off I decided it would be better to try and get through to this bloke so he doesn't kill himself or his team. He is a very young guy with little experience, recently promoted and placed in a very stressful position and has simply stuffed up. I spoke with his OC and he will be sent back to TK for a period of retraining, counselling and mentoring.

I am looking forward to speaking with Zoe and the kids and can't wait to hear their voices. I am so tired at the moment.

21st of June 2011 - Tarin Kout

Today was a busy day; it started with writing the report on yesterday's tasks and ensuring I had a number of significant observations, facts and recommendations to get across to the combat team.

I am missing Zoe and the kids terribly. I will ensure I call them when I get back to base and have a good chat. I hope the kids are well, I spend a lot of time thinking of them playing and growing in the quiet hours and have found myself dreaming of them a lot lately. They need their father and I need them.

We had a memorial for the EDD's today and I thought it was good although I was called out on a IED job and missed the majority of the service. They unveiled a memorial plaque and read a number of appropriate poems to suit the occasion. CPL John Cannon was there as the lead handler, this guy knows everything there is to know about Explosive Detection Dogs and is a great asset, he will be critical in growing and developing the EDD trade for the Australian Army.

22st of June 2011 — Tarin Kout

We dealt with three IED's and a cache today so a fairly busy day all told. I am shattered and need to get some sleep. The decision on the level of command for the EOD assets was made today, they are mine and cannot be messed with by random Majors. I answer direct to a full Colonel, so happy days.

I had an awesome chat to Zoe today and we must have spoken for around an hour. We spoke about the future, the kids who are great although the boys are constantly fighting. We spoke about the kids schooling and the plan for the holidays. We spoke about my parents and their expectations about me remaining in the Army and that Zoe had a chat to Dad expressing her wish for me to get out and he said he would be really disappointed if I discharged. I mean come on mate! it's not like I haven't already committed a large portion of my life to this cause. Two deployments to Afghanistan, two to South east Asia and years of service to the detriment of my family life. I think at 34 years of age I can make my own decisions about what is best for me and my family. I know he means well and just wants the best for me but from my point of view comments like that are hard to hear.

All my lads are doing well and bedding in for a long tour. I am getting a lot out of teaching the Afghans, how to blow stuff up, It's a lot like giving a complete stranger a hand grenade and hoping they don't remove the pin and drop it in your lap. Not being able to trust them is just a reality after all the Blue on Green incidents we have faced. I have to stand next to them every day with weapons and explosives. If any of them did want to kill me it would not be very hard to do it! From my perspective they are good soldiers and I am enjoying this part of my job. Even if one of them did shoot one of ours in cold blood the other day.

I am also enjoying working with the Yanks, they are a real laugh. We have a new CO now also a good guy who is a larger than life Texan, he listens well and is very approachable but loud in that typical American way. I really respect the support their nation provides them, so openly patriotic it makes many Australians seem prissy with our political correctness and over the top urge to please everyone and not upset the minorities. Interestingly if a politician openly spoke out against defence in the USA they would probably sack them.

26st of June 2011 – Tarin Kout

The last few days have been good. The new US EOD Team are settling in and we got them on an air move after another Rocket attack around lunchtime to exploit the point of origin. The Troop commander is good although young and inexperienced. She came and asked me for some advice today as she is having a few issues with leadership in her troop. I gave her some advice and she seemed to appreciate it. I just hope it goes well for them. They have an experienced senior SGT with a fair bit of operational experience so he should steer them well although having a junior female commander is obviously causing some friction.

Gav and I are getting some serious work done and have achieved a lot in the past two weeks. All teams are out and on the ground and operating well. SPR Ball broke his wrist in a vehicle accident whilst driving the Bush Master through some tricky terrain and is being returned to Australia, I pray this is the only injury my troop will deal with this deployment. I need to find a new driver for that team so that is an issue. Simmo lost his Grandfather during the week so that was a bit of bad news for the troop. Life goes on back home and we are stuck here with no influence or ability to assist during difficult times.

I am so proud of Zoe, she is a determined strong woman and I am very blessed that she fell in love with me. I would not change my marriage for all the money in the world. She is pressing hard with work and starting to see some success. I miss her terribly. I just hope she doesn't take too much on.

I started a new initiative to target the IED network operating in our AO and reduce the amount of ordnance, weapons and IED components amongst the local population through the implementation of hand-in pits around the patrol bases targeting local nationals who want to hand in weapons and explosive ordnance. I am hopeful that it will be successful and that it will remove a significant amount of devices before they are placed in the ground.

27th of June 2011 – Tarin Kout

Had a helicopter op this morning responding to an IED a few k's from MNB-TK although was woken early by the call out it was a victim operated IED, pressure plate so I blew the main charge and recovered components for the WIT guys and went home.

Things are good at the moment but very very very busy. It would seem there are never enough hours in the day and the EOD jobs are constant. The lads are good and we even celebrated the Waterloo dinner the other night. Although a week late and no 'piss' to speak of, it was a good night and I took a few yanks along for the experience. Afghan local dining and no hangover so not your typical Waterloo.

I love the concept of the Waterloo dinner though. A few engineers got together to have a dinner at Gallipoli needed an excuse to get on the gas so used the anniversary of the Battle of Waterloo as the perfect cover. What Waterloo had to do with engineers I am not sure?

Anyway they decided to get pissed. Throw in a story about the construction of Watson's Pier and a random Sig "who was in charge of the build"! and hay presto the perfect excuse to get pissed up and annoy the British. You have to love Engineers they will find an excuse to get on the turps any way they can. Very loose beginnings to what is a now an honoured tradition. Although I am sure the Corp history would try to make the event sound more regal and officially important than it really is.

Gav and I are enjoying working together again and it is good to have him here. I constantly take the piss out of him and he gives it back just as much. I have upset a few people but in the main have gained the respect of the higher and lower HQ staff and they know they can come to me for the right advice at the right time.

30th of June 2011 - Tarin Kout

The past few days have been extremely busy and life seems to be going by in a rush. We dealt with a number of IED incidents and had a vehicle strike in a Bush Master today that resulted in severe damage to the vehicle but no casualties so things are good.

Tomorrow I start the Train the Trainer course for the Explosive Hazard Reduction Course (EHRC) and have a number of US and AUS pers to train. It should be good and I hope the students get something out of it.

I had a severe pain in my chest today that worried me a bit, I continued to have minor pain and discomfort throughout the day but feel ok now. If I get it again tomorrow, I will have to go to see the Doc but I don't want to because I think it may result in me being out of action for some time. I think it may have something to do with exhaustion and stress. I hope I get better soon. I am a bit worried about the whole thing.

I am thinking of Zoe and the kids a lot and thinking of life outside defence it all sounds wonderful and I know there will be challenges but I am not afraid like I was last time I put in a discharge. I am keen to embrace the challenges of life on the outside and think it is definitely time for me to start a new life focused around home and family.

2nd of July 2011 - Tarin Kout

Yesterday was finished off with a game of poker with about 10 CAPTs. It was a lot of fun and a welcome distraction to the day-to-day grind of activities that usually occupy my time.

Indirect Fire (IDF) again yesterday morning not sure how many that is since I have been here but a few. Not worth worrying about though the way I figure it, if it is your time it's your time. There is not much you can do about being in the wrong place at the wrong time with IDF.

Today finished with a bang! I responded to a very unfortunate incident that occurred at the heavy weapons range in TK, two Sappers from the Trade Training School were injured whilst firing an RPG when the rocket pre detonated injuring them both significantly. The incident was captured on two video cameras and one of the lads lost an arm along with multiple other injuries. They have been sent to KAF for treatment and on to Germany as the injuries are bad. No protective equipment and no tourniquet so they both lost a lot of blood at the site.

They are not yet out of the woods but will hopefully pull through. These non-battle casualties are often the hardest to deal with as they could have easily been avoided. A real shame that one incident has now resulted in two soldiers being maimed for life and will potentially cost a few others their careers.

4th of July 2011 – Tarin Kout – Independence Day

Today was exciting, exhausting, dangerous and a little terrifying. I was awoken at 0430 by yet another IDF incident and quickly responded to the Point of impact that contained a 107mm Rocket Unexploded Ordnance (UXO), with a US EOD Tech as my number 2, WIT (CAPT Nick Trotter) and a team of 5 dismounts to respond to the incident site approx. 800m East of MNBTK. We put in the cordon and I conducted my approach only to discover the item was not an unexploded ordinance (UXO) but had functioned as a white phosphorus (WP) round and therefore was relatively still intact and looked like a UXO from the Intelligence Surveillance and Recognisance (ISR) assets viewing it. We quickly conducted a post blast and returned to MNBTK and started driving around the airfield back to the Command Post approx. 2.5 km in an open land rover and a White fleet land rover. On our way back we heard a 107 round pass overhead very close, we slammed on the anchors and jumped out of the cars onto the ground digging a trench with our eyebrows.

Not 5 seconds later the next round hit approx. 30m to our flank on the airfield and BANG! the blast wave hit us pushing all the air out of my lungs and ringing into our ears. Super heated fragments of steel went screaming overhead through the vehicles, exploding glass fell as the frag impacted into the cars not 50cm above our heads. As we realised what had happened we quickly identified if anyone was injured and amazingly all 8 of us were relatively unharmed.

When I think about it that was quite a significant near death experience and I can recall the fear whilst waiting for the next round to fall on top of us the siren still sounding, Incoming, incoming, incoming. I recall clambering under the car and thinking did Trots' put the hand break on as my head was very close to the tire. I hit the ground immediately. I am so proud of all the individuals involved as their immediate action to hit the deck saved their lives as any hesitation would have been devastating and resulted in certain casualties. Another round landed in the distance and we began yet another post blast exploitation as we were already on scene.

I feel good surprisingly, just tired after responding to a number of IED's and 2 IDF's in one day and then doing admin on top. I am tired and worn out today and looking forward to a decent sleep. I hope we don't get hit tonight I could really use a sleep in. Not my first near death experience but I was in the open and had nowhere to go and it was about as close to a blast like that anyone would ever want to be.

The US EOD Tech LT (nick named Checkers) is new to theatre, I took her on this morning's job to get her some experience and she got more than she bargained for. Indirect fire (IDF) and UXO jobs are fairly standard and easy, however, nearly dying from an IDF attack always leaves its mark. I spoke to her later in the day to see how she was holding up and she was still shaken. She is suffering from ear pain and can't equalise in one ear, and that is a fairly standard blast effects injury and should pass with time. I think she will be ok at least I hope so. I think she will make a good leader and I will continue to try and help her along her way.

My ears are still ringing from the blast!

8th of July 2011 – Tarin Kout

The past few days have been very hectic I dealt with a CW IED yesterday and have been swamped with reorganising the EOD dispositions across the AO and trying to appease everyone. The reality is EOD is a finite asset and we can't be everywhere so you just have to hit the areas with the most action.

Zoe was annoyed today and asking when I am returning, she seemed as tired as I am. This deployment is starting to take a toll already and with the Explosive Hazard Reduction Course (EHRC) starting tomorrow I will be busier than a one armed bricklayer in Baghdad. I am looking forward to the course but not with the amount of admin still to be produced over the next few weeks.

Task Force (TF) Paladin confirmed today they would give me tactical control (TACON) of the two US EOD teams in the Area of Operations (AO) and the Headquarters (HQ) element to allow me to better coordinate the Coalition Force (CF) EOD asset across the whole area of operations (AO) with more freedom. A big win and I am happy with the current working arrangements of the US teams; however, I need to get them confident enough not to blow in pace (BIP) everything they come across so we can exploit some evidence. The last job they did involved a Vehicle Born IED (VBIED) in the main street of TK which resulted in a kid copping some secondary frag. Not a good result when they have so many options to try and render safe the device but I understand their reluctance only just driving in country.

10th of July 2011 – Tarin Kout

So things are good. I spoke to Zoe today after a few days of no contact and she was happy to hear from me. She mentioned she was sorry for focusing on the negative during our last talk and I just told her she had every right to vent and it was all-good. I miss her and the kids a lot and unfortunately they are all sick at the moment including Zoe, which would make it very difficult.

She is progressing with her business and I am so very proud of her. She is making a huge sacrifice to get this up and running all for me to be able to leave the Army without complete financial burden and be with her and the kids. She really is an amazing woman and I am truly blessed to have her as my wife.

12th of July 2011 – Tarin Kout

The past two days have been extremely hectic and the IED incidents are increasing rapidly across the AO. The ANA training is in full swing and we had the first Demolitions practice today with the Afghans "it was a blast!". The students are very responsive and seem to be picking up the concepts well. We have two US Navy EOD Techs helping out with the training between missions supporting US SF elements. These guys are awesome and add a great sense of humour to the mix. One of the guys Chris Andrieu, reminds me of Johny Dep in the movie pirates of the Caribbean and makes me laugh, he has such a great attitude to training the Afghan people and is great fun to be around him in such a crazy place. Its people like Chris that make being here bearable as when your with them you almost forget where you are!

I spoke with Zoe today and she is still sick but doing well and in good spirits. I really want to get an opportunity to talk to her for more than 5 min to connect and talk about how things are going at home. I feel like I have not had an opportunity to really talk to her in ages and I feel as though I am failing in my responsibility to her and the kids.

Still doing massive hours daily and I am

starting to get very tired. I need to get the work hours under control or I fear I will burn out over the duration of the deployment. 10 months of Mondays!

14th of July 2011 – Tarin Kout

Today started with a bang I responded to a call out at the 5th Kandak Combat Service Support Brigade and arrived to find three shipping containers full of old degraded very unstable ordnance and IED components. I spent a few hours isolating and making safe everything from PMN mines to 107mm Rockets, mortars, RPG's, Grenades, Recoilless rifle rounds and IED containers of all types including Remote Controlled, Victim Operated and anti-handling items. Crap fight but I managed to secure a load of stable stuff for the ANSF EOD training. A massive variety of crap that you just can't get your hands on back in AUS for training so the job worked out well.

Had a meeting with the provincial Chief of Police PCOP for the ANP EOD Team relocation. One of the most memorable personalities I have met. He is known as MK, Matiullah Khan, a 6ft 4in towering imposing man as tough as nails and staunch in character. He was a self-confessed warlord and extremely wealthy through the successful running of a drug trafficking and extortion ring. He controlled the major road networks in the region with his private Army and no one, including coalition forces, travelled on the roads without paying off or fighting Khan and his forces. He was accused of mass murder, rape and abduction as well as many other human rights violations. Eventually he was made Chief of Police and inherited a large force to add to his existing private Army. He doubled the number of Afghan National Police almost overnight by placing uniforms on his private army personnel.

Note added: We would go on to meet in person on a number of occasions in his well defended compound in TK and discussed the future training of his Police personnel in counter IED operations to improve their survivability and basic awareness as he was losing people daily through IED attack. Eventually we would go on to train a number of his personnel although I always felt like we were training a militia force who held the local population to ransom to the whim of a ruthless leader. But that is Afghanistan. Matiullah would became one of the lead Australian contacts for development projects in the region and was paid very well for the privilege. This former illiterate cab driver turned millionaire would go on to command a seat at the presidents table and would later be targeted for assassination and killed by a Taliban suicide bomber in Kabul.

I am very happy with how things are progressing but I am tired and these long days are killing me.

18th of July 2011 – Tarin Kout

The past few days have been hectic, we have been rocketed 3 times in the past four days and had a few IED incidents. Getting smashed with admin but keeping my head above water. Wallaby 2 (my second Aussie EOD Team) came in yesterday and we did a few emergency repairs on the vehicle overnight to get them back out by 0600, so the days are still long. Got about 5 hours sleep last night.

Little Eden is a princess and getting over the flu. Nearly One-year-old, I can't believe the photos she is growing so quickly into quite a little character. I miss them all very much. Mum and Dad stayed with Zoe for the weekend and from the sounds of it she really enjoyed the company. I think it was a bit of a downer when they left. They said they would visit again soon. Just want to be there to hold her and tell her it will be ok. She started crying on the phone today and that really upset me.

I can't wait to get back and get on with the rest of our lives. Apparently Zoe had a few heated discussions with Mum and Dad about getting out of the Army. I don't think they understand how difficult the past few years have been for us. Sure dad spent time away but this has been constant for four years now and it is wearing thin. My priority is now firmly set on my family and supporting their needs, Army needs to take a back seat for a while and if they can't do that then goodbye.

19th of July 2011 – Tarin Kout

Had another near death experience today and I mean near! at 1230am today a 107mm rocket impacted directly into my chalet as I slept. The rocket landed approximately two meters from my head and exploded on impact when it struck the sandbag and steel roofing protecting our shipping container accommodation.

Thankfully it detonated on impact and only slightly breached the hardened bunker because if it was set to delay I would not be here right now. The blast was so loud the concussion wave ripped around the container bouncing off the walls and throwing my brain into a state of confusion, I didn't realise what had happened for a few moments.

A few bits of frag bounced around the steel lining of our container; however, both myself and my room mate were ok although a little shaken and slightly concussed by the blast and my ears were ringing again for ages, I remember trying to regain consciousness fighting to bring my eyes into focus and struggling to see in the dark room through the smoke whilst my lungs filled with the familiar smell of explosive residue. As I regained complete consciousness I remember a fear setting over me that I could suffocate inside this metal box or it could collapse on us and we could be buried alive, I was choking on the smoke for a few moments and there was no light, I made my way on the floor over to the heavy steel door of the container, it was damaged by the blast and we could not open it initially although it didn't take long for the people outside to get us out and I remember thinking why the heck of all the areas this thing could have impacted did this one hit my sleeping accommodation? literally within a meter of my head. I realised if the fuse had of been set to delay I would not even be here today, one simple turn of screw and bang myself and my room mate would have been pink mist, but as luck would have it the rocket fuse was set to point detonate and exploded as soon as it hit the roof above the container, the majority of the blast and frag being captured by the sandbags on the roof. The Over Head protection had saved our lives.

My thoughts went to my family and the idea of leaving my kids fatherless and my wife a widow, I tried to push the thoughts from my mind as I knew they would only bring fear and pain. Yet again I had walked away from what could have been the end to my life. I questioned why I had survived, was there a hedge of protection over my life? I knew Zoe and a number of people back in Australia were consistently praying for me and I felt a sense of peace knowing somehow God had me covered. I had an unfair advantage, and a sense that I was going to continue to be ok and would return home to be with Zoe and the kids. So I put the experience behind me and moved on.

After this incident a number of people started calling me 'the rocket man' because I had three close calls with rockets impacting in my close vicinity over the past two weeks. The name calling was just a bit of fun but it frustrated me, I think more from the point that the incidents shook me a little more than I was letting on and somehow acknowledging them made it too real. I was able to simply put the incidents to the back of my mind and move on but as people consistently brought it up, it made it all to real again. It reminded me that I could be killed at any time and it was not something I wanted to think about.

21st of July 2011 - Tarin Kout

The past two days have been filled with activity, EHRC is into the practical assessment phase and things are moving along well. I have been working with the SOTF-SE Navy EOD Techs lately and I have been enjoying that. The team leader is Garry Simpson and his number two is Chris Andrieu Both awesome guys and extremely professional and knowledgeable in their trade.

23st of July 2011 - Tarin Kout

A total of 10 IED incidents across the AO today and the fourth PMV strike on MTF vehicles since their arrival in June. A busy day, we continued with the testing on EHRC and binned a further 2 students for failing to make the grade. The way I see it, it is an Afghan solution to an Afghan problem, we are not be creating Australian Explosive Ordnance Reconnaissance (EOR) personnel we are making blow in place bandits, but if they are not at a level where I think they have a fair chance of survival and are not likely to kill themselves or others I will pass them.

War is definitely a lonely place for soldiers. We have little companionship other than your mates around you and if you become withdrawn or insular it can be a very bad place to be. That is why I think Defence in general attracts so many extraverted people; because you could not do this job alone.

26st of July 2011 - Tarin Kout

Another 3 days down, The EHRC is finishing up this week, which is awesome, as I need some time to focus on some other projects; it has been good but is taking a lot of time and effort each day. Looking forward to the graduation and seeing the guys get excited when they receive their certificates. I had an interview today with some Channel 9 media crew up at the IED lane about the training and ops we are doing. I think it went ok at least I hope so I don't want to look like an idiot on national TV. Should see in a few weeks.

27st of July 2011 – Tarin Kout

A US CAPT Turned up to my compound this afternoon with a 107mm Rocket and said what do I do with this? I asked him where he got it to which he replied "someone dropped it in a field for us to pick up" I asked him if he had considered the fact that the item may have been a come on and contained a Trojan device in it to which he replied "yeah we thought it was a bit dodgy and were concerned about picking it up". I told him in the future to call EOD in order to mitigate the threats properly and he left. Some days I wonder what goes through peoples' minds.

Also conducted an Explosive Ordnance clearance of a burning 300 man ANA camp to clear C4, small arms and RPG's in the fire so the fire fighters could get in. When we arrived we spoke to the ANA and found out where the majority of ordnance was held and went to the cordon. I informed the fireguard that the ordnance was inside the burning area to which the Big fire fighter looked at me with dinner plate eyes and said, "you guys are going in first yeah?" I felt like saying "no way in hell mate, there are RPG's in there and you have all the breathing kit". But I just looked at him nodded and we went in. It reminded me of a T-shirt I saw once "EOD TECH'S, BECAUSE EVEN FIRE FIGHTERS NEED HERO'S". Classic, Checkers and I looked at each other and laughed and went through to complete the task.

All in all, a busy day. Very tired and need a good nights sleep.

30ˢᵗ of July 2011 – Tarin Kout

I was involved in the biggest attack in Tarin Kot since the beginning of the campaign on Thursday 28ᵗʰ July 11. I raced to the Tactical Operations Centre after hearing an extremely large explosion followed closely by another and witnessed two large plumes of smoke rise over the Tarin Kout city district. It was the start of a very complex attack on the major Govt. compounds in TK. A simultaneous attack on both the Governor's Compound and the KAU Compound starting with 2 x Suicide Vehicle Borne (SVBIED's) to breach the compounds followed up by 2 Suicide vest wearing fighters at each location and a number of infantry attacks. A further 2 Vehicle Borne (VBIEDs) placed on approaches in town to target our forces as we reacted to the attack from our base on the outskirts of town.

I responded USEOD from TK along with USEOD from TOBAR and quickly realised we needed more assets on the ground so I reacted myself with a US EOD Tech and WIT as a third EOD capability as Gav took command in the TOC. When we entered the town I identified a VBIED on a motorcycle at the TK roundabout and we quickly got to work rendering safe a time device attached to the bike. The RSP was delayed due to no air de-confliction, as there were four layers of air supporting the ongoing attacks in the Gov and KAU Compound a few blocks down the road.

Once we received de-confliction we completed the RSP on the motorbike and headed into the Gov compound to respond to a SVBIED reported in the main building. On the ground I split the asset and left EOD 2 to start on the compound and I split with a small security force to the sight of the SVBIED. There was gunfire coming from various locations around us and it was difficult to differentiate between the Afghan National Army guys shooting wildly and the Taliban fighters. As we passed a major compound I witnessed the front of the building collapse on four or five American soldiers as two suicide bombers detonated themselves inside the building as the soldiers readied to breach the compound. People rushed to the aid of the people but we had to continue on to our task location in the Governors compound.

We advanced slowly through a series of alleyways and buildings expecting to take more fire around each corner and then we arrived at the sight of the first Vehicle Born IED blast. The sight was huge, a real mess, as directly across the road from the blast was a primary school with dozens of wounded and dead kids. I quickly identified the blast as a suicide driver due to the remaining body parts and blast pattern. I distinctly remember being filled with a rage and anger at the sheer magnitude of loss of innocent life as I saw the severed head of the suicide bomber that lay on the ground amongst the shattered car and rubble.

The blast was enormous. I started to clear the scene when I identified a suspect vehicle with a number of explosive charge containers in the back of the vehicle. I thought, oh no! we have another VBIED and we need to get behind cover.

We established a cordon and I set up a pull. As we crouched behind a wall, small arms fire broke out again around us and we hit the deck. We were literally between a rock and a hard place, in direct line of fire from the ongoing fire fight but covered from a second suspect VBIED. I decided to conduct the pull so we could get out of there and get to some decent cover. As I was conducting the pull I observed a number of ANSF personnel shooting at an insurgent on a nearby roof top and then watched as they advanced onto his position and filled his body with lead.

They then threw his limp body from the roof, a three story fall, as their fellow soldiers proceeded to kick his lifeless body as it lay on the ground. I remember thinking that Afghanis are such a brutal race, but then again I could understand their anger, I had just felt very angry seeing the severed head of a Taliban suicide bomber. I completed the job on the second vehicle and we continued with the task of post blast analysis of the site and moved back to the building to assist with the Compound clearance.

As we moved back towards the compound where all the shooting was happening it was clear, the building was on fire and that the Taliban were still in the fight. Australian ASLAVs along with US Armoured vehicles had surrounded the front of the building compound and had driven the Taliban fighters deeper into the building. We coordinated with other ground assets before entering the building to clear it of ordnance and Taliban fighters. I was first through the door on the ground floor and as we entered the hallway I cleared the first room on my right. A Taliban soldier lay motionless on the floor clutching his AK47, he was wearing a suicide vest and had taken a number of bullets to the chest and torso. I had to check his vitals whilst holding a gun to his temple not wanting to take the risk that if he was alive he could set himself into a large ball of explosive flame and take anyone with him. I indicated to the team to continue and we cleared the remainder of the ground floor of the building.

As we proceeded up the stairs it became increasingly obvious the building was not in good shape and could come down on-top of us at any moment. The fire continued to rage around us as we cleared to the top of the stairs. I entered the first room on my left clearing top to bottom, left to right and as I went to step further into the room the person behind me grabbed my webbing and pulled me back. Checkers, My number 2 a US EOD Tech, yelled at me to stop as my foot came within inches of a grenade buried under sut and ash. Another close call, I said "I owe you one mate". I had very nearly stepped on the grenade and it would have taken my legs at the least and quite possibly killed me at worst, we continued through the building clearing room by room, body by body, until we made it to the roof top. I saw the blood stains and drag marks from where the Afghan Army had shot and dragged the Taliban Fighter across the building before throwing him off the edge, As I looked down I saw the twisted motionless body laying on the ground three floors bellow.

The building now clear, we began to mark and place charges against all the UXO in the building. I started on the Suicide vest clearance and UXO clearance of the compound. The task was difficult due to the lack of CF security as we had a total of 2 EOD, 2 WIT, 1 Eng Searcher and a heap of ANP and ANA who we could not trust with reports of 2 additional attackers moving toward our location, specifically targeting first responders. We had a few close calls with cordon breaches but everything went well in the end.

I set up a number of pulling lines onto the vest along with a few pull knives designed to cut the vest from the body and release it when we pulled it from a safe distance behind cover. You never simply move a man wearing a suicide vest as he may have had a chance to arm the vest or set a booby trap in his final moments. As we pulled the vest the body got caught up in one of the knifes and I needed to go back in to cut the body free manually. I was happy now that there was no booby trap as the body had been moved significantly, however, I was greeted with the soiled backside of an upside down Taliban Fighter who was wrapped in wires, strapped from his wrists to his waist, and I needed to cut the switches from his body. It was not uncommon for an individual to soil themselves in their final moments and the scene didn't bother me at the time. I cut the device free from the body, and completed our search and documentation of evidence.

We conducted a clearance of the two bodies that remained in the compound and a third outside along with a number of 40mm HE grenades, F1 hand grenades and RPG rounds that had failed to function during the firefight. We then conducted a further clearance of the surrounding buildings and enemy. I observed the remains of a Suicide Borne IED (SBIED) that had initiated inside the building causing the building to catch fire. We were finishing up as the sun set and the shooting ceased except for some occasional shots in the distance as the ANA pursued Taliban stragglers through the city streets. The second US EOD Team turned up and informed us about the fight at the KAU Compound; it read like a mirror image attack of the Governor's compound we had witnessed with 2 x SVBIED and 2 x SBIED's followed by infantry small arms and RPG fire.

I realised we had completed a total of 8 IED incident responses in amongst the mayhem and only just achieved our objective by dark. What a day, what a relief to be alive and that none of my team had been injured. The US had a total of 6 WIA due to stacking on a wall and entering the KAU compound as the Suicide bomber functioned his vest but it looks like they will all survive. There were a number of ANSF casualties but all in all an unsuccessful raid by the Taliban, although resulting in significant civilian casualties but not achieving any of the assassination objectives they were after, although they came very close to the deputy governor; he was chased onto the roof where the final fire fight took place and he was rescued via a ladder.

As a joint Afghan and Coalition force incident we shut down a significant Taliban deliberate offensive operation . I can honestly say I am very proud to have served alongside some great Australian and American soldiers on that day. Their professional conduct and courage made us a successful fighting force and made the operation a success.

The next day was recovery as we arrived back n TK around 2100 and debriefed immediately.

1st Aug 2011 — Tarin Kout

Back into TK to review the sites of the previous days mayhem. We were also called back to deal with a Vehicle Born IED. When we arrived on site I remembered walking past the vehicle on our way to the Governor's compound the previous day. I would have passed within 2 meters of the car and noticed it had tinted windows and was quite heavy at the back. As it turned out it was another VBIED designed to target us as we responded to the attack on the compound. Fortunately for us the vehicle never detonated, if it had it would have killed numerous coalition force personal, potentially including myself and my team.

3rd of Aug 2011 — Tarin Kout

Had a busy few days; went through a bit of a hard time remaining positive, getting very tired and a little fed up with things but after a big sleep-in today I feel much better.

Responded to an ANP vehicle strike two days ago that turned into a night clearance with US security and US EOD team. I lead the op as I was apparently the only one that knew how to do a post blast at night when there was a suspected secondary IED. The US C/S nearly rolled a vehicle on the way out with the mine roller attached and ended up ditching the mine roller attachment so we arrived at the scene well after dark. We dismounted a few hundred meters short, conducted isolation and married up with ANSF security. There were two ANP KIA and a few injured — a fairly messy site due to the vehicle being a utility with no armour and the blast crater was commensurate with a 20kg blast. I recovered a pressure plate and some fragments of the container and cleared the site for secondaries then got WIT in to assist with the post blast. All in all, a good job and I enjoyed working with the US EOD Team again and we got home and completed the report.

6th of Aug 2011 – Tarin Kout

The past three days have been fairly quiet in comparison to last week. It's been a good chance to recharge and get into some administration work. I also had a good opportunity to talk with Zoe and the kids, which was awesome. They seem to be doing well and enjoying the company of Mick and Barb who are staying for a few days.

I'm so proud of my team, they are all just getting on and doing their job, a minor admin issue to deal with every now and then but most of the time they just get on and do the job without complaint. Thats one of the advantages of having so many senior soldiers under my command, you don't get the day to day behavioural issues associated with younger soldiers when there is a SGT equivalent in every small team. I feel really blessed to have such a strong team.

I saw Charlie on Skype and thought he was Joseph due to his new haircut he looks so grown up and big. I couldn't believe it, all his little golden locks are gone. They look so much alike and Zoe kept saying how much he looks like me.

Did another interview piece for the media yesterday and set an explosion for the lead journo of the Channel 9 crew. They loved it and were very happy with the result so it should make a good story. The story is based around the EHRC and ANSF training. I shared a few stories with them and they were very happy to have a chat and interested in my experiences so that's good I suppose. I am not too keen to do any more media interviews as they tend to draw a fair bit of heat and I don't mind staying low key but for some reason they all want to talk to EOD. The Channel 10 piece even referred to the Hurt Locker before crossing to an interview with me, rather embarrassing.

10ᵗʰ of Aug 2011 – Nilli – Tarin Kout

I spent the past two days in Nilli the Capital of Daykundi Province Afghanistan and it was a welcome change of scenery to the past four months. I was called in to blow a few hundred kilos of TNT and Ammonium Nitrate that was confiscated from the Nilly Bizarre and I got there to find a Hazarian population living in complete peace and harmony, these people, with a little help from a small detachment of US Special forces, had managed to drive the Taliban from their land in the months and years past and now don't allow anyone that is non Hazarian to reside in the capital. As a result the place is a booming economy with abundant resources and construction at every turn and day to day life is largely isolated from the war that wages around the rest of the country. It is somewhat protected due to its geographical location, nestled in a valley high up in the mountains, with very limited access in and out. Our only access in is via helicopter and makes for an interesting ride. There is still the occasional Taliban attack, but nothing on the scale of other areas in the province.

On the first day I conducted a reconnaissance of the safe disposal area and then we went to the local Bazaar no body armour, just pistol and a few guards. The locals were amazing and very friendly and the kids were incredible. We changed over about $20USD to local Afghan currency and went through the markets purchasing every toy we could find, then we gave them to the kids who were in hysterics; they loved the attention and gifts and even the old men were laughing. This visit really replenished my spirit as I have been waning of late due to all the death and destruction. The local people of Nilli epitomise the heart of the people of Afghanistan that we are fighting for. A peaceful, stable and happy environment in which children can live their lives without fear of IED's or shooting.

On the second day we meet with the local ANP EOD Team whom I am trying to get relocated to TK for mentoring purposes. Then we went to the SDA and disposed of 4 x 107mm rockets, 400kg Ammonium Nitrate and 90kg of TNT. A very large explosion in a valley surrounded by rocky cliffs. It was great and the local elders and political reps came out to thank us and witness the destruction of the explosives. A great day. We flew back via Chinook just before lunch and I feel good although like I am back into the mundane drudgery of war again after visiting a little mountain resort.

15th of Aug 2011 - Tarin Kout

The days are really starting to fly now the past five days have gone extremely quickly probably because we have been so busy. So much for Ramadan, we have had a number of significant strikes against AUS Bushmasters lately including one that injured two search team members. They are recovering ok but will certainly be sent back to AUS, one with serious spine issues and the other with open fractures and lacerations to almost every limb after being hit by a very large charge Command Pull (CPIED). This trend is worrying me as it very difficult to mitigate against this threat and maintain mobility. The enemy is becoming more and more proficient in attacking our forces.

We have also seen an increase in attacks on ANSF and local nationals including a few particularly nasty incidents involving children again. My lads have done the post blast clean ups and from personal experience I know this can leave a lasting impression on the mind. I will keep an eye on them over the coming months to ensure they are all ok.

Zoe and I celebrated our 7th wedding anniversary yesterday over a conversation on SKYPE, rather disappointing not to be at home. I sent some flowers but they did not arrive until today. A bit disappointing as the florist did not deliver on Sundays. Information I found out about after I had ordered the items of course. I think Zoe is feeling let down but I plan on getting a nice surprise for her in Dubai on my way home for ROCL.

The idea of going home for a few days leave has revived me as I leave in 14 days so I have something very tangible to hang onto and look forward to. When I return in mid Sep I will have just over three months to go until my next ROCL and then only a few weeks until home for good.

18th of Aug 2011 - Tarin Kout

Had a positive Bio match on the jerk that set up the CPIED that injured our lads the other day so now we are going hunting for this fella. Should be a good kill when we catch up with him. This will have a big impact on the AO as this guy is without doubt a member of one of the most effective insurgent groups operating in the AO.

I am sitting here writing this 'off my face' at the moment as I injured my back and could not even walk for the past 10 hours. I have what was diagnosed as 3 bulged disks in my upper back resulting in immense pain. I reported to the Role 2 last night and received some Morphine for the night and then saw the Physio today whom put my spine back in alignment. Instant relief but ongoing pain and stiffness should go away over the next few days I'm hoping.

20th of Aug 2011 – Tarin Kout

Another quiet two days in MNB-TK, finished a few reports and caught up on some admin, nothing too serious happening. It's been a few weeks since we have had any IDF so the war is going quite well.

Spending some time with WIT and the exploitation guys and we have had a few BIO matches lately that is also good.

I watched little Eden walk across the living room on SKYPE today and was amazed at how coordinated she is at such a young age. She yells out "Daddy" at the top of her voice when she sees me on the computer, it is so cute. I miss the kids so much and can't wait to see them.

I will get each of them a really nice gift when I am in Dubai. Something very special, I also want to get Zoe a nice anniversary gift to celebrate our 7th year of marriage. I can't believe we have been married for seven years already, Time really does fly and it is way too short to stuff around doing something you don't want to do anymore. I have loved my career in the Army and all the friends and experiences I have gained although I look back and simply don't feel satisfaction from it in the same way I used too. I truly believe I was meant to do something more, something great, and that is exactly what I intend to do alongside my wonderful family. When I speak to me fellow soldiers so many of them are amazed to hear about my family and that I have three kids, I am so lucky and blessed in this life and it is time to give something back to my wife and kids.

I think I will struggle at first settling back in at home with three screaming kids in the house and I am even a little nervous about returning home on ROCL. But I know I love them and they love me and I pray for patience and understanding when I get home so they can see how much I truly love them all and have missed them. I never want to leave their side again.

22nd of Aug 2011 – Tarin Kout

Seven days until ROCL and I can't wait I am so looking forward to getting home and seeing Zoe and the kids, I could jump out of my skin. Had a busy couple of days, lots of little jobs on.

Last night we lost a Sniper from the MTF whilst on a patrol in a fairly bad area known as Khaz Uruzgan, a very non-permissive environment. Poor bloke got blown 80m when an IED went off he lost a leg and an arm was CASEVAC to MNB-TK but died some two hours later. Matthew Lambert, 26, a private in the 2nd Battalion, Royal Australian Regiment (2 RAR), serving with MTF 3. It was his first deployment to Afghanistan.

We stood up EOD and WIT to go to the site and conduct exploitation but TF ATTACK decided they did not want to fly us in there due to the threat on the ground. 25 odd Taliban with HMG and RPG capability. Stuff it, I was ready, but it would have been a hot insertion. In the end I think the decision was the correct one as we would have had very little security on the ground and potentially lost a few more soldiers in the process of getting evidence to determine the exact cause of death to a soldier who we know was killed by an IED. A bad day for MTF and a day which marked the 11th IED Strike since MTF 3 deployed, it would have been 10 but a PMV struck another one this afternoon.

I did a UXO disposal task up at the heavy weapons range this morning, just a few Russian 82mm Mortars that had misfired during an ANA Mortar practice. The funny thing was when I arrived there was five LNs in the impact area collecting the frag for scrap metal. They even stripped down all the armoured vehicle hulls on the range and stole them as well as taking down the perimeter fence. So I was standing there thinking 'how can I get rid of these blokes?' when a SF operator turned up with a suppressed M4 and said 'do you want me to get rid of these blokes for you?' I said yeah mate sure how do you plan on doing it? He fired a safe warning shot which had the desired effect. The sound scared the piss out of them as they mounted their bikes and took off. Classic I said mate that was very effective! He said that's the only language these pricks understand. Then I went forward and blew the ordnance. Far out! I laughed when I told the story to Gav on my return to the shed.

Yesterday we got a call-out to the Black Hawk landing pad as two 2.75in Rockets had hung fired in the rocket pod so we recovered them and headed out to the range with the Yanks and gathered all our stock pile rubbish like recovered DFC's, YPOCs, Grenades and all sorts of small arms and did a stack. Got a great video.

26th of Aug 2011 - Tarin Kout

3 days until I get out of this crap hole for ROCL and I can't wait. I Conducted a handover with Gav today and I am happy he has everything under control whilst I am gone. My biggest fear is that one of my lads will be injured or killed whilst I am away. Touch wood! nothing will happen and I will return without incident.

I think the crap will hit the fan at the completion of Ramadan as Eid is due to finish around 4 Sep and then all the Taliban will come out to play. We had a Hoax DFC on a motorbike out the front of MNB-TK today that indicates to me they are attempting to watch our tactics and procedures and adjust to conduct a successful attack using SIEDs to target our EOD assets and first responders. I think the kids will be very excited to see me in a few days.

31st of Aug 2011 - ROCL

I ended up doing another job on my last day in TK, I dealt with 2 x bags dropped at the Engineers Gate to MNB-TK and recovered 5 x PMN AP Mines, not a bad haul on the final day. The last few days were taken up by meeting and greeting the ROCL Team: Wayne Schoer, Zelco, Weino and Matty Allwood. All went well and I completed my Handover with Gav. I am a bit concerned about the lack of driver situation for Team 4 but other than that I think everything should go fine during my absence. I am very happy that Gav knows what he is doing and what is expected of him and I have every confidence in him.

I am now sitting on a plane flying back home, the flight has been intense, firstly on a C130 from TK to KAF and through to the Aus base approx. 6 hours' travel. Then a day and night in the main base waiting and a 3am start today to depart Main Base for Darwin at 630am. The flight then left Darwin to Sydney and now we are on our way to Brisbane where I will meet a driver to take me to the Gold Coast to see my beautiful family. I am very excited to see everyone and keen to enjoy a few lazy days at home. This is my first of two ROCL trips and although the travel time is extensive I am very happy to be headed home.

13th of Sep 2011 – ROCL finished

Currently waiting for the flight out of Brisbane to depart on my journey back to Afghanistan. Typically, the plane is delayed and now we have been of loaded from the plane back to the terminal.

Well my leave period was great although we did not do much, just hung out at home watched a few movies and took the kids to Sea World and a few parks. It was wonderful to see the kids and I picked them up from school on my first day back. Little Eden has grown so much in my absence and is literally running around the house, she gave me a huge kiss and cuddle and seemed very happy to see me. Joseph was so excited when I picked him up and cuddled me so hard like he would never let go. I also went to his school when he received an award for 'Awesome reading and writing skills'. He is so cute and a bundle of joy. He is like a newborn calf stomping around bumping into things with his skinny frame. Charlie was also happy to see me and when I got to his school I couldn't see him right away because of his haircut. He ran up to me, stopped and looked at me, then produced an uncertain smile and gave me a big cuddle. I really missed them all so much. Charlie said I was not to go back to work for a long time this time and that I had to come home soon to take him to the Zoo. I feel a bit bad we didn't get to do all the things I promised like going to the Zoo but we had no car as our car broke down, but we did have some fun and I did enjoy their company.

Zoe looks amazing and is so skinny and beautiful, she spoilt me with food and wine and cooking and we splurged on dining out and enjoying each other's company and really reconnected. I love her so much and really love our life and the potential of our future together. We did have a few fights but we got through them. I think my temper is heightened and my patience reduced due to the stress of deployment and it will be hard to adjust to normal life again.

I suppose the biggest decision we made on my leave was to find a home to buy and make the Gold Coast our permanent home. I am very excited about the prospect of living there and starting our new lives together. Zoe with the business, and me doing reserve work and building. I truly believe God is blessing us and I think we can really make a wonderful life there and the kids enjoy the area and the school so that is important to me.

Now it's time to get my head back in the game on ops and focus on keeping the Troop safe and coming home in one piece.

16th of Sep 2011 - Main Base

Zoe has been working so hard on her new business and I have faith in her really making a success of it, she deserves recognition after all the hard work she has been doing to make it a success. I know the reason behind all her hard work is to provide some financial freedom to give me the chance to get out of the Army once and for all and I respect her for putting so much hard work into it as all she wants is for us to be together as a family.

19th of Sep 2011 - TK

I woke up today, my second day back in TK, after another terrible sleep. I have started having night terrors again and they seem to be getting worse. I am a bit concerned as I am actually getting up out of bed and walking around and talking half asleep and half awake. My roommate had to call out to me last night to snap me back to reality and I went back to sleep. I must be waking up around 15 to 20 times a night and seeing terrible things in my sleep. Mainly the kids I have witnessed injured and killed by IEDs. I really hope I get a fix on this soon as I don't want to be in the field with this sort of thing happening. It happened in 2008 after a significant incident where an entire family was killed and I woke up looking for my weapon on a few occasions. I am a bit concerned I will grab it and use it in a confused state and possibly injure someone or myself. Not to freak out but it is very concerning when you don't have control of your own body and mind in a semi-conscious state and can actually see people around you that aren't actually there. Bugger this. I guess it was brought on by ROCL where I let my guard down and started processing stuff again. I need to turn it off or I won't be able to function, as I need to over here. I need to focus on the here and now and getting the job done.

As far as work goes things are ok. Wayne has kept the ship sailing since Gav was sent home due to his wife Wendy having a heart attack. I can't imagine anything worse than getting news like that when deployed in a place like this so far away and not being able to do anything. Poor bloke is hurting back home at the moment as Wendy has since had a second heart attack and now has a blood clot close to her heart. I am praying for her recovery.

A lot of the admin has dropped behind but that was to be expected with only one guy here holding the fort. The lads are well although one of my teams had a close call with an IED vehicle strike but thankfully resulted in no significant injuries. The boys were thrown around a bit and they suffered some minor cuts and bruising and concussion; however, the Bushmaster did its job and deflected the majority of the blast away and saved their lives. This vehicle is responsible for saving so many lives in theatre and the people associated with the Bushmaster project should be proud of the impact they have had on saving lives throughout this campaign.

I worry about the brain injuries suffered as a result of these IED strikes, the body is put under extreme pressure and it has to have some long term effects. I only hope it doesn't come back and bite us in the future. There continues to be a fair number of incidents daily and I had my first job three hours after getting off the plane yesterday so it is still busy. It realistically won't slow down for a few months yet when the cold weather starts to set in.

22th of Sep 2011 – TK

Last few days I have been settling back into the job, lots of admin to catch up on but things are ok. I think the dreams have stopped I had a good sleep last night for the first time in a week so that is good.

Not much to report at the moment fairly quiet out and about but a lot of reporting that things are about to get crazy. I am ready for it.

26th of Sep 2011 – TK

The past few days have been ok, just getting back into the grind. The post ROCL Blues are setting in a little but I am still remaining focussed, my drive is waning a little though. I received my PAR today and I must say it was a very good report and would no doubt secure me a sub unit command; however, that is not to be as I am not currently interested in furthering my career within Defence and now I am focusing on getting my resume out and about.

I can do anything I set my mind to and overcome any obstacle placed in front of me. Feeling good and over half way done on this deployment.

29th of Sep 2011 – TK

I am worried without a stable second income. Leaving the Army could be a huge risk. Two mortgages, three kids and a wife to support, the pressures are mounting and I'm not sure I can risk getting out of a secure career even though I want to.

I love my family and I have faith in God to see us through this time of uncertainty.

I must be confident in my own ability to perform in the private sector.

30th of Sep 2011 – TK

Today was a really good day from a work perspective, I received notice that the Singaporean EOD Training Team I have been requesting is in full effect and that two pers will arrive in two weeks as the recon party for the remainder of the team due to arrive in Jan 2012. A huge win for us which will allow us to focus our efforts on the mentoring piece outside the wire whilst the Singaporeans focus on continuing the initial training piece inside the wire for the Afghan Army.

Tonight I saw the Tour De Forces play in TK at Poppies and it was amazing. We saw Red Gum play, including some great tracks like, 'I was only 19' and 'Waltzing Matilda', a good comedian who had two brothers in the Army and a young Aussie Rock Band, can't remember their name but they were very good. But the highlight for me was running into an old mate, LTCOL Robinson, 'Unky Robo' a champion of a guy who was inspirational to me when I was at SME and was a great support during a difficult time in my life when I lost my best mate Andy Scott who hung him self in his Dads shed that year.

Listening to the songs about Vietnam made me think a lot about my own difficulties in dealing with the Dreams and anger issues that seem to haunt me every time I go home and let my guard down. I hope one day the dreams will stop but I know in the back of my mind they wont and I will have to just learn to deal with them as a part of who I am. I will try to use them to become a better person and hope to Christ it does not affect my family in a negative way and that I can learn to cope effectively and not let it rule my life or define me in a negative way.

4th of Oct 2011 - TK

Work is ok but home is breaking down. I told Zoe about the extension for the deployment out to Feb 12 and let's just say she is not happy. I completely understand and feel terrible about the whole thing, she made some really good points about the kids needing their father her needing her husband and friend and that the entire thing was just driving a huge wedge between us. I miss them all so much and just feel helpless as does Zoe and I know this trip will leave some lasting scars on us as a family. Zoe is burning out and it is simply not fair to expect her to raise three kids on her own. The kids suffer, she suffers and I suffer and it really makes me ask the question why? Is it all worth it? What am I actually achieving by being here?

All I want now is to go home, get out of the Army and get on living a normal life where I can take my kids to school, to the beach and have fun with them and bless my wife the way that she blesses me. Zoe told me today the bank will not lend us the money to buy the house .I am not too fussed about as I am happy to hold onto some money and get out of debt for a while. I really liked the house but it is not to be and I am sure God has another plan for us. I pray that God continues to bless our lives and above all things keep everyone safe. I can't wait for the day I return home for good.

Zoe wants me out now but thats just not going to happen, there just simply is no one to replace me and I am not saying that in a boasting way but the SQN has told me they can't even support my second ROCL at this point. 11 months is too long to be away from your family.

10th of Oct 2011 – TK

Arrived in Nilli on the 8th Oct to start an Explosive Ordnance Clearance Task on the range and do some work with the US SF ODA guys. The US SF have been using the area for a few years. A fairly easy task but I decided to bring a few Yank EOD Techs to help just to have a break from TK and the mundane existence that that life offers. I have Dustin, Amanda and Tyler helping and today we cleared a fair portion of the area and disposed of a number of items including, HE Frag grenades, mortars and small arms. Nilli is a fantastic place no need, for body armour or long arms just cruise around and do our thing. It is like a holiday in comparison to TK and the people here love us.

Today we delivered a bunch of tables to the local school and the kids were so happy. We also did the usual handing out of lollies, which always draws a crowd of kids. Tomorrow we plan on heading into the market to pick up a few supplies for dinner as we are cooking and then we will head back out to the range to finish the EOC task. In the afternoon I plan on doing a few fireball shots for a photo shoot up in the mountains and then prepare to visit the Chief of Police to discuss EOD Training in TK for his local team. So we should have a few busy days before heading back to TK on the 12 Oct 11.

I am constantly thinking about the security of my guys in the forward operating bases and hoping they are doing ok. I'm very confident in the teams to do their job but the constant threat to life weighs heavily on me.

13th of Oct 2011 – Nili

Still in Nili after three days and enjoying the change from TK. Today we took a drive to a village about 2 hours north to inspect a partially constructed school and had lunch with the village elders. The experience was great and we have decided if we are going to be stuck in Nilli for a few more days we will drive back out to finish the construction work that the contractor bailed on. The people are awesome and so friendly; the hospitality shown to us was amazing. You completely forget you are in the middle of a war-torn nation and feel like you are on some kind of Aid mission sent to help the local people. This is the type of place travellers would love to visit and would make for some amazing tales.

We also delivered some more desks to a local school in Nilli this afternoon and I was a bit disappointed with the craftsmanship as the desks were constructed by local kids in TK going through the Carpentry school, so tomorrow I am going back there to fix the desks and make them a little stronger and ensure they last for the kids. The kids are amazing and so happy to see us each time we come through.

Zoe is such a strong and amazing woman; she is not only looking after the kids alone, working but also sorting the purchase of a property, sale of land and evaluation and rental of our Ipswich property. What an amazing woman; I am truly blessed and I will not take it for granted. Any time I speak with anyone about our situation they all say the same thing. How does she do it? I don't know how you guys stay together with all the pressures deployments and the Army place on you.

I truly love her and the kids and feel like it is completely unfair on them and I owe them so much more. I just want to be home for them and live a normal life and it is incredibly clear to me that the Army will never allow us to do that so it is time to make a change.

I will get out when I get home and I will submit my discharge paperwork before I leave Afghanistan. I told my boss today about my plans to discharge and he agreed completely stating that the Army is not set up to support families in my situation.

18th of Oct 2011 – Nilli

Eight days in Nilli is a bit more than I expected to be spending here, however, we are preparing to move out by helicopter today. Our time here has not been wasted and we have achieved a lot in the past week. We completed the initial ordnance clearance task and then started working on construction of a few things around the base and then to a remote village to build a roof on a local school. We also constructed and delivered school desks to two local schools.

Had an interesting week and it breaks up the day to day in TK. We lost a local kid here the day before yesterday after he fell into a flour press and a man was severely injured in a blast in a separate incident, lost a leg, testicles, head trauma, internal blast injuries and severe lacerations but we revived him and he should survive, I assisted with first aid and Evac and was unfortunately covered in blood from the incident. Other than those two incidents this place is very safe and peaceful. I spent yesterday delivering demolition safety lessons to locals who use black powder for blasting and then reviewed their local blasting techniques, so it has been rewarding. I am ready to get back to TK now and back into the high tempo stuff.

22nd of Oct 2011 - Nilli

I feel like crap - today my stomach is all in knots from something I ate, (probably the Goat I bought in Nilli). Started another cse today for the Afghans and it is really taking it out of me. I had an interview with the Australian War Memorial today as well and it was fairly interesting but the guy kept asking about dead bodies and how we deal with them and do we get night terrors etc. I just told him yeah and when he asked for more detail I said he should talk to my wife who really has to deal with it. I talked a little about coping strategies and stuff but tried to focus the interview towards EOD.

25th of Oct 2011 - TK

I have spent the past three days in pain trying to pass kidney stones. At first I thought it was just a stomach bug or food poisoning, however, after spending an entire night in pure agony and half the next day I decided to go to the doc. At first they were about to cut out my appendix but a US surgeon changed the diagnosis to stones. I spent one night and two days on a hospital bed on drips and morphine but other than the stone moving lower it has still not passed. I feel it low and deep in my bladder It is defiantly sitting low and needs to come out but at present it is just a low pain that emerges at irregular intervals like a good kick in the nuts.

Other than that the next EHRC has started and I was forced out of bed today to get things rolling. I find it difficult that things simply fall over if I am not there to sort them out. I am missing Zoe and the kids a lot at the moment and I think being ill doesn't help.

30th of Oct 2011 – TK

Yesterday was a very terrible day for us as a deployed force. It started around 0700 in the morning when I was getting ready to take the EHRC out to the demolitions range. We received a message over the radio an incident was occurring involving mass Australian casualties at a patrol base in the south of our AO (FOB Pace Maker), what we later learned as the helicopters kept returning with KIA and WIA was that an ANA squad commander had decided to open up on Australian and ANA soldiers inside the patrol base whilst the members were on parade. The casualty toll included 3 Aus KIA, 5 WIA, 1 Terp KIA, 3 WIA a number of ANA soldiers killed and injured and 1 x insurgent KIA. This member had completed his morning prayer and then engaged the backs of the parade of soldiers with a PKM heavy machine gun. I later learned one of the KIA was a mate of mine, an Engineer I have worked with for a few years now and a legend of a guy, always happy and the type of guy who would bend over backwards to help you.

This kid had so much going for him as a

sportsman who represented Australia in the olympics, a lad who was looking at pursuing a career in the SAS and an all-round top guy. I was very saddened to hear of his death and went to my chalet to see his brother and close mate who are also deployed to see if I could offer any help. What can you do for two guys who have just lost a brother and a best friend? These guys have lived in the room next to me for the past six months and got on like a house on fire. I gave them both a hug and said how sorry I was to hear of the loss.

Both guys broke down and cried and I felt so helpless during this very sad time. The Two other members were killed. were Captain Bryce Duffy and Lance Corporal Luke Gavin. I knew Bryce although not well. From what I knew of him he was a well liked individual with great moral courage, a professional Artillery officer who will be sorely missed. These guys gave the ultimate sacrifice for their country and their mates and will not be forgotten.

1st of Nov 2011 - TK

Today I spent the day on the range training the ANA again thinking not 24 hours ago some ANA person blasted away my mates in cold blood. What are we doing here? Well we get up and fight on and continue the job that our Govt and the Govt of Afghan has entrusted to us. I have taken a few extra precautions but in the end if one of these guys wants to kill us its bloody hard to prevent it. Maybe our best defence is just becoming friends with them. The last thing I want is to die a hero after being shot in the back by people I am trying to help!

3rd of Nov 2011 - TK

Been a terrible few days and I have not been in the mood to write. We had the Ramp Ceremony for the lads the other day and it was a sad but fitting send off for the boys. Been getting straight back into work and was out mentoring ANA teaching demolitions on the range the very next day after the shootings.

8th of Nov 2011 - TK

Today was another bad day for us. I just finished reading an article detailing the dangers of mentoring and the number of murders and attacks committed by ANSF on CF over the past 12 months. Tonight another ANA soldier attacked AUS forces in a patrol base, this time injuring 5 personnel 3 AUS and 2 ANA. This nonsense is only going to get worse. I do not see a future in mentoring that will be able to successfully mitigate this threat. We will see more and more AUS casualties over the duration of this campaign as a result of these incidents and I only hope and pray none of my personnel fall victim to this horrendous form of attack.

The article I read detailed many of the reasons why ANSF forces may be driven to commit these crimes. Typical answers were cultural, social, moral and ethical differences between these two groups. We will never get along and to think we can is flawed. We are different in every level of our social, cultural, moral, ethical and spiritual views. These are not isolated incidents; up to 10% of all CF shooting deaths are as a result of ANSF engagements, referred to as Blue on Green incidents. This is a significant threat and we can try to adapt and improve our defence, but we will never defeat the urge of ANSF individuals to kill us instead of working with us. There is a deep seeded hatred for infidels and that is what we are, the way we are perceived and the way we will always be perceived.

When your motivation to kill is driven by theological views and upbringing it is easy to understand why these individuals take to shooting us in the back. To them we are arrogant, disgusting humans who don't deserve an honourable death. They will shoot us if we urinate in an area where we can be seen, swear, search their homes, look at their women, stop their vehicles or offend them in any way shape or form and they will simply justify it through the Koran. This hatred is evident in every day to day encounter and is so deeply embedded into their every being that no matter what we do or say it won't make a difference. We can apologise for causing offence, make rules and regulations to respect their messed up society and values, apply ridiculous levels of political correctness and blame ourselves for their actions and try to appease them in every way but this will not change their view.

A good example that comes to mind is when an ANA soldier drew down on us after we tried to stop him from cruelly killing a puppy. He had cut off its ears for fun and was kicking the animal to death. This act was extremely offensive to us and we intervened and as a result he was willing to shoot us. On the contrary, when we shoot dogs that attack us in the fields they threaten to kill us for shooting a person's property. These people do not understand this view of property over an animal when compared to killing an animal for fun, they have their beliefs and values and they do not match our own. Another example is the treatment of women and young kids. In their culture it is socially acceptable to beat a woman to death for practically nothing and to rape young girls and boys; however, we find these acts repulsive in the highest order. We will never adapt to their philosophies because they are barbaric, immoral and wrong. We are ordered to apply understanding and patience and fight a war with rules, restrictions and ROE; however, they are bound by no such rules and will continue to kill us over minor disputes and altercations or just simply because to do so is to die a martyr and go to heaven with your virgins.

14th of Nov 2011 - TK

Met Tony Abbott today. dressed the guy in a bomb suit and had a laugh but other than that life goes on in TK and sorry I didn't have much time to speak - Tony I have important stuff to do.

15th of Nov 2011 - TK

Another long day at the range, running the C-IED working group, dealing with visitors from Paladin and JTF 633. Very ready for sleep.

23rd of Nov 2011 - TK

Well I stopped writing for a while, as I was not feeling much up to it after losing our mates recently. I feel a bit better now and having completed the EHRC I feel much better. I was struggling teaching these guys on course thinking about one of their fellow soldiers gunning down our soldiers in cold blood and then another incident at a separate PB only days later wounding 5 more.

I decided to change my tact with them, try to befriend them and went out of my way to treat them with respect and it really worked. One of the Aus SGTs on the course had a number of run-in's with the Interpreters and it boiled over on a few occasions and it was so easy to see how these green on blue incidents can evolve from literally nothing but a failed understanding of each other's cultural and social beliefs and simply offending someone in this situation can lead to murder.

14 out of the original 20 students passed and each student personally thanked me for my instruction

and taking the time to train them. I felt proud of the course and changed in my view of these individuals. I don't think as Australian soldiers we are particularly good at mentoring these people and generally we perceive them as uneducated, dirty and ill-informed religious extremists. These pre conceptions can be very difficult to break through and on a whole I think we are perceived as infidels who swear, fart and behave generally extremely inappropriately and they see how we see them and are genuinely offended by it. This is carried over in everything we do, as we get frustrated when they fail to follow simple instructions and we swear and carry on and belittle them in front of their colleges. If this occurs, they become extremely agitated and I believe it is simply incidents such as this that drive many of the green on blue incidents not an alliance with the insurgency or the Taliban.

I read a piece of graffiti on the bathroom wall the other day that said, "no wonder the ANA kill so many of you Australians, and it's because you are a bunch of arrogant people." At first I was extremely offended as an Australian our friends had not even been buried and here was some dick badmouthing them. Then I thought about it and thought maybe this Yank has a point, however poorly displayed. A few days later under the quote were a response, which read. "That's rich coming from a Yank there have been over 30 something US soldiers killed in Blue on Green incidents during the campaign". Again a good point but per capita and in such a compressed period we Australia need to look hard and long at what we are doing to fall victim to these incidents which show no signs of stopping. Not that I think we should blindly accept all the unacceptable social and cultural differences these people display, as they are fundamentally wrong. You can never fully trust these people and never let your guard down.

The IED's have slowed somewhat but we keep getting a few incidents each day and have had a number of rocket attacks again. I went out to FOB Hadrian the other day to do a reconnaissance and see my team out there. Blue Graham and Allan Reilly running Wallaby 2 with Nutssy, Guthridge, Ling Ling and Newman. Good lads but typically my troublesome team. The base was attacked with small arms and an RPG fire during the visit which was a brazen attack not normally seen in the area. Things are changing constantly, just when you think you have a good understanding of what's happening, things change. Like specific IED cells operating out of Balluchi and Chora a very typical cell with an effective and reliable MO now changing it up and targeting CF's in a different way. I am concerned with the number of come on devices we are seeing in Miribad, Balluchi and the Dorifshan and think we need to be very careful as the enemy is actively gathering intelligence on our TTP's and probing for weaknesses.

28th of Nov 2011 - TK

Just got back from yet another 107-rocket attack that caught me in the open again. Not to close but a bit a frag flew overhead. Not sure how many rocket attacks that is but definitely into the double figures.

I submitted the Honours and awards for my troop this week and I hope they all get up as I hate seeing all these staff officers getting recognition and the guys doing the hard yards on the front line every day missing out. We will see.

Not too long until ROCL and I am really looking forward to seeing Zoe and the kids. I miss them terribly at the moment and feel like I am missing out on a lifetime of events in the kid's young lives. I hope they don't develop any resentment towards me and accept me back into their lives as their father. This is a real fear for me.

29th of Nov 2011 – TK

I watched the US Army throw a good officer under the bus today and I was extremely disappointed to see an individual junior commander relieved of her command by an organisation that has displayed very little loyalty or support. Checkers was told today that she would no longer be in command of her EOD Platoon in TK and a new LT was sent in to replace her.

This event unfolded due to one of her soldiers being found smoking marijuana. LT Plachek failed to inform her command immediately as her PL SGT told her he wanted to get the soldier back to TK and find out the extent of the issue. In the time it took to get the soldier back from a field operation the team leader radioed through to the higher HQ and informed them of what had happened. As a result, her immediate commander who has proven to be a useless and spineless individual laid out LT Plachek as a liar and a scapegoat.

The entire incident has eroded the trust in the PL and destroyed a good junior commander's career and more importantly her faith in herself as a leader. I think this incident will continue to follow her in her career and destroy any chance of her having a successful and fulfilling career. It is a real shame as she has been pivotal in establishing the command relationships between AUS and US EOD and moving forward in the development of an ANSF EOD capability in the province.

She has done what I would consider a great job and has proven to everyone she is a capable and dedicated EOD operator and officer.

Fortunately for her the COMD in TK, COL Aickem, has recognised her achievements and is going into bat for her but it is too late as she has now been relived from her command and will see the remainder of her deployment out in KAF. I felt sorry for her, as she is a good kid and has learned a great deal during her deployment and shown great promise. She was also the number two EOD Tech for myself on a number of jobs including the big attack in TK where she proved her worth under fire and in a very difficult and dangerous circumstance. I have nominated her and her platoon for a commendation for their efforts whilst a part of the CTU EOD Task Group and only hope this sheds some light to the command group at Paladin that this officer was unfairly relieved of her command.

I think I have changed my view of women in combat roles after working with her, as I would take any EOD Technician with her skills and determination in the Australian Army. Maybe there is hope for women in EOD although Amanda is fairly tough and often acts like one of the boys; I guess you would have to in order to survive in an environment such as this as a woman.

My faith in the US Army is diminished as a result of this incident and I only hope we, the Australian Army, would show more loyalty to our junior officers than was given to LT Plachek.

3rd of Dec 2011 – TK

The rogue ops continued today with a few cache recoveries assisted by our friends from FHT. We recovered 6 Type 72 Chinese AP mines and 2 PMN-1's from a cache and cleared a few previous cache sites along with a cave that was littered with human defication at its entrance. Not an overly enjoyable job but a rewarding one when you come up with a good size cache that you know puts a dent in the enemy's ability to target us.

I have been thinking a lot about the Blue on Green stuff again and particularly as I am interviewing a few interpreters for the job of ANA EOD interpreter. We need to be able to trust these guys and I have already seen that trust misplaced at great cost to Australian and US lives. This is a decision I will not take lightly.

Not long until I am home with Zoe and the kids for Christmas and I can't wait I am so excited to see the kids open there presents and smile, a happy 'complete' family. I still need to get presents and hope that I will be able to get something from Dubai.

Been working very long hours and feeling the pinch now, I really need to recharge the batteries. Keys and Jenno are back from ROCL and Keys got to see his newborn son for the first time. It must have been wonderful for him. I am very fortunate that I have such a great bunch of guys working for me. I did a job with keys today and enjoyed his company. We just joked around all day and did the task like it was nothing, like stacking brick to build a house, they just become routine after a while, no thrill or deep fear just another job.

I am often asked how I feel when completing an EOD task and I always answer the same way. Your training just kicks in and you push the fear and doubt aside and crack on and do the job. In truth now it's just like doing any other task. I don't feel the levels of fear I used to; however, in saying that I do not become complacent, I am very meticulous and extremely cautious about my work for good reason. Complacency will get you killed faster in this game than anything else.

6th of Dec 2011 – TK

Been on a lot of rogue ops lately, every day for three days recovering caches and blowing up UXO and IED's. Today we had a huge cache find containing a massive amount of ANAL, mines, mortar's, IED components and grenades. This find will definitely leave a mark on the local insurgent network and when we got back to base tonight we got a hit on the ISR platforms I have been pushing for and spotted two IED emplacements with Heron (UAV) leading to numerous Compounds of Interest (COI's) to target in coming days. All in all, a very good day.

I would love to sit here and write about all the details of the ops I have been conducting over the past few weeks but the truth is I can't. Every part of what I am doing is beyond anything I can write about here. But the important thing is I am enjoying my work again and having a real impact on the enemy and saving lives so I am happy.

Tomorrow we start mentoring the new ANA EOD Team and I am so keen to make them a success as the first ANSF EOD Team to be mentored in the province.

Less then a week before I go home to see Zoe and the kids for Christmas and I am so excited about it. I really hope they accept me back without too much disruption to their lives. I lay in bed very sad at night lately just thinking about all the precious moments I am missing in their young lives. Time to sleep and get up to do it all again tomorrow.

8th of Dec 2011 – TK

lot of IED's and finding a many of caches, which have to be having an impact on the insurgent supply lines. The new US Route Clearance Package (RCP) struck another IED today making that 4 IED strikes in the two weeks they have been here. I sat down with the comd element last night and went through a number of Tactics Techniques and Procedures (TTPs) for improving their survival and chances of finding devices; however, at this stage they seem to be slow learners. Todays strike resulted in 1 x CAT A casualty with a broken back. The strike was on a route near a previous identified IED emplacement so the RCP should have been searching through not simply rolling along waiting to blow up.

I had to sack a Terp today as he has proven sub standard with his translation skills and when we are dealing with explosives I need him to be able to communicate clearly or it is a safety concern. It's a shame because the guy is a good bloke and was keen to work with us. His replacement is an 18 year old kid who looks about 15 but has great language skills speaking Aussie, Pashtu and Dari so should be great. His name is Abdul but we have named him Bazza.

11th of Dec 2011 – TK

Ready to go home on ROCL for Christmas with Zoe and the kids and I can't sleep I am so excited to see them. Just finished packing, after a long day conducting training and handing over all the work for two weeks. I hope Wayne and Zelco do a good job when I am away and don't let things fall over. I have my concerns but hey at some point I just have to let go and try not to think about this place and all it's issues for a few days. Just get home and enjoy the time I have with my family.

15th of Dec 2011 – On the Plane

Well I am sitting on the plane on my way back to Australia for ROCL, I have mixed emotions at the moment mainly in regard to what I am going to do once this deployment is over. I really just want to jump ship and tell the Army enough, no more, I must spend time with my family now. But I know nothing in life is that cut and dry. My biggest fear is that Zoe will say no more; it's them, or us meaning family or work. I really think I could make a go of things on the property at Byron. Sure I am scared but hey we have a little cash and we could get by so what's the big deal. Not everyone lives like this. A life where you don't see your family and kids, a life where single mothers raise young families waiting for fathers to breeze on through every once and a while. This is not the life I see for my family and it is time to make a change.

Sometimes I feel so lost in all this confusion. I need direction to guide me down a path. I feel like I am drawing closer to those crossroads in life again, this is not an unfamiliar feeling and I could name a few of the top of my head. Cross roads, milestones whatever you want to call them but they are defining moments in one's life when you make a decision that effects the path your life will take and it can be so critical in overall happiness, life experience and fulfilment. Some of these moments in my life have been: High School, Joining the Army, Overseas Travel; University, RMC, Marriage, children, deployment and now getting out of the Army.

I have truly enjoyed my career in the Army and would recommend it to anyone considering it; however, it comes with the following warning; This game is for young single people and is not conducive to a happy successful marriage and family.

This is not being bitter or twisted it is simply a factual observation of my experience. The truth is so many senior officers in the Australian Army are single for a reason, they chose career over family. This is not the image of an Australian soldier that I associate with and as much as Defence wants to think they are family focussed, and looking after family's number one, they are kidding themselves.

The only important thing to senior officials in Defence is there own careers. This is evident in everything we do these days, from politically correct decisions gone mad, to over reactions on incidents resulting in all of us looking like fools in the eyes of the media and the Aussie public. This is no longer an organisation I wish to be a part of. I will always hold a great deal of pride for my historical involvement but we are simply moving down separate paths.

I hope Zoe and the kids enjoy my time back at

home with them and that I don't upset them too much when I leave again.

I read an article in a Defence magazine, (Land, sea air), or something similar, written by a sniper from MTF 3 who spoke about his first patrol after the death of his mate struck by an IED. The article was very interesting in that he spoke openly about how he felt; his fears, his job and his mates. I was very impressed by this article and hope many more young Aussie Diggers can draw from his experience and writing.

27th of Dec 2011 – Back at the Airport in Brisbane

Well I am getting ready to board the plane and head back to Afghanistan for the final push of this deployment after spending the past 10 days with my wonderful family.

It is even harder returning this time as I had such a nice time at home with Zoe and the kids. We went to Lindeman Island for 4 nights of relaxing in the sun before heading back to the Gold Coast and chilling out at home celebrating Joseph's birthday and Christmas. I really enjoyed spending the days with the kids and felt like we all reconnected really well. My fears about the kids not accepting me back were unfounded and little Eden was such an amazing pleasure and so affectionate. Charlie was on his best behaviour and Joseph had a blast hanging out with his dad. Zoe and I reconnected well and I love her even more today then when we first met.

There is a lot of decisions to be made between now and when I return to Australia in Feb 12. When do I discharge, how do I discharge, do I take LSL, do I apply for other jobs, what do we do with the land in Byron, Where and when do we look at purchasing another home and where do we live when I get back? So many unanswered questions about our future but I feel good about our future as a family and I have less fear about getting out and trying my hand at civilian life.

28 Dec 2011 - Main Base

Just spent 1.5 hours waiting for some AT in a bomb suit to deal with a suspect bag, welcome back to the WAR ZONE' oh hang on we are in Main Base Dubai, I guess they do this every few weeks IOT try and justify their war pay.

Just spoke to Zoe before; I am missing her and the kids a lot and just thinking about getting home It's always harder returning after ROCL and I think because of Christmas it is even harder this time. Although I would definitely recommend trying to get a leave over a special holiday to be with your family, the time is crazy and rushed but it is also a time where your families emotions are all heightened and often a time filled with stress so if you can be there it definitely makes a difference. Zoe told me the house feels empty now that I have left and that makes me feel nice as I know I am a valued member of the family and although they get on and continue their lives without me my absence is noted and quality of family life is improved when I am around.

30 Dec 2011 - TK

First full day back at work and it started just the same as when I left. We had a call out to TK early for an RC-IED strike post blast followed up by a VOIED strike on an ANA vehicle resulting in 4 KIA and finished with a Post blast back in TK of a suicide bomber on a motor bike resulting in 2 KIA one of which was completely cut in half by the blast, quite a site to behold. I actually think these two were Taliban and suffered an own goal. Classic win for the good guys.

The admin has been left and more piled on in my absence and it would seem Wayne and Zelco were flat out with the day to day. But it's ok I know the day to day is flat out and I would rather be busy then bored.

I had another night terror last night the second in a row and I am a little concerned, but if previous experience is anything to go by I should settle back into a routine soon enough and the dreams will cease. I hope so anyway as I again found myself in the hall way last night looking for people that are not real, in a state of half dream half awake trying to convince myself that I am dreaming but I can feel my heart pounding in fear and can't quite convince myself that I am dreaming. I manage to get my self back into bed without waking my roommate and having to explain another dream or make up some lame excuse that I was looking for something. I think to myself where is my pistol and tell myself not to grab it in my sleep and start firing shots randomly into the night at a ghost figure that I can't remove from my sight.

31 Dec 2011 – TK

Well it's just ticked over 1200 back in OZ and I managed to call Zoe who was sleeping to wish her a happy New Year. I wish all my family and friends a wonderful and happy 2012 and wish I were there to welcome in the New Year. However now I am going back to work as we just had another call out.

1 Jan 2012 – TK

Goodbye 2011 and welcome to 2012. This new years eve was significantly insignificant in Afghanistan, Ops continued as normal we dealt with more IEDs and pulled more caches out of the ground and the war continues without pause. I went to bed before 1200 and awoke around 6 in the morning to start a new day which seemed no different to the day prior; however I had a warm feeling in my heart when a thought occurred to me that this year will be the year I change my life and focus on my family and start living life to enjoy life and not letting life pass me and my family by just looking forward to when I come home or when the next course is finished or when I will be able to sleep in my own bed with my beautiful wife but simply living in the moment and enjoying my life my family and my friendships.

We said farewell to COL Smith tonight as he departs for home some 5 weeks prior to his unit and I feel for him in having to leave early, knowing his team will remain behind to complete the deployment without him. He is what I have referred to as the perfect boss, a strong and diligent leader and a knowledgeable, approachable man who listened to advice and acted in the best interests of his people. I can easily say he is the best commander I have had the privilege of working for.

Wayne and I presented him with an EOD Troop coin and I thanked him for his leadership and support with achieving so many of the things we have achieved as without his continued support we would most certainly not have achieved the things we have with mentoring, C2 and the establishment of TG633.10.8 EOD Troop. I am sorry to see him depart as I would have liked to receive my number 2 Afghan campaign medal from him on our departure. I will ensure that his support of EOD will be remembered in the legacy we leave behind. COL Smith thanked me for my efforts and went into some detail as to how impressed he was of our achievements and my personal achievements including the incident on 28 July 2011. I was honoured that he mentioned this and it made all the hard work, suffering and pain worthwhile. He reminded me of why I do what I do and that it does matter. It is funny how we just need to be reminded now and then that what we do is important and makes a difference.

2 Jan 2012 – TK

Not a good day today. I woke up at 5am to go on a cache recovery OP where we found and disposed of 375kg of Potassium Chlorate. I returned to MNB-TK at around 1300 to discover one of my teams, Wallaby 2, had been involved in an IED strike and three of my men were wounded. 2 x Cat C and 1 x Cat B. I went to meet with both LCPL Newsman and SPR Linwood who seemed a bit banged up but in good sprits and were obviously ok. I then asked about CPOCD Graham (Blue Dog) who had been flown to KAF for observation and treatment. I was informed that he was fine but suffered multiple fractures to his lower limb. I will go to KAF tomorrow to visit him before he is Returned to Australia (RTA). It is a great shame that he will RTA with only 5 weeks to go as he has had a strong and dedicated deployment and developed so much during his time with the EOD Troop. He is a great bloke and a dedicated leader and EOD Tech and I am happy to have served with him on this operation. I am sure he will be sad to be departing early and not returning with his team which he has dutifully lead throughout his time in Afghanistan.

7ᵗʰ Jan 2012 — TK

Crazy few days I flew to KAF to see Blue Dog off to Main Base and AUST. He was in good spirits and although he was pissed off to be going home without his team and the troop he was ok. His leg will require significant surgery, pins and rehab but he should recover ok within 6 months the doc said so not as bad as it could have been.

The past few days have been spent doing admin, reports and preparing for HOTO as well as training the incoming searchers from MTF 4. I can't wait to get out now and just seem to be counting down the days.

I have been quite sick the past 2 days with a bad cough and flu but seem to be recovering ok now with the doxy double dose treatment. Zelco is off in two days and the new team arrive in a little over a week, so just trying to keep ticking over the days.

9 Jan 2012 – TK

Not to long now getting all the final admin sorted and looking back at all the achievements from the deployment. I am happy with the Troop and all the individuals in it; deploying to Afghanistan as an EOD operator for 9 months is not an easy task and they have all stepped up to the plate well, I couldn't ask for anything more.

Zelco Paskov "Z" left today after extending to backfill me for ROCL and I have to say for a guy that did not get a start on the run on side he has performed very well. A Navy diver who knew nothing at all about land operations and has taken every challenge thrown at him head on I thanked him for his dedication, commitment, loyalty and service, You're a good man Z and Navy is lucky to have you, I would take you at 20 EOD SQN any day.

I get promoted to MAJ in two days that should be interesting although I hate parades and we will be formed up in the GYM at MNB-TK to receive my promotion from the new CJTF 633.

11th Jan 2012 – TK

I received my promotion to Major yesterday, I felt a little nervous and keep answering the phone today with Captain um! Major Cullen. I guess it will start to feel right after a while.

I felt really bad for Zoe today as I rang her early in the morning her time to hear the news she made an offer on a house which is very exciting, the house is in a nice area and the right price; however, she then told me the house has Termites in the roof. I asked if she had organised a pest inspector and she told me she had but the guy we used last time was not available and that she had booked one recommended by the owner. My alarm bells started ringing and I really put a downer on things. I feel terrible but we really need to be sure the property we buy is not a dud. The last thing I need is another house that is falling down and in serious need of repair. I have been talking with a number of civil Engineer and builder mates about it and received some varying advice and I will talk to Zoe about it again tomorrow. I just feel terrible, as I know she is working so hard to put our lives on track and give us direction. I love her so much and respect her and I don't want to hurt her feelings.

13th Jan 2012 - TK

More admin today and starting to get used to the MAJ thing. I feel good about leaving TK and Afghanistan in a better way then when we found it. I think this country has a very long way to go before it will see peace, if ever. And before the Afghan people become united in it's fight against the Taliban.

I am currently trying to establish a three man ANP EOD Team in TK from Nilli. This is not an easy task and you may think well they are ANP so the ANP can look after there life support issues such as accommodation, food and transportation. Well no, to put it simply this team is from Dey Kundi province and no one in TK wants to help them even though they are ANP and an EOD Team, this is due to a number of factors. Firstly the Afghan people have a belief system based on tribal law, i.e. if you are a part of my tribe I will care for you if you are not then you can die in the cold. You may think that the ANP is a national tribe but you would be mistaken. The comd of the ANP in TK has nothing to do with the PCOP in Dey Kundi or anywhere else in Afghanistan for that matter and if this capability is not going to remain in TK as a part of his organisation then he wants nothing to do with it. The other factor and probably the most important is the fact that the Nilli ANP personnel are Hazara (Persian) decent from the Mongols, and the Hazara people are not well liked in Afghanistan as a whole. They are overwhelmingly Shiite Mulims and comprise the third largest ethnic group of Afghanistan, forming about 18% of the total population. Over half a million Hazaras live in neighboring Pakistan and a similar number in Iran.

They have been persecuted for many years and although they live in peace in Nilli they will be beheaded if we place them in TK itself. Therefor I need to find accommodation locally within MNB-TK and in a location where they will be protected from their fellow countrymen. So as you can now see simply moving 3 people from one area to receive critical training and mentoring in another area is a complex and difficult task.

22nd Jan 2012 - TK

Snowing in TK wooohooo, soldiers and snowball fights go on. Still handing over and everything is going well other then 2 EOD Troop who were supposed to arrive in TK today; however, due to the snow storm no flights in or out. That's what you get when you plan a RIP in the middle of winter. Classic.

25th Jan 2012 - TK

Counting down the days now only 13 days to go. Held my last C-IED working group starting stock take and final hand over so I can't wait to see the back of this place never to return.

1st Feb 2012 - TK

Today we blew up around 1 Tone of explosives on the range, which was fun and a good stress relief. I have been feeling very stressed over the past few days and I couldn't quite put my finger on why. I think it is a combination of sorting out all the handover stuff, getting all my people back into TK ready to go home and the thought of returning to work back in Aus.

Well my final team arrived in TK today from

Hadrian and I was very relieved to have the entire troop back in loc ready to go home.

I have reached a realisation point in my career that the Army doesn't care about my family or me and they just simply want to get every drop of blood out of me that they can. Well it's time to give the army the big finger and get out.

Looking forward to getting up tomorrow completing my hand over and stock take and getting one step closer to getting out of here. One week to go today before I get on a plane and start the 4 day trip home.

For the past two hours I have been reading comments from the public about an article written on DFRDB and CPI indexing Defence pensions. To say I am pissed off would be an understatement, With all the nonsense that is going on in my head at the moment feeling depressed, scared, like I have no control over my emotions and generally feeling horrible I then read comments from "the general public" that infuriate me even more. The reality is we live in a country where the vast majority of people don't care about the sacrifices Defence Force personnel make for their freedom, nor do they know, or want to know, anything about it.

To you the general public I say this: you are ungrateful whingeing people! If you have not served in the Defence Force do not comment on this issue and do not confront me with your left wing rhetoric I will end you. And when you need a hand whether it is as a result of a natural disaster, peacekeeping or war, do not fear because braver men and women will sacrifice themselves to support your rights, protect your homes and families and carry the burden of your freedom, the freedom that gives you the right to do nothing but whinge.

3rd Feb 2012 - TK

Today my Nanna passed away. I am very sad for her passing and sad for my mother, I wish I was there to celebrate in her life at the funeral; however, I'm not. Rest in Peace Nanna and say hi to Poppa for me.

4ᵗʰ Feb 2012 – TK

Had our medal presentation today and although I am very proud of all the members of 1 EOD Troop I was disappointed that the commendations and awards I submitted for members of the troop were not presented today. This is either because they were not accepted or have not been processed yet, either way I think it is a typically disgusting ADF response to honours and awards for exemplary service of our personnel and the lack of recognition astound me. Members of CTU were presented with commendations during their medal parade a week ago and some of the individuals who received those awards should hide in shame for example ..... a logistics SGT who for every dealing I had with him was an incompetent buffoon; but I guess a log SGT who can't do his job is more deserving then an EOD Technician who puts his life on the line every day, for the safety of others, is not deserving of recognition as this is the job he signed up for. Its days like this I am ashamed to be a member of the ADF.

11th February 2012

Home!!!! alive, in one piece and ready to start my new life.

I found it interesting going back over this diary and reading about my thoughts on PTSD and how I thought I had all the answers. Life is always easier as a casual observer looking in than as the person drowning in the problem looking out.

10

Darkness Falls

Pride goes before destruction,
and a haughty spirit before a fall.
Proverbs 16, 18.

I was so happy to have him home, so ready to share the reigns of par-
enthood and ease the burden of life I had been carrying for nigh on a
year, I felt invigorated and complete, having my teammate home. We
were a complete family unit once again. Ironically, Andy broke his foot
a few days after his return and ended up in moon-boot for six months.
At least I had him home for moral support if he wasn't good for much
else for the moment.

We bought a small house in Mudgeeraba, which we viewed as the
realisation of our new beginnings and things looked bright. I knew
Andy was fearful of leaving the Army, lacking confidence in his ability
to do anything else, so I compromised. If the military could give him
a 'cruisey' posting in Canungra we would make that work. Unfortu-
nately, even when Andy threatened resignation if he didn't get such a
posting, he was offered an even more demanding job that would see
him in South Australia for 6-8 weeks at a time.

He was disillusioned by the military's lack of care and foresight
even when he spelled out the hardship and toll it was taking on his
family. He had the wisdom to recognise that enough was enough and
finally resigned. We sold our share of land in Byron Bay to Andy's mate

as the situation had become quite complicated with his marriage and we now felt we belonged in the Gold Coast and really wanted to have a real go at placing roots here.

It is safe to say that after 17 years in the Army one becomes somewhat indoctrinated, some people would call it brain washed or fanaticised. I probably would have fallen into this classification, certainly from the perspective of an outsider looking in. The Army was my life, it meant more to me at times than my own family. I was prepared to die for the cause and prepared to lead others to fight against any enemy I was told to, because I trusted in the organisation implicitly and I was a part of it.

That's what they want us to do. We learn to fight, kill and survive in difficult conditions, under difficult circumstances and to say yes to orders given from above. I would not say without question, but at times, close to it. I was just a small part of a big organisation and my personal ideals or agendas were not as important as that of the Army. Essentially I was, as required by any military force, an apolitical soldier. I did what I was told and got on with the job. For the most part I only made waves when I thought I really needed to.

On my return, I was highly motivated to make a break from the military and I was ecstatic to be home with my wife and kids. Life was good for a few weeks and I soon received a new job opportunity, which gave me the motivation and confidence to hand in my discharge and sever ties with Defence.

I retired from the Army at the rank of Major having served 17 years in defence of my nation, I was proud of my service and proud of the organisation I had served in. However, I left with a knot in my stomach as I could not shake the feeling that in some way I was deserting my mates and my duty. No matter how much I told myself I had done my part, I still felt like I should do more. This feeling would stay with me for years.

*****

When I left the Army, I really struggled with re-defining my sense of purpose in life and finding a sense of personal satisfaction in the knowledge that what I was doing was making a difference.

'A man without purpose is a dangerous man!' - Hugo Strange, from Batman, was very real.

When someone would ask what I did, I wouldn't know what to say and I would resort to a statement along the lines of 'I used to be in the Army!' I no longer had a label or job title to define who or what I was. I was living in the past and hanging onto an idea of something I no longer belonged to.

Things started to look brighter initially as we undertook renovations in the home we called 'ours'. We found we had a common passion in renovating and took great pleasure in the bold redesign of the once old home to a modern, bright space we were happy to call our own.

I proudly stood by as I watched this reluctant, but capable man grow in his confidence, in his ability to do something outside of the Army. The satisfaction he was gaining from working with his hands and completing the task at hand was good to see.

The usual frustrations occurred as Andy failed to see his need to help out in anyway with the home or the kids, and anything he did do, he viewed as a favour to me. I struggled with this concept as he was now home and available. Why was it not obvious to him what needed to be done? This required us to sit down together and actually negotiate duties and obligations.

He started a new high paying job in the private sector which entailed him working from home. That had its own challenges as you can imagine. We'd gone from having him absent to having him home all the time, but we also had to find the balance between work, rest and renovating. We stepped on each other's toes constantly as he struggled to adjust after having lived as a single man for a year. The noise and responsibilities of three children around him 24/7 were so totally different from what he was used to.

The original reintegration of our lives together as I said before, proved to be challenging. The army, in fact actually gives you some training on how to cope with it and the signs to look out for, but there was no training for this. This was unchartered territory, because Andy had left the army, they told me he was no longer eligible to receive resources.

When I enquired about some helpful DVD I'd been informed of, I was horrified and disappointed at the complete lack in duty of care toward an individual that had practically sold himself out to the military. Thank God he got out when he did!

Six months after his return I realised I was still walking on eggshells around him and shying the kids away to give him space and things were getting worse when they should have been getting better.

I started my new job in a position as the Explosive Ordnance Disposal Manager for a company based out of Sydney. The role was in a Training and sales position for EOD related equipment for Defence, Police and various specialist civilian sector agencies.

I quickly found my feet and thoroughly enjoyed the challenge of a new and exciting career outside the military and I threw myself into my new role. I travelled extensively within the first six months, even spending time in the United States of America rubbing shoulders with current and former defence personnel, law enforcement personnel and Government officials.

The job required long hours and dedication and suited me to a tea. I was still able to use my extensive knowledge and unique skill base in a sector that appreciated the skills I had. I found the job relatively easy as all I really needed to do was sell quality EOD and military equipment, that I understood implicitly, to police and military units around the country and overseas. I didn't even take my long service leave I had accrued over the years preferring to get stuck straight into the new job as I couldn't think of anything worse than sitting around for months twiddling my thumbs.

Everything was going well for a while as I kept my mind busy with the challenges of a new job, new home and family. However, things began to change as I became increasingly tired. I had not had a good night's sleep in months as a result of night terrors and hallucinations and I was becoming more and more agitated, aggressive and detached. On top of the stress of settling back into the roles of being a father and husband and starting a new job, we moved into a new home and I was in the throes of some major renovations. I realised I was not handling stress in the same way that I used to. Life was pulling me in every direction and I was failing to keep my head above water. I started to notice things about society that bothered me as well. I really struggled with the day-to-day, mundane suburban existence, watching the world go by, people going about their lives with no thought for what was happening in the world.

Did no one care that people were dying daily fighting the evil on the other side of the planet? Did anyone understand that their freedom was not actually free? It was paid for with the blood of our soldiers! But isn't that the point of living in a great country like Australia, the general public get to take their freedoms for granted without question, as a right not a privilege, because we have a military and a police force to ensure our freedoms are protected. The issue for me was that most people don't even consider that the military and police are the reason they have the freedoms. Without the people in uniform their world would be a very different place.

The world is not peaceful, kind, accepting, politically correct or even friendly! I have seen it first hand. The world will bite you in the butt, chew you up, and spit you out given half a chance and our freedoms are actually much less secure than the government and public perception would have us believe. I understand it is a good thing that the average person in society would not even consider that a soldier fighting overseas has anything to do with his or her own life. I think that is inherently a good thing, however, it still pissed me off immensely and I let it fester under my skin until it became an ulcer that made me resent the society that I was living in, the very same society I had gone to war for, to protect.

I became increasingly angry at the smallest of things. Someone pushing in line at the checkout, someone cutting me off in traffic, or someone bumping into me in the street. Even someone looking at me or smoking in my vicinity was enough to get a rise out of me. My anger gradually grew to the point where I could no longer control it. I felt like I was bottling up all my frustrations and anxieties and that they would simply burst. All of a sudden I was at peak anger, 0-100 in two seconds flat, screaming obscenities, chasing individuals, hitting and kicking cars and assaulting people for no good reason. I would quite literally blow a fuse and feel completely overwhelmed with anger. It would take me hours to calm down from a slight altercation or agitation. After a number of minor and not so minor altercations I came to the realisation that I was becoming dangerous and that I was not in control of my actions.

*****

Andy continued to drink well beyond excess without question or conscience regularly. It was much later that I found out that he would actually hide the amount he was drinking from me. Again, I became his drinking conscience. I hated playing this game, but felt I was the only one responsible enough to help him manage the amount he was drinking as he couldn't. Truthfully he couldn't control his drinking because he didn't want to. He was self-medicating once again, staying up to all hours of the night, eating and sleeping poorly, it was a complete recipe for disaster. We argued all the time and the arguments seemed to get worse as he continued to make very cutting accusations, without a thought for any consequence. I began to feel the undeserved growing resentment he was feeling toward me.

The unyielding, unreachable man he had become was a complete stranger to me, and I struggled to imagine a future with him. I distinctly remember feeling bewildered at my inability to make him see my viewpoint and couldn't fathom his bizarre reasoning. He would usually take off in the middle of an argument leaving me to fear the worst. Although suicide was never mentioned at this point, I was always fearful of his frame of mind.

I now know he was doing anything and everything to push me away. He would return and usually the argument would be left unresolved and the whole scenario would be swept under the carpet. As a fixer this went against everything in my nature, but I was so emotionally drained most of the time that I had to learn to pick my battles.

To say our relationship was struggling would be the understatement of the century. Andy required intimacy from me to feel loved and secure, but I required love and friendship in order to be intimate. It was a catch 22. After each argument and there were many, I struggled more to find my reset button, even after there was some semblance of reconciliation. I felt like my heart was being chipped away bit by bit, unable to see how it could possibly be repaired. It felt like Afghanistan all over again. He was still unavailable and completely unsupportive yet, he was here.

Resentment began to grow inside of me as a result of feeling his resentment towards me. He was taking for granted that I would always be there for the kids no matter whether he felt like being around or not. This made me feel completely disregarded and completely taken advantage of.

There were moments the resentment I felt towards Andy even rippled out to the kids. I felt extremely alone, because I gave my everything to protect the kids, 'bubble wrapping' them with a mother's love and they would never even realise how much energy it took.

My mind was playing games with me, making me wonder how the kids would remember their childhood, how they would remember their mum and how they would remember their dad. Would they want a relationship with me when they got older? Would they want to be free from the woman I had become? I found myself going into all sorts of weird tangents. Spiralling into depression.

Andy's disconnect toward the children and myself was very clear and escalating fast. He began to feel disillusioned with his job and was beginning to show anger and resentment towards me. I knew that in his mind it was I who made him leave the army and he voiced as much.

He believed, if he had still been serving he wouldn't be going through the struggles he was going through. His vivid nightmares returned and I watched him sink fast into depression and he began to distance himself even more. He seemed to want to get away from us all the time, it was hurtful and confusing knowing he didn't want to be around us.

On one occasion he told me it was because he just couldn't handle the kids. I was hurt and angry on their behalf and told him it was unacceptable, unnatural and unfair and that he had to fix it! On one rare occasion where we were actually talking constructively I told him he needed to see someone, because things were getting out of hand.

*****

It was about this time he began to see a Psychiatrist who confirmed our worst suspicions and diagnosed Andy with Post Traumatic Stress Disorder and Major Depression.

I began to fear the looming clinic visits as Andy always came back in more of a mess than before. It was as if the visits compounded and amplified his condition and he came back embodied in the condition even more! I hated the place, and on the occasions I visited the Psychiatric ward I could only feel the darkness and hopelessness. The Psychiatrist wanted to keep Andy in the clinic for 6 weeks but I refused to let him stay, baffled how the suggestion of removing him from reality would actually fix anything?

From what I knew they had no idea how to treat PTSD other than to throw random experimental drugs at it, he was no better than a lab rat in there. As a compromise he was signed up to an outpatient program which I believe, had some benefit but he was prescribed various comatose drugs which only seemed to make matters worse.

At least before this time Andy would show some form of emotion even if it was extreme anger, now there was nothing but a stupor. At other times the drugs seemed to make his reactions worse and he seemed to lose his temper more erratically and uncontrollably. It seemed like a game of trial and error to see which drugs actually suited whom. For most of the time he would sleep for hours on end only rising to eat.

This was no solution. I refused to believe this was the only alternative to dealing with the anger, bad behaviour, bad dreams and self-medication.

Andy knew my attitude toward the meds and at one point decided not to tell me that he had been prescribed four different drugs at once, one for dreams, one for anxiety, one for sleep and one for mood disorders. It should be noted that each drug was prescribed for specific conditions but the physicians were unaware how Andy would react to them.

I sensed something was wrong when I saw him go into this strange stupor and start having cramps and sweats. He was having negative reactions to the drugs so decided to stop them all at once. This was a really bad idea as the body can actually go into shock and shut down. The result was that he had to go back to the clinic for a complete detox. It was at this point the psychiatrist identified that he had a dependency to alcohol. Finally, the doctor and I agreed on something!

After this last experience with medication we were on the search for alternative medications. I managed to convince the doctor to allow Andy to give alternative therapies ago. Against his beliefs he agreed and we went on the search for alternative therapies.

Andy had to resign from his job as he was advised he couldn't work anymore. This was one of the hardest things of all I believe he had to deal with. Not only was he struggling with a lack of identity and purpose since leaving the army but now not only could he not provide for his family, he would be dependent on a government pension.

He was stripped of all pride, he was ashamed of his dependence and his lack of ability to provide for his family! Things were to get a lot worse before they got better.

My own anger returned as I looked at the direction my life had taken. This wasn't the man I married, I hadn't signed up for this type of hardship and truth be told I didn't think I could take anymore. Feeling robbed of the carefree optimistic girl I once was and now I had lost the man I had married too!

His struggle was evident to everyone and everyone would ask how Andy is doing. 'He needs to take it easy, he's doing too much, he looks tired', they would say. In my mind I screamed: 'What about me? When do I get to rest? When do I get a break?' It felt as if I had been working overtime non-stop ever since he had left for Afghanistan and the reprieve that was supposed to come from his return never came.

The strain just escalated as I was now dealing with the emotional abuse he would throw at me and was exhausted from protecting the kids from his erratic mood swings. I resented him for the damage he was doing.

Comparing the current existence to his previous absence, made me realise that this new reality was much harder than when he was away. When he was away I could make myself hope for better things when he returns, but now there is no hope of reprieve. There was no time for wallowing in self-pity and this was not part of my character either as I preferred to just get on with life.

I found it particularly frustrating to watch Andy suffer from de-pression. In my mind there was no time to feel sorry for oneself. As far as I was concerned, he needed to just open his eyes to see that we need him, think positive thoughts and he would be able to move forward. I had always managed to give myself little pep-talks, even when I felt I was spiralling into what I suspected was postnatal depression at one point.

PTSD was with us for life the psychiatrist said. Did this mean that I had seen my future with this stranger? Once again the burden of sole parenting on my shoulders was unbearable. Joseph was at one point asking, "why doesn't Daddy laugh anymore?" It was heartbreaking to watch my children look at their dad with growing awareness and caution, not quite knowing how they'd be greeted.

It was around this time, I found out I was pregnant with our 4th child. My already failing grip on sanity was tested even further. I felt guilty and at the brink of despair when I found out I was pregnant again. I just couldn't fathom taking any more on my plate. I spent an entire night crying out with feelings of desperation and fear.

I'm a fighter and a fixer so we weren't going down easily, I did my best to help Andy believe in some small way I could help fix him, but every triumph where we'd experience some peace and happiness would be seemingly sabotaged by his volatile emotional state, one step forward, four steps back seemed the never-ending cycle of this journey.

One such an occasion was Anzac Day, we had made a commit-ment to try and change the morose theme it was known for and tried to reinvent the day as a family day where we could remember the lives lost and the freedoms gained in a positive way. A day that didn't end in drunken stupors and fights.

The day started out well, we went to dawn service and had lunch, but then Andy decided to stay and catch up with mates for a 'few beers'. (I had long since recognised that as code for 'piss up'.) One of his friends had said it would be good for him to have a drink and talk about it, but I knew better.

Everything came to a head on ANZAC day 2012. I decided to go to the Dawn Service and then get a few drinks with friends. A few drinks turned into a few to many and before I knew it I was punching on with some random bloke at a bar in the early hours of the morning. Trying to punch respect for soldiers into a guy in the early hours is not a productive way make a point. I was put into a cab and sent home.

When I arrived I couldn't find my keys so I walked around the back of the house and broke a door to get in. After stepping on dog poo in the back yard, I proceeded to walk it through the house spreading it on the carpet, over clean clothing and even into the bed until I was woken up by Zoe asking what was going on.

I was so drunk I don't even really recall much of what happened next, although a fight ensued and at some point I went through a glass sliding door and fell asleep in the front garden in the rain. I was really starting to make a habit of messing my life up and I needed a wakeup call fast.

Long story short he came home well into the early hours of the morning, stomping dog poo angrily throughout the house with little regard for sleeping children. Limping in his still moon-booted leg, blind drunk and furious. He'd had a fight with some random person who had stated his opinion, which obviously Andy disagreed with.

I was furious to say the least and disappointed. When would he learn that alcohol was not his friend? He slept it off, but was in poor form the next day, sinking deep into his head, not coping with anything and becoming once again completely withdrawn and unable to communicate, fighting to quiet the destructive voices inside his head.

He sought solace at his parents' farm, wanting to spend time away in solitude so he could reflect. All I got was that he was going away, again, leaving me with the kids, again.

My mother, bless her, would council me from a place in her heart, relaying from her experience and wisdom, telling me that all marriages were the same but I couldn't hear it. All I heard was that I needed to be the bigger person, because Andy couldn't be. This pained me coming from my mother thinking that at least she would be my ally. In the depths of my despair, no body understood my pain, nobody saw the grief and death I was feeling inside. Writing this now and looking back at myself, I find myself selfish and unlikeable. And truth be told whilst I was so busy focusing on my pain and my feelings, I was unable to see Andy's suffering as anything other than another excuse for him to be selfish.

*****

The Army will train a person to become extremely effective at dealing with complex, difficult and dangerous situations. As a result, soldiers will react quite differently to many people in stressful situations. We are trained to run towards the danger not away from it. Advance to contact, enter a burning building, run towards an explosion and chaos. It is often referred to as the fight or flight response and as a soldier we are taught to always go on the offensive. Fight, don't avoid the danger, run towards the danger, burning vehicle, gun fire, explosion or screaming people. Don't run away.

I was truly indoctrinated to the point that when I left the Army, I found it very difficult to quiet myself in any situation. I was always on guard, constantly checking my surroundings, looking for indicators of a threat and trying to read people around me. Everyday situations became increasingly difficult and draining. I found myself wanting to be alone, avoiding crowds and busy places as I was constantly on guard, I simply could not turn it off. It became exhausting and it was easier for me to avoid society all together.

As a result, I started to withdraw, I didn't want to go to parties, social events or meet up with mates. I didn't even want to talk, preferring my own company over anyone else's. I started to become a recluse and I buried myself into my new job. I required alcohol to socialise and even to function in any setting.

Things went from bad to worse when I was in Melbourne attending a conference. My family life was a mess and I was happy to be away from Zoe and the kids for a few days focusing on work. I was great at not being present for my family mainly due to the fact that I often felt like I didn't have a lot of value to add to family life.

Zoe was an exceptionally competent mother and had the house and kids on a tight schedule, I would try to help or interject my own ideas or personality into the mix, but I would always seem to muck things up, break routine or cause issues. So I was happy to just go to work and provide the money, remaining at arm's length from everything that was going on in the house.

At the conference I was speaking to numerous ADF personal regarding our company's equipment and training opportunities when I was approached by an individual who told me he was sent to warn me to be careful about how I was approaching the ADF as clients and not to use my influence or network to gain commercial business.

The problem with his statement was the fact that he was essentially telling me not to do my job! My company hired me for two reasons: one, because of my unique military experience; and secondly, because of my connections within Defence. I knew this and so did they, however, I never stepped outside of my professional obligations and as an active reservist I still had ties to Defence. I had not even been out a year and the C-IED network within Defence is a very small organisation. So of course when I spoke to people within defence I knew them, on both a personal and professional level. However, I never breached that confidence or stepped over any lines, in fact I took care not to.

I was extremely offended by the assertion that my integrity had been called into question and I stewed on it for days. It gradually wore me down and started to eat into my confidence. I began to question the integrity of my job, the value of the company and my role in life now, as nothing more than a peddling merchant. I started to see no value in what I was doing and it broke me.

I would not say it was this specific event that pushed me into the abyss, however, it was the catalyst from a build-up of many smaller incidents that finally broke me. My mind started slipping into a deep depression, fuelled by alcohol, and I began to tear down everything around me starting with my employment and my family.

Depression is a sinister little devil. It will enter your mind as nothing more than a negative thought that is fuelled by insecurity, fear and loathing, and starts to grow into an all-consuming beast that devours every aspect of one's life.

I was entering into the eye of the storm and to top it off my hallucinations and vivid dreams had become a nightly event. I could no longer handle stress in the same way I had done in my previous career and I began to crack at the seams. Even simple mundane tasks becoming too difficult to bear. I withdrew even further into myself refusing to talk to anyone spending more and more time alone and getting angry with everyone and everything. Nothing made sense anymore, I was questioning my value to society, my value to my family, my value in humanity. I had lost the one thing that I was good at and now I had nothing bigger to believe in or be a part of.

What I have come to understand about PTSD, is that it effects everyone that is associated with the person suffering, not only the sufferer.

I started to destroy every relationship in my life by shutting down from friends, not answering phone calls, text messages or emails. Not socialising to a point of complete withdrawal from society. Then once I was at home I would start to push my family away, shutting down to conversations, seeking independence and solitude. Angry outbursts became a regular occurrence and shouting at the people I loved the most in this world became normal.

I was so self-absorbed that I did not have time to notice anyone else in my life or consider how my behaviour may be impacting the people around me. My kids became a problem to me and my wife became an enemy.

After a while I began to hate myself in a way I had never felt before, negative speech filled my every waking moment. Thoughts of: I am worthless, I am no good, I have no purpose or goals, I am a burden to everyone around me, filled my mind throughout the day. After listening to negative self-talk for some time I started to believe it and as a result all I wanted to do was push the people I loved away from me to protect them. I figured if I could break away from my family they would be better off and subconsciously I began to work at breaking down my marriage and my relationship with my children.

One of the scariest thoughts I had during this time followed a particularly vivid night terror and hallucination. I woke up in my bed and saw a young child at the edge of the bed, she was severely burnt and had her right arm severed by an explosion. I jumped up and grabbed her reassuring her everything would be okay. I lay her down on the bed and grabbed a shirt from the ground. I started to bandage her stump to stop the bleeding as the child whimpered and screamed in pain.

At this point Zoe woke up and asked me what I was doing, she shook me and told me to release our daughter as she was screaming, I looked at Zoe and firmly told her to stop! That I needed to stop the bleeding or she would die. All I saw was a young Afghan girl with horrific injuries in extreme pain. Zoe now grabbed our daughter from my arms fearing for her safety as I slowly came to, eventually realising the young girl was not an Afghan blast victim but my own daughter.

I had a number of hallucinations since returning home, however, this was the first time I had put one of my own kids at risk of physical injury. I had on occasion pursued people throughout my house tackled and wrestled with objects in the lounge such as light stands and chairs believing they were intruders.

After this incident I realised my own family were at real risk and that I had absolutely no control over my actions as I could no longer determine reality from fiction. I thought I was losing my mind!

I considered going back to the Army and getting my career back on track, repenting of my decision to leave, and wishing to be taken back into the secure fold of the military to provide me with the purpose that I so desperately needed. I was lost in a way I had never been lost before and I very quickly found myself at the bottom of a bottle, now a functioning alcoholic at best. I was hanging onto work but my desire to grow and work performance had already decreased and my boss had noticed.

Zoe was at her wits end and I was doing nothing to save our marriage; I simply didn't care enough, consumed by my own depression, tired of never really sleeping due to the constant oppressive attacks of nightmares and visions and reliving events in my mind. I had not slept properly for over six months and my mind and body were taking a toll.

Eventually Zoe had enough and insisted I see someone and get some help. At home I became increasingly irritable, not quite fitting in, not being able to find my place as a father or husband, seeming to fail at every turn and driving a wedge between myself, my wife and kids. I increasingly felt like I didn't fit in.

The night terrors continued relentless and at first Zoe was very supportive, compassionate and considerate. However, as the bouts of sleepless nights and increased tiredness compounded, it only added to the stressors on our relationship.

Some nights I would wake up completely gripped by fear; I thought if I moved I would be shot by a Taliban sniper or rogue Afghan National Army person just waiting outside my bedroom window for me to sit up in bed. I completely expected to hear the crack, thump of a bullet leaving the muzzle of a rifle as the hot lead entered my body and tore through my vital organs. I would lay there in fear for hours, not moving, not sleeping, just in fear.

Things were going from bad to worse on a daily basis. I was now drinking excessively every day in an effort to silence the noise in my head and get some sleep. I figured a drunken sleep was better than no sleep at all. Throwing alcohol on this problem was like throwing petrol on a fire and the home situation rapidly deteriorated. I was steadily drowning in a well of depression and self-pity.

I had never really experienced depression before, sure I had been sad and unhappy at times but I never felt life was really bad or not worth living. Up to this point, I actually had quite an upbeat, outgoing personality, that was quick to bounce back from adversity. I was completely unprepared for what was to come.

Before too long I was out of control. I had no control of my own actions and I knew it. This feeling of loss of self-control was extremely confronting to me as I had always had to maintain some level of control for my work, if I didn't, then there were consequences. However, now those consequences seemed irrelevant.

I was angry that no one seemed to care, no one understood, no one could help me and even if they wanted to I wasn't going to let them. I found it increasingly hard to silence the negative self-talk and started to spend more time isolated in my own self destructive thoughts. I would constantly hear myself say, I am worthless now, I don't have any purpose in life, no one needs me. What good am I?

The first time I had a panic attack I actually thought I was having a heart attack. My chest tightened, my breathing became difficult, I became light headed and extremely anxious. I had never experienced anything like it. Me? The guy who walked down range to stand over large explosive devices brought to my knees by an emotive response to a negative thought. I just couldn't make sense of anything.

Zoe knew I was struggling more and more every day and she would try to break down the walls and talk with me, but I found it so hard to open up. I didn't want to share what I considered to be my burden, with her and let her carry that on top of everything else she had to deal with.

I started to consider suicide as a solution and even planned out how I would end my own life in detail. I started to think about it constantly as the negative darkness consumed my weary brain. I hated the idea of suicide, having lost my best mate early in life to this act and seen it effect a number of people in Defence and my personal life over the years. I knew it would tear my family apart and was a coward's way out, but none of that seemed to matter as the darkness descended upon me and became too much to bear. I had found the end of myself and I was found wanting.

I was no longer strong enough to find a reason to fight and I came very close to ending it all seeking silence for my tormented mind.

Seeking help for PTSD and Depression was probably the single hardest thing I have ever done in my life. My worsening condition was so blatantly obvious to everyone around me although I did not want to admit that I had a problem. I thought acknowledging it would simply make it more real and sentence me to a life of ridicule and shame. I felt weak and like a complete failure as it was, I didn't want others to know about it as well. I would tell myself over and over again, this sort of thing only happens to weak people. I was so very scared of revealing the demons I was facing as it would remove the veil of deniability that 'everything is okay' and 'I'm fine'. Admitting I had a problem was tough. I would go over typical sayings like 'just get over it', 'build a bridge mate', 'toughen up princess'. I would tell myself everyone has problems, I'm no different, just deal with it. But I could not. The panic attacks became more frequent, brought on by stressful situations and gradually even brought on by very little.

The day I walked into Psychiatric Hospital I was completely broken and I saw no other solution. I was admitted into the Hospital for a PTSD 12-week program. I was heavily medicated from that point on. The realisation that I could no longer cope was like being hit by a freight train. Bullshit! I would tell myself, harden up, what is wrong with you, get your shit together! This shit does not happen to you. You have a strong mind, some degree of intelligence and certainly are not weak in the head. But the reality was far from the defiant voice crying out in my mind, I was broken and needed help.

Excerpt from my diary in Hospital:

"I sometimes think if I did not leave the Army I would still be operating at a suitable level and would simply have pushed my memories and issues to the deepest darkest passages of my mind to never see the light of day. It makes me think, how many of our serving people are suffering this pain in silence? Instead I find myself fighting a new battle, a battle with the "Black Dog", a frightening and formidable foe that depression is. This enemy in my view has been responsible for killing so many people. People I know and some who have been very close to me. I feel like a victim for the first time in my proud life and it frightens the hell out of me."

"To feel like a failure is not to admit failure, to admit you have a problem is not failure, it is the start of a long battle that I intend to win and the hardest admission I have ever had to face in my life. A word of advice to those unwary souls who are concerned to look inward and reflect on their lives and what it means to be a man; be careful because you may not like what stares back at you."

I resigned from my job as I could no longer complete my duties and I became dependent on my wife and on the system. I was extremely fortunate that my employer supported me during this time as well as the Department of Veterans Affairs (DVA). Some amazing work by a local advocate rescued us from losing everything we had worked towards financially. I was placed into the huge machine of DVA's incapacity assessment procedures and felt helpless to do anything. My life now so completely out of control I could not stop it spinning.

Emotionally I shut down completely, even to the point of losing empathy for my own children. The thought of my mind returning to that place sends shivers down my spine. I remember thinking to myself, this is how a psychopath must feel when they kill someone, just no emotional connection to anyone or anything. It's not that I didn't want to feel, I wanted to feel more than anything, but it was as though that part of my brain had simply turned off and I didn't know how to turn it back on.

I pushed Zoe and the kids away emotionally to the point that most wives would have left. However, Zoe just took blow after punishing emotional blow and would not give up on me. It was not easy for her or the kids, she lived in a constant state of fear and chaos, not knowing what husband would greet her at any given moment.

I would shut her out by simply not communicating and isolating myself in a drug induced hibernation for days at a time only rising to eat or drink. On the occasions when I felt well enough to socialise with anyone it was always an effort and I would try my best to fake my responses to people around me, aided by Valium and various other medications.

I soon developed an addiction to Valium or Benzo-diazepam as it was the only drug I had access to that would dull the noise in my head, making me feel okay while not turning me into a complete zombie. As a result, I developed a daily intake of between 4 and 6 Valium and begged my psychologist to keep prescribing them to me as it was the only thing that suppressed the rage inside me.

The truth is I felt I needed the drugs at the time to function as I could not handle the day-to-day running of life. Just being around the kids would set me off. They would try their best to keep the noise down and play without fighting; but kids are kids and they make noise, fight and play.

Zoe would do her best to keep the house running and the kids at bay, she was exhausted as she was constantly in a protective role of the children in her need to shield them from me. I was in such a bad way that I could not even stand to be in the house when they were home at times and would avoid the house in the mornings before they left for school and avoid the home in the afternoon when they returned, simply because I couldn't handle the noise. Losing my temper and screaming at them all would inevitably make me feel even worse. I didn't want to yell and I didn't want my kids to hate me so I would avoid them during the really hard times.

Without Zoe holding everything together I would have been completely lost. I thank God for her every day because there is no doubt in my mind that if she had left me at that time, I would have killed myself immediately. Her strength, endurance and tenacious love for our marriage deserves recognition and respect, she is without doubt the strongest most resilient woman I know and I am so very lucky to have her as my wife.

It was Zoe who sat with me each frightening night that I would have my dreams. It was Zoe who would continually try to build me up and get my mind back on track and it was Zoe who sat up praying with me for healing and reprieve.

It was Zoe who insisted I get help for the sake of our marriage and our children and it was Zoe who shielded our children from as much of the pain as she could.

For a long time, Zoe tried to fix me in her own way. Out of her love for me she would try to talk through issues with a patience that I admire. She spent hours thinking about ways to help me find peace and encourage me to embark on various activities such as surfing, exercise or spending quiet time keeping my mind active and out of the darkness.

She purchased various helpful books, DVDs and CDs in an attempt to better understand what I was going through and provide me with tools to battle the negative thoughts in my head. Zoe tried to be there for me in every possible way, cooking meals, washing clothes, cleaning up and taking care of the children, she loyally never left my side in my time of need.

Unfortunately, my perception was that I had become just another problem that she felt she needed to deal with and fix. Zoe grappled with the idea that she could fix me for quite some time. However, inevitably time would prove I was beyond the help of a loving wife.

I think I knew she couldn't fix me from the outset and I would get increasingly agitated by her loving gestures and advice and started to develop resentment towards her support, based on the idea that she was now the head of the family and I was simply a problem that needed solving.

I couldn't provide for my family, I couldn't function as a father and I was failing miserable at the loving husband routine. And now, Zoe was taking over all the roles I was not capable of performing. I would look at how well she coped with turmoil and chaos and I would feel like a burden to her and the kids, thinking they would be better off without me around. It felt like my manhood was being stripped away by the fact that my wife was so capable, and my resentment grew. Things became increasingly bad between us and I left the house, sometimes for days at a time, although never at the request of my wife, she only wanted me home where she could keep an eye on me and monitor my behaviour. Keeping me in check, ready to step in if things got out of control.

The situation developed into a state of frenzy where I did not feel at ease in my own home and I was crawling out of my own skin to be alone and independent. We had some enormous blues resulting in very hurtful and angry things being said to one another, things that can't be unsaid or taken back, but things that can be forgiven.

I remember the day I looked Zoe in the eyes and admitted that I wanted to die. I saw the fear set in and what I believe was the confirmation of something she already knew. She became so angry, upset and scared. She held me in a way I felt she would never let me go. We both cried that night for a long time as I fought to hold onto the love that burned inside me for her. It was still there buried beneath layers of pain and turmoil. I felt like I was being tortured by an obsessive beast that I had no control over.

I was completely broken as a man and I had no answers to help get me out of the despair I was facing. Admitting the depth of my despair to my wife was one of the hardest things I have ever done. It was a moment mixed with utter shame and a feeling of complete failure mixed with a strange feeling of relief based on the idea that I was no longer hiding the truth of my situation. I needed my wife in that moment more than I have needed any other person throughout my life and she was there for me; a rock standing by me even at the point of collapse. I came to the realisation that I could not fix what was happening to me and that I needed to get help from someone or something else.

*****

Zoe was also getting to the end of her strength with constant disappointment in our relationship and her exhausting single parenting role. She fast became disillusioned with the sharp turn our lives had taken and could look to the future with none other than foreboding. She had lost the compassionate, romantic man she had married and couldn't imagine a future with the insensitive in-compassionate, unmoving man I had become. My optimistic wife was now a shadow of her former self. When she became pregnant with our fourth child, that was at her breaking point. She cried the whole night telling me, that now not only did she feel as if she was raising our 3 children on her own, she would now have to raise another and she didn't think she could do it, as I had become completely unreliable to her and the children. She was so beside herself she told me it was easier when I was in Afghanistan. She struggled with ongoing feelings of abandonment even though I was now back home.

Thankfully when she was at her breaking point, she turned to God for help, admitting she couldn't go on anymore, she had reached the bottom of her reserve. She prayed for strength during the hardest times, knowing she couldn't do it in her own strength and if she did we wouldn't make it. She knew she couldn't do it alone, but with God she could overcome anything life threw at her. She drew comfort from God's promise that he would never give us more than we could handle.

It was not long after this she came to me with her revelation that she could not fix me and that she didn't have to. She had been trying so hard to revive the man that she had married and tried to recover the life that we once had that she had lost herself in the process. She told me she could no longer try to fix me because she knew she couldn't. She said she had a responsibility to focus on the children who needed her more and the impending arrival of our unborn baby. She told me, she would no longer be the driving force behind my battle but she had to give that role to me. It seemed to her every time we took a step forward, a poor decision on my part took us three steps back. She said that one such occasion was that Anzac day, where I decided to meet up with some mates in the evening. I drank beyond excess and got into a fight. I came home in the small hours of the morning incredibly angry. This anger led me to a decision to take off to my folks farm in Goulburn for a week.

Zoe told me that she saw this as nothing other than running away from her and the kids yet again. It would be weeks before I returned to any form of coping again. It was slowly dawning on me that alcohol was not helping my condition.

I automatically took offence to her telling me she was taking a step back and that it had to be my responsibility to get well. I took it as her telling me she no longer loved me and that she was giving up on me. What I later realised is that she was in-fact giving me that independence that I so desperately craved, by removing the responsibility of my healing off of her shoulders and putting it onto my own, where it belonged in the first place.

This was a defining moment in our new unchartered relationship. It was the dawning of something new and significant for us both. The effect of release was so powerful on Zoe that she later told me she was actually able to laugh at something for the first time in a very long time.

After a few days of cold shoulder, we spoke for hours about how we could move forward together. Her revelation gave her peace that what was happening, was not within her control and that she had to trust in God for healing and repair.

She took a huge step back from the way she was dealing with me and realised in her longing to protect and support me, she was smothering me and driving a wedge between us.

This was not through any fault of her own, but simply a result of the situation and my mental health. My idea of communicating was ignoring or grunting and I realised if we had any chance at a future together, I needed to become better at communicating with my wife.

We decided to focus on the truth of what we had and that was a strong love for one another. We both realised that this problem was not simply going to go away and I needed to seek help from outside of my marriage in order to save it, or lose it all.

*****

I was miserable, and my despair grew. I can recall many times when I would lock myself in my room, crying that aggrieved deep painful cry that comes from the depths of loss and mourning. Walking around at the shops in a complete daze, my mind constantly going over the hurtful arguments that we've had. Some of these arguments got pretty ugly, and Andy would punch holes in walls, I would throw things at him (and I was a pretty good shot too).

I learned to recognise when I actually goaded his anger, and learned when I needed to walk away. I learned to let stuff slide, I learned to sweep things under the carpet, too many things. Sometimes this was impossible, there were moments when Andy would hunt me down to vent his anger. I would lock the bedroom door and push furniture against it in a vain attempt to keep him out. He would punch his way through, just to say his piece, so blinded by anger. His violence would scare me, although I never felt threatened that he would actually physically hurt me. He always managed to control himself enough not to, but the message of angry hate was in his eyes. They weren't his eyes. Those eyes belonged to someone else and they scared me.

*****

Finally, around this time, Andy started to see a Christian Psychologist and we were reminded that we didn't only have to rely on the world's 'band aid' approach to his sickness, but overcoming in Christ was a very real and powerful possibility. A glimmer of hope started to glow on the horizon.

It took some time before Andy could accept the forgiveness he was offered as he was unable to forgive himself, he carried such a burden of self-hatred and condemnation on his shoulders. He struggled with the concepts of grace and redemption.

We spoke about the strong spiritual experiences Andy has had during his life and he explained that this was completely different from what he had experienced in the past.

I had been brought up a Christian and although I had convictions, I don't think I really knew the full extent of strength and peace I could draw from in Christ. Then again I had never really been through anything that was as emotionally testing and draining as this was proving to be. I was so used to handling everything myself and listening to myself in my anger and despair that I had forgotten to listen for God's voice. At this point there was no other choice. The choice was between life and death in my circumstance. Looking back, I recognise that I had to walk through the fire to draw closer to God.

During the times where I became so overwhelmed with despair and frustration, and I had gotten to the point of depletion, I could do nothing else but fall to my knees at Gods mercy. The only place I seemed to find solace and reprieve. I found a reservoir of strength, forgotten to me and a peace that went beyond all comprehension came over me. I knew we would survive, I also knew there was hope. It became clear that my only hope of survival in this thing was to call out to God for help. For far too long I had been trying to do this in my own strength and I began to draw comfort from scriptures like John 16:33 These things I have spoken unto you, that in me ye might have peace. In the world ye shall have tribulation: but be of good cheer; I have overcome the world. KJV.

It was during these times that I could see when my focus was on myself and my feelings I was unable to have compassion towards Andy, who was actually really struggling. He hadn't chosen this illness, he wasn't deliberately hurting me, or the kids, he couldn't help it. I had to consciously remove myself from the situation in order to help him, because my current tack wasn't helping anyone.

I realised that I had been carrying the burden and responsibly of Andy's illness on my shoulders and knew that as a result I was crippling his healing. My need to fix him was stopping his authority in taking control of PTSD himself and as such he was defined by it. The burden on me was too great physically, I needed to release him so I could focus on the kids more fully and the pending arrival of our new baby, determined to bring her into a happy place.

It was shortly after this revelation I decided to tell Andy that I needed to take a step back, and that I needed to give more attention to the kids and my welfare being pregnant. As you can imagine, it certainly didn't go down very well. He took it as me saying I'd given up on him and that I didn't love him anymore. I tried to explain my heart, that I was in fact giving him the freedom and responsibility he needed to get better.

That was a turning point in our lives, as I watched Andy grow in his faith and subsequently learn to battle and overcome PTSD and depression. PTSD ceased to define him as an individual but rather became just a part of him that he had to learn to manage and conquer. There was a long way to go in the healing process for him as an individual, for us as a couple and for us all as a family.

There was no immaculate healing although we prayed and we prayed hard. But with that too came revelation that even Paul had a thorn in his flesh and like Paul, Andy was learning that his thorn kept him needing Christ and that his true strength was in Christ, his attitude toward his affliction came close to an appreciation- 2 Cor. 12:9 and he said unto me, My Grace is sufficient for thee: for my strength is made perfect in weakness. Most gladly therefore will I rather glory in my infirmities, that the power of Christ may rest upon me. KJV

I now began to view this life changing turn with hope, believing Gods Promise in Rom 8:28 And we know that all things work together for good to them that love God, to them that are called according to his purpose. KJV

I knew that behind our hardship there was purpose and design beyond what we could fathom, and Andy's story would be used for good. I knew he'd be on this journey today, writing this book, because I knew his struggle, our struggle would be a powerful story that needed to be told. It needed to be told to those who hold no hope, to their partners who feel that way also and their children and all who are impacted by PTSD and the 'Black Dog'.

I honestly believe without a doubt, that without God, Andy and I wouldn't be together today, Andy probably wouldn't be alive today, whether through self-harm or most likely some senseless heroic act, because he'd still be in the military.

PTSD sufferers and those around them get used to a cycle of life where things go well for a time but inevitably the seas will get rough again. The only difference for us was that with Andy's growing faith those rough seas become further and further apart, so much further apart in fact that when an 'episode' did occur, it was so unexpected it would feel like the rug was completely pulled from under our feet. I would pull through completely shell shocked wondering where the hell the fall came from. There were times I had thought it was all over and the worst was finished. I know for Andy the pain was like he was a dog going back to his own vomit, he somehow kept making the same mistakes even though he had learned to recognise the triggers. Each experience left us feeling completely deflated.

*****

One of the proudest moments in my life and I dare say his parents' life, was the timely witnessing of Andy receiving a Commendation for Distinguished Service award by the Governor General. It gave us the opportunity to see him publicly recognised. He had become one of the best in his field and was now being recognised for his contribution to his country. Although it was hard for him to receive as he thought himself unworthy of the accolade, I believe it helped him to complete this chapter in his life and gain closure ready to begin anew.

I knew one of his worries was that he had let his father down when he left the Army, and in truth his father had expressed his disappointment believing he still had so much more he could give to the Army. Knowing this, I asked his dad one night in front of Andy if he was proud of his son, he said yes, I asked: 'does he know that and have you told him?' He looked a rather uncomfortable Andy in the eyes and choked up as he told his son he was proud of him. I believe that was a defining moment in that father and son relationship.

*****

In October 2013, our little Ireland finally made an appearance five days late! To say her pregnancy was the hardest would be an understatement. Not only did I no longer have any confidence in my body's experience in pregnancy as I thought I was going into labour many times and hadn't. I also struggled with thoughts of inadequacy at how I would be able to handle the responsibility of another life, given the circumstances.

She finally prompted me of her impending arrival when I was home alone with the three children. Andy was out of range and his mother who had been staying with us to help out was in Brisbane. After a string of angry expletive voice messages to Andy, I had come to the understanding that I would be having her by myself. As I prepared to hop in the shower with images in my mind of the news stories to follow of the "heroic woman gives birth alone in a shower whilst looking after her 3 other children" Andy arrived home.

We left the children in care of my sister-in-law and rushed to the hospital to give birth to Ireland about half an hour later. When I say we gave birth I mean me. Within moments of her arrival, she looked us both directly in the eyes almost like she recognised us and we were smitten. I looked at her and felt immediate love for the child I had secretly dreaded having. I remember thinking "oh I love you!".

Ireland was simply a pleasure and quickly found her place in our home. She was to prove to be the missing piece to the puzzle we never knew, was lacking. From the moment she was born I felt a fierce love for this child I had fought to make the world a happier place for. God gave Andy another chance with her and their bond is special. This special little doll that engaged everyone with her eyes, brought a special peace to our household at a time when it was most needed.

The Christmas that followed surrounded by my family brought with it feelings of contentment and resolution that the coming New Year was going to be different from the last. We would get through this, for the sake of our growing family, we had to.

*****

Although we had hope, the darkness still won occasionally. Andy's battle with his mind was fought daily as he struggled with dark thoughts and anger. I too had to reset my outlook daily and had now learned to control my part in the arguments and recognise when to step back.

Sometimes, it still proved too much for me and I failed miserably. I'd like to say that it ended with words alone and that I had enough self-control not to hit him, but I didn't. There were moments out of complete exasperation and frustration, in a desperate attempt to snap him out of his hurtful heartless spiel that I would beat my fists on his chest.

One night, not long after Ireland was born, I was exhausted, Andy had told me his brother and their four kids were coming to stay. I had told him I was so anxious about it, feeling completely ill-equipped to handle entertaining guests, given my new-born baby and Andy's frame of mind. I couldn't understand how he could be so insensitive to completely disregard my feelings as a new mother. We argued for a few hours but the crescendo reached its peak, just before midnight. I remember at one point grabbing the laptop and a beer and dropping them in his lap saying that music and alcohol was the total of his con-

tribution to entertaining guests. Knowing full well the cooking and cleaning and babysitting that was required not only for my own children but another four to boot and I was completely overwhelmed by the prospect. Predicting the long hours of drinking and loud laughing that were commonplace every time Andy got together with any of his brothers or mates, often not climbing into bed until daylight. Too many times, in fact every time I would spend the following day completely exhausted from no sleep, looking after the kids quietly while the dads slept it off. Anticipating the worst of the situation but precedence stood blindingly in my face, and I had my own sleepless nights already to contend with; with a newborn in the house.

I was so upset because he called me a bitch over and over (even in front of the kids) saying I was completely inhospitable and that he chose his family over me. At the peak of the argument where we were both beyond any reason, I tried to get passed him so I could lock myself in the room with Ireland. He kept slewing ugly hurtful insults at me and blocking my way, pushing me back at one point and I caught my toe on the carpet (it hurt for months so I'm pretty sure I broke it or something).

At this point I was so angry and frustrated I ran at him and swung at him in rage landing a surprisingly effective right hook on his cheekbone. I remember time slowing as I looked at the swollen vein throbbing just under his eye where I'd landed the blow with a mix of horror and awe, shocked at what I had just done.

The ringing doorbell knocked us both out of our reverie. His brother's family had arrived. It was midnight. I ran to the bedroom and locked myself in for the night unable to face anyone. Early in the morning he came in to wake me. He hadn't slept but had spent the night reminiscing and catching up with his brother.

He apologised as he remembered the hurtful things he had said to me, he told me he didn't mean them and that he would always choose us first. Shamefully, but a little smugly, I observed that he had a black eye. I asked him what he told his brother? We joked about the transparent reason he'd come up with that was apparently unquestioned.

The time together spent with his brothers' family was actually great and there were some wonderful memories made as the cousins spent rare time together.

Andy was sensitive to my needs and struggles with Ireland and

*was conscientiously supportive domestically. It made a huge differ-
ence. We talk about it now with some amusement, but at the time, our
relationship had sunk to new depths and we really didn't know how to
get out, though I think some level of growth had occurred as Andy witnessed how overwhelming solo entertaining and the general running
of a household with four children had become.*

*The only outlet he seemed to find was in surfing, I tried to en-
couraging him to break the negative late night sleep cycles by kicking
him out early in the morning for a surf. He would come back a completely different man. It was on the water that he could renew his mind,
meditate and put things back into perspective. This became a good
part of our routine. I would remember to go to God for my strength at
times, but I knew Andy was still struggling to do everything in his own
strength, and whilst he was doing that, he would always fall short.*

*Andy continued in his struggle to find a new identity and began almost
frantically seeking purpose in helping everyone and everything whether it was neighbours, church or mates, which in itself was admirable
but he was finding it difficult to know when to say no and to recognise
his own limitations.*

*More often than not we would be sacrificed in his endeavour not
to let others down, invariably we were let down. I was often put in the
position where I would have to stand in and say something, of course
this wouldn't go down well, as I came across as controlling and jeal-
ous. Thankfully I had a great ally in our Pastor Miles who developed
a great friendship with Andy and who recognised Andy's need to slow
down and step back.*

*I encouraged him to take the time to give back to the family and
the opportunity to rebuild the strained relationships particularly that
with his youngest son Charlie, and find purpose in being a father. He
struggled to find enough self-worth in this. We fought each other on
principles such as my controlling hand in the home, to which I argued
that he had made me that way. His past and present absences and con-
sistent unreliability meant I had to maintain control and take charge
and now am struggled with relinquishing it to him without merit.*

*****

A turning point for Andy I believe was when he volunteered to speak at the boys' Anzac service at school. With such eloquence he delivered a heartfelt speech that although censored for the school audience hinted at the dark deep suffering felt by many of our present and past soldiers. The underlying passion and loyalty behind their sacrifices.

So many people in the 1000 odd audience were so moved by the speech that he was asked again to speak the following year and also be a guest speaker at the local Mudgeeraba dawn service. Prior to the event hearing him prepare his speech and discuss his own reflection on his time served made me reflect on my self worth and how others saw me.

I could say I still have moments where I feel like I'm taken for granted, but knowing all wives probably feel that way, even when I know I've been through a lot, and stuck through a great deal for Andy, for our kids, when many other mums, wives, would've checked out. I'm not looking for a medal, or even recognition.

There were my own mental battles through this experience as I've seen Andy get a lot of gratitude from friends and strangers for his service and his sacrifice. This has often left me feeling a little disregarded, not because of a need for recognition but more because I actually wonder if anyone has noticed or appreciated my pain, my scars, my sacrifice for our marriage and our Kids. Does anyone actually understand why I am who I am today? It seemed as if my sacrifices were recognised but merely expected as part of the package of being married to a serviceman.

My sacrifice was fueled by my strong love for my kids and my husband, and my hope is that when I die it will be with the knowledge that I had done the best I could with my circumstances. God knows my heart and I want to hear "well done my good and faithful servant".

I was quite humbled when a few people approached me after Andy's speech and thanked me for my service and my sacrifice to this country. I could only answer them truthfully, "it wasn't in my strength." On Father's Day 2014, Andy went in to have the long awaited shoulder reconstruction. The surgery went well but he struggled with the aftermath of the pain and the drugs, and not being able to surf.

I watched fearfully as he fell back into his depressive withdrawn state. Trying to lift him out of it was to no avail. Depression was making a comeback.

After a week or so we went to church and he had a complete breakdown, he couldn't stop crying, and I couldn't console him. He told me he thought he needed to go back to the clinic because he didn't feel right, but I fought him on it, arguing that it would make it worse.

We sat together as he sought solace locking himself in the spare bedroom. I tried to get him to focus on me, but his eyes had taken on that familiar shade of black I now is associated with his depression and anxiety. He struggled to focus as he looked at me with dilated pupils, I could swear the pupil engulfed his whole eye and actually shook.

He admitted to me then, in the deep depths of his depression that he wanted to die and had actually made plans on numerous occasions. I felt sick to my stomach as I realised that it wasn't that he didn't love us or that we weren't worth living for but he thought we'd be better off without him as if he wasn't worth enough for us.

My heart broke for this man that was so weakened by this affliction, and I hated to see him so exposed. Somehow I found the strength to overcome my own grief and I told him he needed to fight, he needed to fight for us, for his kids, because we needed him and we loved him. I saw light flicker in his eyes and knew all was not lost, that he was still struggling but was not giving up.

11

Road to Recovery

And so began the Journey to reclaim a life that PTSD and Depression stole from me. This journey would prove to be the most difficult and tumultuous journey I have ever embarked upon, however, I am still here today as a result of taking these first steps in seeking help and coming to terms with the fact that I needed help.

I was admitted into the Currumbin psychiatric hospital for a 12-week PTSD program. As part of my treatment I was placed on various medications including anti-psychotics, to treat my violent and aggressive mood swings and outbursts. Now I am not a huge fan of drugs, I don't even like taking Paracetamol if I have a headache, however, having gone through this excruciating process, I understand the vital roll these medications can play in saving people's lives. My own opinion is that these medications, although completely necessary in the short term, provide no long term cure and are simply akin to placing a Band-Aid on a severed artery.

My own journey through the minefield of medications saw me take in total some eight different drugs over a two year period. Some treating the symptoms of my condition quite effectively accompanied by side effects that were often as difficult to cope with as the condition itself and included things like, extreme tiredness (also referred to as zombie-ism), rashes, muscular cramping and joint pains, extreme mood changes, insomnia, stomach cramps, diarrhoea, dry mouth, erectile dysfunction, numbness, loss of memory and drooling.

One of the most upsetting side effects of PTSD for me was my almost complete loss of short term memory. I could not recall the simplest of instructions or remember what I was doing from one moment to the next. At one stage I was unable to read for a period of around six months as I would simply read the same few words over and over again eventually giving up in frustration.

I began to realise my condition was also having a very real physical effect on my body as well as my mind. I had had numerous panic attacks, profuse sweating and stress rashes break out over various parts of my body and now my brain was not responding to normal daily activities in a way I was used to. It was incredibly frustrating and added to my overall anxiety and lack of wellbeing. However, over time, what I began to realise is that PTSD and Depression are simply injuries like any other, they must be treated if they are to improve and if left unchecked can have catastrophic effects.

I began to focus more on my mind and reinforcing positive images and thoughts in my mind, rebuking negative thought patterns. Sometimes I succeeded and sometimes I failed; however, each time I failed I simply dragged myself back up and started the fight again. Climbing out of a black pit of Depression is a seemingly impossible task that starts with one positive action, that positive action for myself was a revelation provided by the words of the Apostle Paul in his second letter to Timothy. I was lying in my bed in the psychiatric clinic thinking to myself: 'I have lost my mind. I am plagued by constant hallucinations, seeing things that aren't there, I am on all sorts of drugs to keep my mind at a point where I don't want to act on the constant urge to kill myself and I have lost all emotional connection to the people who mean everything to me, being my wife and my children'.

I thought to myself: 'I may well end up in this horrible place in a drug induced state for the rest of my life.'

It was at this point that I picked up my bible and turned to the following scripture: *For God has not given us a spirit of fear, but of power and of love and of sound mind.* (II Timothy 1:7). As soon as I read this scripture I realised I was made with a sound mind and that I was in-fact not going crazy. I would never admit to myself that I was crazy from that point on and I have stood on that scripture as the basis of my recovery, with the knowledge of truth that God made me with sound mind and therefore nothing could take that away from me.

Over the course of the next 12 months I went through a roller coaster of emotions as I began to feel moments of clarity and peace followed by complete chaos and darkness. At times I felt like I was only hanging on by my teeth.

One particular day my young daughter Eden ran over to me as I sat at the end of the bed my head in my hands, she pushed her way into my arms and cuddled me. I felt the numbness of emotion slowly give way to the love this little girl was showing me, unconditional, undeserved love, slowly but surely the barriers began to break down in that moment, my baby girl had managed to reach me on a level that no one and nothing else could. I felt alive again in that instant and felt my heart swell with emotions that I thought were long dead.

Suddenly, I was overcome with love for my little girl again, I returned her hug thinking I don't want to let go in case this feeling that was lost vanishes again. I am not sure why it happened that way but I am so thankful for Eden who in that moment saved me from myself through simply loving me.

Our fourth child Ireland a beautiful healthy little girl was born in October 2013. I distinctly remember the joy of her birth and her looking up into my eyes for the first time. I had glimmers of hope during moments like this and occasions where life seemed survivable again, I had every reason in the world to live and share in the upbringing of my children, although, Depression and PTSD still had a firm hold on my life.

After a short glimmer of hope I soon found myself again in a position of pain, torment, suffering and despair. I was on numerous, constantly changing, medications in an attempt to find the right combination for my condition. In addition to this my family situation was extremely strained. Zoe was losing strength in her will to support me through this difficult time as she was burning out raising four kids on her own. Now dealing with the demands of a newborn and with my mood disorders. My children didn't know which father was going to greet them from one moment to the next and I was still abusing alcohol as a self-medication tool, simply being around me made both Zoe and the kids constantly on edge.

Then came the turning point!

In the last days, God says, I will pour out My Spirit on all people; your sons and daughters will prophesy, your young men will see visions, your old men will dream dreams.18 Even on My servants, both men and women, I will pour out of My Spirit in those days, and they will prophesy. ... (Acts 2-17-18)

At this time, I was receiving counselling twice a week, I would see a Psychiatrist, whose simple solution was to load me up on various anti-psychotics and mood stabilisers. I was also seeking help through a Psychologist who operated from a Christian Faith frame work.

This man had a very unique and different approach to my psychological care than what I had heard from the larger medical community. Rather than reinforcing the mindset that my condition was permanent and incurable he simply stated that through faith in Christ all things are possible and that mental healing was one of those possibilities. For the first time in a long time, I started to allow myself to believe there was hope at the end of the darkness and started to believe I could get through this tormenting time in my life. A slight glimmer of light was established in the darkness.

Jesus used this man to do something amazing in my life and in one day reignited my relationship with God that for some reason although I did not feel it was any longer there, it was simply dormant. The simple realisation that I did not need to carry the burdens that I was carrying alone, as Jesus could carry them for me was a revelation that saved my life.

My new Psychologist had an easy demeanour about him that I felt allowed me to open up and trust him. He has a trade background as a blacksmith and a heart to help people. He is strikingly easy to be around in that he has a very unique way of presenting himself as calm, patient, non-threatening and engaging.

My initial impression of this man was one of confusion as he is a man of significant stature without being domineering or authoritarian. He was quintessentially opposite to the stereotypical Army person in almost every way. He listened and did not lead discussions but rather opened the door to honest conversation.

I did not initially really know how to relate to this man as he was very different to me in almost all aspects of his personality. However, over the next four years our relationship would develop into one where I would consider him as a mentor or life coach as much as my treating psychologist. His slow and easy demeanour allowed me to gradually break down walls, communicate openly and begin to deal with the emotional chaos that was occurring in my mind.

This reminds me of one of our early meetings. We had started to discuss death and chaos and direct some of the incidents I had been exposed to in Afghanistan and I was becoming increasingly agitated and anxious. So he decided to conduct a few calming and releasing exercises I would later learn was also called a blood cleansing exercise. He asked me to close my eyes and concentrate on my breathing, slow deep and deliberate. He continued to talk me through quietening my mind and body and allowing myself to relax and let go. This was a difficult process, but I gradually released and lowered my guard as this stranger spoke quietly in the background confessing the blood of Jesus over my mind, body and spirit to heal and cleans me of my pain and suffering. I imagined myself on a beach, listening to the waves as they slapped against the shore, feeling the ocean breeze across my face and smelling the salt air. I remember looking into the sand dunes and I saw something that would change the path of my life forever:

I saw a cross lift up out of the ground, at this distance it was hard to make out if there was anyone on it so I approached the cross and saw him as plain as day. Jesus nailed on that cross, as I looked up at the image of Christ on the cross I felt completely overcome by love and warmth and I passed out. I woke up, I imagine only moments later, and I looked at my treating psychologist who was sitting in his chair and was now looking at me with a smile on his face.

This experience was so different from what I had experienced earlier in life in South America, which was a drug induced state that left me confused with an out-of-body experience. When we were in Darwin, it felt like I was being attacked by the devil, whereas this experience was the complete opposite. I was overcome with peace and love and didn't feel any fear during the experience itself.

It was only afterwards, when I was overcome with fear and confusion as to what had happened. I witnessed something incredible and so detailed in a way that I had not experienced before and it confused me. I was not sure how to understand what was going on and I asked him what had happened. He simply remained calm and explained I had experienced an encounter with God and I had had a significant physical reaction to that experience. He explained how my body had shook quite violently and then rested back in the chair completely limp. He asked how I felt and reassured me, everything was okay. The session was nearing completion and I left still very confused about the entire experience.

I remember leaving and thinking to myself I'm never going back. I got home and explained what had happened to Zoe who looked at me with a smile on her face as she exclaimed "it sounds like you were slain in the spirit", I said "what the f... is that?" and she continued to explain that it is a loss of consciousness that has reportedly happened to people who have been overcome with a spiritual encounter. I asked if it had ever happened to her, hoping this would in some way lessen my distress, however she had never experienced it personally although had witnessed it on a few occasions. I spent the remainder of the day and into the night researching this phenomenon in a perpetual state of fear and disbelief. I had experienced something very real although I could not explain it nor grasp the reality of it. I trawled through youtube.com videos and articles of people claiming to have had similar experiences, only to question each video I watched or article I read, and tell myself these people were crazy and in turn believing I was also going crazy by association. I started to question the reality of what had happened to me and wondered if I had simply imagined the entire thing, although in my heart I knew the truth of that experience and I would never let it go. Looking back, this encounter was all about surrendering to God, I was releasing my guard and my tight grip obsessed with controlling every aspect of my life and started breaking down the walls and through the vail.

I eventually worked up the courage to ask my pastor, Miles, about this phenomenon and he explained what had happened to me. He was a great comfort and provided some much needed guidance and support normalising the experience and explaining it in terms that I could better comprehend.

He said the spiritual world around us is as real as the physical and that we were made in Gods image, his Spirit. He went on to explain that there were many things that we could not understand or explain about the spiritual world. However, this did not make it any less real. He explained my encounter was simply a spiritual encounter and that I could either embrace it or fear it. God is only good and if I pursued him I had nothing to fear.

This conversation was a turning point for me and allowed me to view my spirituality in a new way not bound by fear of the unknown but more from a position of wonder and amazement and was the launching pad for a more spirit filled life to grow inside me. I had decided to surrender my own understanding over to Gods understanding and my life over to Jesus. This process happened over a period of time as I gradually became more comfortable with my own limited understanding of God and spirituality and I cut down the preconceptions I had formed over the previous 36 years.

I continued to see my psychologist and benefited greatly from his advice, gradually I allowed myself to feel forgiveness and allow God's grace into my life. The idea that Jesus died on the cross so that I might live rested on my soul and gradually to hold pushing away the hurt, pain and resentment. My mind was slowly becoming freed from oppression and turmoil although the journey was far from over.

A Mentor and a mate!

I was also fortunate to have another positive influence in my life at this time, Edmund Liebenberg, a burly tough man in his 60's. Looking at him I saw a strong, abrupt and determined man of little compromise and I respected him for it. He had a history of operational service in the Rhodesian SAS and on occasion, would share amazing tales of his time in the wilds of Africa, fighting against a cunning and dangerous enemy.

This man was also a very knowledgeable Christian and I warmed to him immediately as his background and our shared faith drew us together. I would confide some of my darkest fears in this man who would openly share his own dark past as we would sit for lengthy periods sharing memories over a beer or two. He would share his wisdom and understanding of scripture in a way that I found extremely fulfilling and educational. I respected Edmund as a man and it helped me to deepen my knowledge of the Bible and consider my own circumstances in a different light.

Looking back, it was the relationships I had formed and allowed to grow, that helped me through this difficult time the most. I had a handful of people in my life I was now slowly willing to open up to and talk to. Just having an ear to talk to was such an incredible help to me during my darkest days.

I decided I needed to make a concerted effort to break free of the oppressions of PTSD and Depression. I was taking my medication, reducing my alcohol consumption, eating well, exercising, trying to socialise, going to church and fighting for a better life through pursuing Christ as my strength, rather than fighting for life in my own strength. I was doing what I thought to be all the right things to get better and improve my life. The good days were slowly starting to return, socialising more, communicating with my family and enjoying occasional moments of peace.

Then I was hit with another relentless wave of nightmares followed by a slide back into Depression. I had been down this path before and I should have been able to recognise the signs, however, I felt like I was free falling without a parachute. All the progress I had made over the past months was washed away in an instant and I was back, trapped in the darkness with nowhere to turn.

Below is the letter I wrote to myself during this time and I think it gives an interesting insight into my mindset at the time.

A letter to myself:

I want to start with a definition that I believe is perhaps the most important string of words the human ear could ever hear.
"Grace is one-way, undeserved love"
I feel undeserving of God's grace!
I feel empty, run down and out of energy to fight!
I feel like life is too hard!

What set me back?
- The bureaucratic process of seeking help through government organisations
- A list of growing names of soldiers I have served with that are either dead, in hospital or suffering from PTSD and Depression.
- Being diagnosed with Tuberculosis
- The idea of not being able to work again
- Not sleeping, adding to increased anxiety, anger and agitation.
- Reverting to alcohol
- Being quick to anger with Zoe and the kids.

Resulting in feeling like I am failing my family, because in reality I am not a loving supportive husband or father and there is evidence to support this statement. I am withdrawn, sad and detached and putting on a happy facade is draining and weighs heavily on my soul.

I am trying to be someone I am not, because I hate the real me. I am afraid of the real me!

This has led to creeping feelings of no self-worth, no worth to others no good for anyone, a burden to my family and friends and all who come in contact with me.

Even the word of God has on occasion emptied me with my lack of giving, selfish behaviour and lack of empathy.

What happened to the strong proud man, the loving devoted husband and the doting father, or the good fun mate I used to be?

I can't even go to watch my son receive an award at his school, because I'm afraid that I will have a panic attack. Yet, I long for the opportunity to detach myself from my family because I think if I'm not there I can't disappoint them.

I find myself wanting to place myself in harm's way so I can die without directly taking my own life as I see my suicidal thoughts as the devil at my heels and I refuse to give that bastard the satisfaction of adding my soul to his collection.

Although I have sinned I am forgiven! I can find peace and freedom in God! I may never forget the horrors I have witnessed and perhaps that is my cross to bear, but they will not define me. I have come so far and I refuse to go back. I will find a new me in Christ undefined by the confines of war, man or sin.

Jesus is with me and Jesus is my strength when I have none.

"Jesus, carry me through this dark hour and deliver me back to my family, whole, complete and full of the Holy Spirit. My life is in your hands from this day until the day I die."

I know I will stumble as Jesus stumbled carrying his cross but I will not quit, I will not lie down. I will be free.

The glimmer of hope through my faith became the only thing holding me up. I had nothing else and had reached a point of complete despair. I immediately started to catastrophise my life as I watched it spiraling out of control, as though I was a spectator to my own demise. It was as if I was in the passenger seat watching myself drive off a cliff and I was powerless to stop it. I would focus on the negatives and an overwhelming fear that I would not be able to handle this mental setback and that I could end up back in a mental hospital with the Junkies and alcoholics whom I resented and despised.

In addition, I had injured my shoulder and required an operation and I was not in the head space to deal with the surgery; however, at the insistence of the doctors I decided to go ahead with the operation.

Surgery went fine, and I was in and out of hospital in a few days. When I got home I found it difficult to rest, my mind would wonder into thoughts of worthlessness and despair and I would sink deeper into an insidious depression. The pain medication was making me feel very sick mixed with the anti-depressants and I found it difficult to focus. The pain would also increase my irritability and make me even quicker to anger. Family life was quickly becoming unbearable.

I have always struggled with the concept of rest and I saw work as a reflection of character, strength, capability and usefulness. I often felt worthless if I was not actively doing something and for me to simply be lying in bed resting, represented complete failure in my mind. Again my good mate Miles, who had become a positive voice of reason in my life, advised me that rest is important and God wanted me to rest, he pointed me to Psalm 23:2 *"He makes me lie down in green pastures, he leads me beside quiet waters, he refreshes my soul."* I tried hard to meditate on this scripture but it simply did not bring me peace. My mind was at odds with my spirit and I could not find rest.

As it turned out God had other plans. Looking back, I believe

God wanted to get my attention in a big way and through breaking me down to a point of submission he would force me to find rest in him.

It was around this point that I had another mental breakdown, I define a mental breakdown as reaching a point where I could not get myself out of the depressive state I was in. Feeling overwhelming thoughts of self-harm and wanting to die. I thought about simply taking a large volume of pills all at once, as life was just too hard. I was feeling sick in the stomach, had headaches, my chest was hurting and my shoulder was in a lot of pain. I was in a state of confusion and strife with the Department of Veterans Affairs and how I was going to continue to provide for my family financially. I was constantly fighting with the Psychiatrist in regards to the cocktail of medication I was on and how they were adversely effecting my body and mind.

At this point I decided my only option was to kill myself or reach out for help one more time. I would completely ignore thoughts of my family doing life without me and convinced myself that they would be better off with me gone. I went to my best mate's house with the idea of distracting myself from these thoughts but I quickly realised this was not working. My friend could not help me and with great reluctance I decided to go back to the Psychiatric ward.

I did not want to go there because I had numerous mixed experiences there in the past and I thought this place was reinforcing the view that I was broken and that there was no cure. In addition, Zoe hated the place, often saying it felt awful and heavy and that every time I go in there I come out worse, doped up to the eyeballs and not even resembling the man she had married.

Going back to hospital went against everything I had been working on through my faith and coming closer to God and believing in the possibility of healing. However, at this point I saw no other option and I was admitted into hospital once again.

After being admitted, I experienced severe stabbing pains in my chest. I did not know what was happening but it was very intense and scary. I jumped out of bed and went into the hallway to seek help from one of the nursing staff and collapsed under the extreme pain in my chest. The hospital staff called an ambulance and I was taken to the Emergency department. There, I was treated for various symptoms including anxiety, however, I knew this was something more. It was not just anxiety as I had suffered from this condition for some time and knew the signs and symptoms intimately.

I was scanned, prodded and blood tests were taken. As it turns out I had blood clots on my lungs and pleurisy. I was extremely unwell and I remained in the hospital cardiac ward for the next few days receiving treatment for blood clots and Pleurisy, (yep, just added a new disease I didn't even know existed).

As it turned out I was quite sick and had a real chance of dying here in hospital. I never pictured myself dying in a hospital bed on the Gold Coast, but for a moment I thought finally the pain will stop and I don't even need to take my own life.

I started praying for forgiveness and preparing myself; trying to get right with God. It was at this point of complete surrender that I suddenly realised I no longer wanted to die, in fact I really wanted to live!

I was bombarded with images of Zoe and my kids and I started praying non-stop as I began to think more about the people in my life and less about myself. I thought, what will my wife and kids do if I die? Who will look after them? Who will love them and watch them grow? I guess at this point my heart changed from looking inwardly at my own pain to looking externally at the people I really cared for in life. It was as if empathy had turned on again.

This was the defining moment in my battle with PTSD and Depression as for the first time I was able to consider others and empathise with the feelings of my family, rather than only concentrate on my own feelings, suffocating in the pain I was in. At this point I made a pact with God. I promised him if he spared my life I would dedicate the rest of my life to honouring and serving him.

I did not expect what happened next! That night, after prayer I felt more at peace than I had felt in days and I slept like a baby. No nightmares, no hallucinations and little pain. The next morning, I went for scans on my lungs as I had done a number of times previously and all the blood clots had gone!

I thought wow, the Doctors thought wow, that's interesting and after several consultations, they decided I could stop the blood thinning medication I was on in order to prevent one of the clots from traveling to my heart or brain. They felt safe to simply monitor my progress for the next few days. They kept treating me for the pleurisy as I was still feeling the effects, (chest pain and difficulty breathing) but the symptoms were decreasing and continued to decrease over the next two days. By day three I was feeling well enough to ask to go home. I was advised to rest and I decided for the first time in my life I would take that advice.

Hebrews 4:10:
For anyone who enters Gods rest also rests from their works;
just as God did from his.

From this point on I started praying and believing in faith for healing, renewal and blessings on my life. I stopped hating myself and started thanking God for his blessings and his sacrifice for my salvation. I started living by faith and in grace. I also attended a prayer group at Elevation Church and received prayer for healing by a group of amazing faith filled people. I believe this also had a profound effect on the rate of healing I would experience over the next few weeks.

Romans 12:2
Do not conform to the pattern of this world,
but be transformed by the renewing of your mind.
Then you will be able to test and approve what God's will is –
His good, pleasing and perfect will.

Shortly after he went for a drive to see Greg his Psychologist. I got a call from Greg saying he needed to go to the clinic. Who was I to argue? I dropped him off as it was no place for the kids. At least he was seeking help, even if in my mind it was in the wrong place.
Ironically within a short period of time he started to have severe

chest pains. These were not concurrent with anxiety or depression and he was rushed to John Flynn hospital. There they discovered he had a number of blood clots on his lungs and on top of this he was diagnosed with Pleurisy! No matter my opinions of the place, if he hadn't of gone to the clinic when he did, Andy could have died. I thank Jesus he went in when he did, but I also see that God was in control of the whole situation.

Andy thought he was dying when he was in there and that was the beginning of a very significant soul searching journey that he is still on today. He came out of hospital a very different man, something had changed, something significant.

He came home with purpose and drive that was previously lacking, somewhat akin to the man he used to be, but most importantly, he came home with a will to live. His focus moved from inward to outward and like a match of tug-of-war we slowly gained momentum, cohesion and balance. Through our faith, we have ultimately found forgiveness. It was those weeks after Andy locked himself away that his new purpose was developed and refined, but what occurred on those sleepless nights is for another story and not mine to tell.

The journey to recovery of his mind and body and the health of our relationship and our family is a long ongoing one, but with love and faith, we have found softness, patience and a wealth of endurance much needed to get through.

It has been hard to prove to Andy at times that I'm on his side, and often to myself to acknowledge that he is not my enemy, but the only way through this is together. For both of us now, quitting is not an option. We are a team and we know we are better together than apart. The past battles have only brought us closer together and made us stronger. We have seen what we are capable of surviving and that gives us so much hope for the future.

I realised too, that all the effort I had spent trying to protect my children from being damaged, although understandable was not necessary. People are always saying children are resilient, but it is so much more than that. This journey is not just Andy's journey, it's not just my journey either, it's my children's journey too. Every experience, rather than damage them, has moulded and shaped them into the compassionate and empathetic individuals that they are today. Who knows what little world changers they will become and just what they will do with the knowledge and depth of Depression and PTSD that they have witnessed, that is otherwise sorely lacking in society today. My faith encourages me yet again that no experience is wasted and that there is a hidden purpose yet to be revealed. This gives me hope beyond understanding and reason. Indeed, as I look back, like the stars that reappeared on my windscreen to remind me of another time, events highlight themselves like golden thread in the intricate tapestry of our lives revealing a purpose and design.

Today, Andy is completely medication free, our four beautiful children are healthy and happy. Joseph is now 10, Charlie is 8, Eden is 6 and little Ireland is 2. We are currently building a new house, yes we have moved three times since our little house in Mudgeeraba. What can I say, I'm still that girl that loves change and adventure? But we are truly living life together and we are a great team, sure we have bad days, but who doesn't? Its okay to feel down, its okay to feel depressed and its okay to be affected, BUT its not okay to stay that way. Andy has to renew his mind each day to keep the darkness out, but in faith he has truly overcome, his is a story of hope, worth being told.

12

Revelations

The following weeks and months after my hospitalisation became an incredible journey of faith and renewal of mind, body and spirit. I started living a life full of joy and happiness I did not think possible. I would embrace my children and lovingly smile at my wife, something she had not witnessed in a very long time. I had found a level of peace and happiness with my family that I had never experienced before. I threw away all the medication I was on including painkillers, anti-inflammatories, blood medication, anti-depressants, and anti-psychotics, much to the discouragement of my various Doctors. This is not something I would recommend to everyone, as coming off this much medication all at once can have very detrimental effects to one's health.

Throughout this time, I have been wholeheartedly seeking God through scripture and prayer and dedicating my life to living by faith. God was rewarding me with love, kindness, happiness and health. He was revealing so much of his message through the Bible, I felt like my cup was overflowing and I could not get enough of his truth. For the first time in my life I am on the path God had created for me all along and I don't plan on stepping off.

My mind is renewing itself in amazing ways each and every day. Even going through the process of writing this book it has continued to untangle the web of painful memories, processing them, clearing space for daily life.

To me PTSD can be explained like this: Imagine a computer that has too much memory stored in it. It begins to run slower as it is overloaded with data, unless the data is defragmented and cleaned out, the computer will continue to get worse. Our brains work in much the same way.

Those suffering from PTSD, store these horrible memories in the back of their minds, never unpacking them completely, due to circumstance and or trauma. Our subconscious does its best to un-cluttered this space whilst we sleep, explaining the vivid dreams and hallucinations. However, unless we actually face these life changing events, unpack them and digest them properly, going through the raw emotions involved, this space will never be clear.

Writing, for me has been a process of pulling on a string and slowly untangling the knotted chaos, one strand at a time. The incredible result has been with each memory pulled forward and faced, my mind's capacity to work as it should, increased. I am not a brain surgeon; but I have walked through a dark valley and I am living proof that you can make it through, no matter how dark, desperate and lonely it feels.

Just knowing that what seems impossible is actually possible, gives me the strength and determination to continue. My heart's desire is that sharing my story will in some way remove some of the stigma and mystery associated with this illness and provide hope for others suffering from this oppressive condition.

I was also incredibly fortunate during some of my darkest days to have an amazing person get involved in my life. This person devoted a significant portion of his time and energy to listening to me and hearing my problems. He provided a safe outlet for me to vent my anger and frustrations with life.

Miles is a very cool guy, fit, happy and energetic. He is an incredibly talented surfer and all-round good guy, father of five and pastor of a church.

Our relationship started one day as I sat near the back of the church watching a short film of five guys hanging out at the beach, surfing, drinking coffee and having fun. I remember looking at this film thinking, I used to be fun, and I used to have friends and then sinking back into my shell of isolation and depression.

Zoe identified the flicker in my eyes and insisted I go and introduce myself to the pastor, who was one of the guys in the video and tell him, I wanted to get into a life group like that. She pushed and pushed until I found myself standing in front of this guy thinking, 'I feel like such a tool,' but I summoned the courage to introduce myself and say I liked surfing. From that moment Miles looked at me and identified something in me that he wanted to get to know and he pursued a friendship with me until I broke and let him in.

Miles openly embraced me into his life in a way I had never known anyone to do before, open, honest and loving. I thank God that he kept pursuing me and breaking down the walls, because if he had not been there over some very difficult times, I know that I would not be writing this book today. He saved my life on occasion by simply being there as a friend when I felt I had run out of options. I believe God placed Miles Paludan along with Greg Gardner and a few other key individuals in my life for their specific purpose, at specific times, to help guide me back to Jesus and salvation, through faith.

His advice, pastoral care and friendship sparked some enormous growth in my mind, body and spirit. This man brought so much wisdom and peace to my life through simply getting me engaged with life again. He encouraged me to get out of my shell and return to the surf. He encouraged me to get involved in life, talk to people and start to let people in. He also showed me that society was not necessarily against me and that I did not need to walk through this life alone. In fact quite the opposite is true. We are made as social creatures who need positive interaction with other human beings to live a full and productive life.

Miles has a unique and wonderful way of breaking down barriers and listening to people. He is exactly what I need in my life; I will always treasure his friendship and I am humbled by the way he lives his life as an example to others.

Over the next year I developed a friendship with another incredibly inspirational man, Geoff Willson, one of Australia's greatest explorers of the modern age. What Geoff has achieved in the past 11 years is nothing short of inspiring. From near death escapes, grand desert journeys and noble Antarctic expeditions, Geoff now holds three world records:

Longest land journey ever by kite across the Sahara Desert.
First ever kite surfing expedition across the Torres Straits between Australia and Papua New Guinea.
Fastest unsupported crossing of Antarctica under wind power. (3,428 km in 53 days)

Geoff took me under his wing and re-introduced me to horses. Something I had not experienced since I was a boy on my grandfather's farm. What started as Equine therapy was so enjoyable that I now try to ride at least once a week and have developed an unexplainable bond with horses. I feel incredibly grounded whenever I have the privilege to ride. In much the same way, paddling out for a surf in an uncrowded beach break helps me to become centred. Nature has an amazing way of grounding me and I am reminded to engage with this instinct as often as possible to promote feelings of happiness, wellbeing and health.

Geoff engaged my adventurous spirit that had been turned off and I am so thankful to him for that. He has a quote that he uses when speaking about overcoming adversity, *"we have an unfair advantage in life through our faith in Jesus."* This statement is so true for me in that I could not do life without my personal relationship with my creator.

In the past year I was saddened by the Death of my childhood friend Johnny.

He is remembered by his son and three daughters. Johny had gone on to live a rather fast and dangerous life constantly battling with drug addiction. His death did not come as a real shock to me, however, I felt real loss at his passing. He was my best friend for much of my life, the best man at our wedding and there at the birth of my first Son. Looking back at Scotty's death, I felt terribly guilty over his suicide and it stayed with me for years. Thoughts like I should have been there for him and if only I had gone to his house sooner or made more of an effort, he would not have killed himself. I did not get the same guilt with Johnny's passing. He was a grown man and at 38 had made his own life choices. I did my best to help him over the years, only meeting with disappointment and regret. Johny fought his demons for many years and his battle was now over.

More recently my life was impacted through another friend-ship in a very big way. I had grown as a person and as a Christian and I was now part of a life group of around ten guys, all normal, fun, energetic young blokes just keen on hanging out and talking open-ly and honestly about life and every day issues. I was now focused on living a purpose filled life constantly seeking God in everything I did. I worked hard to develop healthy lifestyle choices, get off all medication and reduce my alcohol consumption. This life group be-came a very important part of my life as it provided the infrastructure I needed to bond with other guys away from the issues of marriage and children. It provided a place that I and others could speak without fear of persecution or ridicule and made me a better man as I became accountable to others.

One of the guys in this group I had become very close to was Secombe, a young 38-year-old fun, energetic and cheeky character. He was a professional skater in a previous life and into the fast life of drugs, music and drinking associated to the scene in his native home of New Zealand. He was extremely well respected in the skate-board-ing community.

Secombe had three young boys similar ages to my own kids and they went to the same school. We would go surfing together regu-larly and really enjoy each other's company. He was someone I could really click with and his friendship meant a great deal to me. Secombe had a huge heart for helping kids and troubled youth. He had a way of gaining their trust and speaking into their lives to effect positive change. His reach was far and wide and his testimony was shared with hundreds of youth across Australia and New Zealand. He was also impacting my own life in a very positive way.

On the 1st of February 2016 he died suddenly from a heart attack at the age of 38. His death really shook me as I could not understand why a man like this was taken. I struggled in coming to terms with his death as he had so much to live for and his family really needed him. I was requested to say a few words at his funeral and I spoke the following:

> Although I only knew Secombe for a short time, it felt like we had been friends for years. We just clicked and friendship came easy to both of us. I don't typically let many people into my life but Secombe had a way of breaking down the walls and connected with me right away.
>
> That's just the way he was, he was so warm, genuine, humble and approachable, with a massive heart for Jesus. He showed me how a brother in Christ is meant to behave, he just loved people in his own quiet and humble way.
>
> Over the past few months we spent more and more time together, surfing, chatting, going to men's life group and catching up at church. He had a profound impact on my life in a very short space of time and from what I have learned of this man he impacted everyone he came in contact with. Every time we spoke he would leave me feeling happier and more focused on living the life Christ has ordained for me.
> I will remember Secombe as a man of great moral courage, gentle, loving and compassionate, so rich in knowledge and wisdom beyond his years.
>
> Secombe's last words to Shannon at our men's group were as follows:
> 'God never does anything that is not good... We sometimes don't understand, but he only does good.'
>
> His words echo in my mind as I play out the conversations we shared, we have lost a brother in Christ but I take some comfort from the fact that his relationship with Jesus was so profoundly strong.

I heard death explained in an incredible way yesterday:

When God calls his children home he is filling a void in his own heart. The void we now feel not having Secombe here with us is the same void God feels whilst we are on earth and is only filled when we return to him. Nothing can replace the void left behind and life will always feel a little less complete without you but I take comfort in the knowledge that you are home with Jesus.

I can't make sense of your death brother but I know in my heart you heard the words from God:

'Well done, my good and faithful servant!'

Knowing you has impacted my life in a way I will never forget. You have shown me how a man who follows Christ should live, honouring his wife, loving his children and supporting his friends!

Over 700 people attended his funeral and I sat there in awe of the celebration that was occurring to honour his life. He had touched so many people and I was honoured to have known him.

Over the following weeks, the life group decided to get around his family and support them in any way we could. We decided the best way to do this was through finishing off some minor renovations at his home to make things a little more comfortable for Talie and the kids.

Through the simple act of giving in a small way, God revealed himself to everyone involved in this project. Amazing things started to happen as the community rallied around this family in their time of need. Meals were provided, school fees paid, funeral costs covered and generous donations made to help this family. A local pool builder decided he wanted to bless this family and construct a pool, free of charge, extensive renovations of the house were completed.

Through being involved in this activity God has shown me firsthand how being a blessing to others has greater reward than one could even put into words. It has been incredible to see the heart of people in the wider community have such a lasting and dramatic impact on the lives of Talie and her boys.

Secombe would have been very grateful knowing his family were being loved and cared for in this way.

I am reminded that life is all about relationships with one another and if we are able to place aside our prejudices and simply love one another as we have been commanded to do, life can be so richly rewarding and joy filled.

Jesus left us with two simple commandments, they are a wonderful guide to living a full life:

'You shall love the LORD your God with all your heart, with all your soul, and with all your mind.' This is the first and great commandment. And the second is like it: 'You shall love your neighbour as yourself.' On these two commandments hang all the Law and the Prophets.

(Matthew 22:37-40 NKJV)

Since Secombe's death I have been convicted to pursue life with everything I have and to be bold in Christ. Not to hide behind the comfortable vale of religion or spirituality, but to shout Jesus' name from the roof tops. He is a loving God who only wants peace for his children, so listen to him calling you and enter into his rest.

It is this boldness that has provided me with the strength to complete this book. Life is too short to be lukewarm, I would rather be hot and persecuted than lukewarm and accepted.

I have also been blessed to see God moving in a very real way amongst Secombe's family and friends. There have been enormous outpourings of support and generosity including many people coming to know Jesus, because of the circumstances surrounding his death and the way it has touched so many people's hearts.

I feel like God placed Secombe in my life so that I could be there during his family's time of need to be a pillar of support in the same way others were placed in my life during my time of need.

God has revealed his purpose for my life through so many series of events. I know my job is simply to love and help people wherever I can and spread a little light and salt wherever I go.

"I can do all things through him who strengthens me."
Philippians 4.13

If you are reading my story I would encourage you to search yourself and seek out what gives you purpose in life. Identify it and hold on to it, allow it to grow from an idea into something tangible and actionable. Allow it to shine through you, so that people can see it in you and in everything you do. When you have purpose, you have hope and with hope you can live a fulfilling life and achieve your destiny. Without hope we are lost. I encourage you to be 'others focused', because when we are focused on others we become the best versions of ourselves.

Post script

I continue to have occasional panic attacks, angry outbursts and chaotic moments in life since my healing began and on occasion I have ended up back at the Doctors office and even back on medication for short periods of time. If you look at the history of where I was and where I am now, the comparison is nothing short of a miracle. I don't even view those times of relapse as a negative, but simply as a reminder to stay focused on Jesus. He is my only salvation in this life and the next.

When I look back at my story I am able to see how God's intricate design has been woven into my life and the truth is, he has been in control from the very beginning, even in my darkest days. I don't think my story is particularly exciting or unique, but I was urged to write it so that others may find hope in the darkness, through Jesus redeeming love. I am anxious at times about how people may perceive my story and may ridicule me or my family, however, I know by being faithful in writing this book I am walking in line with God's plan for my life and for that I am so very grateful.

One of the driving inspirations for writing this book was to draw attention to the epidemic of PTSD, Depression and Anxiety within the veteran community and in society as a whole and to remove the social stigma attached to mental illness, as this is often the root cause for individuals not seeking help. This hidden disease is nothing to be ashamed of and is simply a mental injury that needs diagnosis and treatment like any other.

Beyond Blue revealed the following statement: *'In Australia, it's estimated that 45 per cent of people will experience a mental health condition in their lifetime. In any one year, around 1 million Australian adults have depression, and over 2 million have anxiety.'*

The Australian Bureau of Statistics reviewed that 1.4 million Australians at any one time have Post Traumatic Stress Disorder (PTSD).

One of the key points I wish to make here is that PTSD, Anxiety and Depression do not have to be terminal conditions and can be overcome through hope, love and understanding. Suicide is not a solution, it is simply a catastrophic end to life that may have been prevented, had the individual received the proper care in time.

I feel like the luckiest bloke in the world that by the grace of God I have been given the gift of a new life. I don't claim to know everything God is trying to teach me, in fact far from it, but I can say with conviction that I am now on a journey that is bigger than I could have possibly imagined. My life is dramatically enhanced through spiritual growth. I cannot begin to explain how good it feels to have hope back in my life, in a way I only recall as a young child, carefree and looking at the world with wonder, excitement and amazement. My gaze is firmly set on eternity.

The best part of the life I am now experiencing is that it is freely available to anyone who is lost, suffering or broken hearted.

Writing a book.

Writing this book has been a cathartic experience for me in so many ways. When I look back at how shut down my brain was, to the point where I could not even read for a period of time, due to my mental condition; I am amazed at the healing that has occurred. Writing down my experiences has allowed me to untangle the knotted spider web of memories trapped in the recesses of my brain and unravel them into single incident memories, allowing me to live more in the present and less in the past.

The concurrent benefit to this process has been an increased clarity of mind and peace with the completion of each chapter. I don't know exactly why my brain has responded so well to this activity, however, what I can say, is that I highly recommend giving it a go if you are suffering from mental illness.

Start by simply keeping a journal and jotting down your thoughts. Slowly, as you feel more comfortable delve into your memories and allow them to come out onto a page. If you don't get them out they will come out in their own way, as anger, depression, anxiety and dreams until your mind can find peace.

"With men this is impossible, but with God all things are possible."
Matthew 19.26

Words and Abbreviations

AA	Australian Army
ADF	Australian Defence Force
A-ExHC	Army Expolosive Hazards Centre
ANA	Australian National Army
ANSF	Afghanistan National Security Forces
ANP	Afghan National Police
AO	Area of Operations
AO	Artillery Officer
AO	Army Officer
AO	Australian Outback
ANAL	Ammonium Nitrite Aluninium
ANZAC	Australian and New Zealand Army Corps
Aussie	Australian
ARR	Army Ready Reserve
ASF	Australian special Forces
AWOL	Absent Without Official Leave
AWTI	Australian Weapons Technical Intelligence
Capt.	Captain
CASEVAC	Casualty Evacuation
2nd CER	2nd Combat Engineer Regiment
CF	Coalition Forces
Child Giant	Bigger than normal child
CI	Corps of Infantry
CPIED	Command Pull IED
CO	Commanding Officer
	Commissioned Officer
Col.	Colonel
CP	Command Post
CPL	Corporal
CPO	Chief Petty Officer
DSC	Distinguished Service Cross
DF	Defence Force
DO	Defensive Operations
DO	Duty Officer
DOCS	Department of Child Safety
EDD	Explosive Detective Dogs

EHRC	Explosive Hazard Reconnaissance Course
EHRT	Explosive Hazard Reduction Technician
	Explosive Hazard Reconnaissance Technician
EOD	Explosive Ordnance Disposal
EOD Manager	Explosive Ordnance Disposal Manager
EOR	Explosives Ordnance Reconnaisance
FOB	Forward Operating Base
hootchie	small plastic sheet use as weather cover
HMAS	Her Majety's Australian Ship
IDF	Indirect Fire
IED	Improvised Explosive Devices
ISAF	International Security Assistance Force
KAF	Kandahar Air Field
KIA	Killed In Action
LtCol	Leutenant Colonel
LRPV	Long Range Patrol Vehicle
MAJ	Major
MMA	Mixed Marshal Arts
MTF	Military Task Force
NCO	Non-commissioned officer
NSW	New South Wales
OP Relex	Operation Relex
OPSO	Operations Officer
PB	Patrol Base
Pers. or pers	personnel
PO	Petty Officer
Poppa	Grandfather
POW	Prisoners of War
PTSD	Post Tramatic Stress Disorder
RACE	Royal Australian Corps of Engineers
RAOI	Royal Australian Corps of Infantry
.RAR	Royal Autralian Regiment (Commando)
RC-S	Regional Command South
RE	Rules of Engagement
RIB	Rigid Inflatable Boat
RMC	Royal Military College
ROP	REstrictions of Privileges
RPG	Rocket Propelled Granade

RSM	Regiment Sergeant Major
SAS	Special Air Service Selection
Sgt	Sergeant
SME	School of Military Engineering
SOTF	Special Operations Task Force
SOTG	Special Operations Task Group
SVBIED	Suicide Vehicle Borne IED
TFU	Task Force Uruzgan
TACON	Tactical Control
TIC	Troops in Contact
TK	Tarin Kowt
TOC	Tactical Operations Centre
	Tactical Operations Command
TTP	Tactics Techniques and Procedures
VBIED	Vehicle Borne IED
WIT	Weapons Intelligence Team
WTI	Weapons Technical Intelligence

Refences

Lonely Planet Travel Guide   (http://www.lonelyplanet.com/)

Australian Government, Department of Defence. "Lance Corporal Jason Marks". Defence.u. Archived from the original on 11 October 2010. Retrieved 2010-09-30.)

Maps:United Nations News Centre
United Nations News Centre1212 × 930Search by image
Map of Afghanistan, June 2011. Source: Department of Field **Support, Cartographic Section;** Afghan Map is from www.geographicguide.com; World map is from worldatlas.com

About the Authors
Andrew and Zoe Cullen

Andy is a veteran of 17 years service in the Australian Army. Retiring as a Major in 2012 having served 6 years as a soldier in the Royal Australian Infantry (RAINF) and later as an Officer in the Royal Australian Engineers (RAE) focusing much of his career in Explosive Ordnance Disposal (EOD). He was awarded the COMMENDATION FOR DISTINGUISHED SERVICE for operations in Afghanistan.

Zoe grew up in the tranquil hills of Byron Bay living in a mud brick home built by her parents. She has a passion for life, family and travel. After university Zoe married into the Army, her own career taking a back seat to Andy's life as a Military Officer.

69406671R00172

Made in the USA
Columbia, SC
14 April 2017